CURRENT RESEARCH IN EGYPTOLOGY 2012

Proceedings of the Thirteenth Annual Symposium

University of Birmingham
2012

edited by

Carl Graves, Gabrielle Heffernan, Luke McGarrity
Emily Millward and Marsia Sfakianou Bealby

OXBOW BOOKS
Oxford and Oakville

Published by
Oxbow Books, Oxford, UK

ISBN 978-1-78297-156-6

A CIP record for this book is available from the British Library

This book is available direct from

Oxbow Books, Oxford, UK
(Phone: 01865-241249; Fax: 01865-794449)

and

The David Brown Book Company
PO Box 511, Oakville, CT 06779, USA-
(Phone: 860-945-9329; Fax: 860-945-9468)

or from our website

www.oxbowbooks.com

Front cover illustration: Footboard from a coffin, c. *900BC, in the collection of the University of Birmingham (The University of Birmingham Research and Cultural Collections, BIRRC – XO728).*

Contents

Papers presented at Current Research in Egyptology XIII and not included in this volume (in alphabetical order)

Khufu's second boat project, difficulties and wishes
Afifi Rohim Afifi
Chief Inspector of Antiquities of the Giza Plateau

Who or What is Werethekau? A Problematic Inscription (UC 16639)
Ahmed Mekawy Ouda
University of Cairo

Late Period Regionalism in Ancient Egypt: a Comparative Analysis of 25th and 26th Dynasty Coffins from Thebes and Akhmim
Allison Williams
University of Liverpool

Cry and Silence: rethinking the nature of the man-god communicative language in ancient Egypt
Amr Omar
American University in Cairo

HALF AN ITERU ONWARD! The "Mycenaean Brigade" at Amarna: Egypt, the Aegean and Late Bronze Age Warfare.
Alexandros Giannakoulas
University of Oxford

Paper-rock Stelae and Sacred Landscapes in the Eastern Desert during the Ramesside Period
Anna Garnett
University of Liverpool

Egyptian Imitations of Mycenaean Stirrup Jars
Birgit Schiller
Humboldt University of Berlin

The Garstang project: an integrated collections review
Claire Ollett
University of Liverpool

The Sphinx: Evolution of a Concept
Colin Reader
Independent Researcher

Coping with Uncertainty: the Use of Faith in New Kingdom Egypt
Daniel Potter
University of Liverpool

The Encircling Protection of Horus
David Lightbody
University of Glasgow

Bushes, Undergrowth: the Word *Šfnw* in Egyptian Texts
Flavie Deglin
University of Lille III Charles-de-Gaulle

Control of the Wild as Elite Funerary Activity in the Predynastic
Francis Lankester
University of Durham

Royal Festivals in Cultural Memory Studies
Gabrielle Heffernan
University of Birmingham

Analysis of the Early Dynastic Naqada Royal Tomb Assemblage
Hayley Meloy
University of Liverpool

Greek or Egyptian, please make up your mind: Ptolemy II Multi-Cultural Presentations
Heba Abd El Gawad
University of Durham

Technological Innovations in the 2nd Mill.BC in Egypt: a Theoretical Model for the Use and Distribution of New Technologies and Materials
Heike Wilde
University of Heidelberg

Too Many Bilbils in New Kingdom Egypt? Implications of Documentation and Publication of Early Excavations in Egypt
Henning Franzmeier
Freie Universität Berlin

The Vernacular of the Letters to the Dead
Julia Hsieh
Yale University

The Late Shabti Group of Iufaa
Jurgen van Oostenrijk
Independent Researcher

All made up? A re-examination of the function of the 'cosmetic spoons'
Katherine Howley
Brown University

Identifying and Recording the Book of the Dead in the Second Pillared Hall of the Tomb of Karakhamun
Kenneth Griffin
University of Swansea

A Tale of Two Suppressions: Reinterpreting Papyrus Mayer A and the So-called 'War of the High Priest' during the Reign of Ramesses XI
Kim Ridealgh
University of Swansea

Mehet-ouret in the Royal Funerary Texts
Loriane Bussien
University of Geneva

Innovative Strength of Middle Kingdom Tomb Decoration – the Meketre Project
Lubica Zelenkova Hudakova
University of Vienna

A Survey of some unpublished Roman demotic papyri in the collection of the Austrian National Library, Vienna
Luigi Prada
University of Oxford

What is the Tale of Woe?
Luke McGarrity
University of Birmingham

The Lion in Pre-and Early Dynastic Egypt – Power and Glory?
Lyn Stagg
Independent Researcher

The Stela of Nebet-Kebeny CG 34117
Maha Yehia
University of Menofiya

Dates and Precursors of the Opet Festival
Masashi Fukaya
University of Oxford

Votive Shabtis of the Twenty-Fifth Dynasty
Meg Gundlach
University of Swansea

New Discoveries from the Middle Kingdom
Mohammed Youssef Ali
Chief Inspector of Dashur and Lisht

The Ears Stelae Chronological Partition: for a New Understanding of the Personal Piety Development
Nathalie Toye
Ecole Pratique des Hautes Etudes

Beyond the Grave: New Kingdom Tombs at Saqqara, Egypt, as Shrines of Cultural Memory
Nico Staring
University of Leiden

Amarna Erasures in Theban Tombs and the Question of Monotheism
Paal Steiner
University of Bergen

Did Min really need all those lettuces?
Pauline Norris
University of Manchester

Cultural Hybridity as a Model for Cultural Change in New Kingdom Nubia: a Reassessment of Egypto-Nubian Relations
Paul van Pelt
University of Cambridge

The Perception of (Real) Place in the Middle Kingdom Coffin Texts
Peter Robinson
Independent Researcher

Tomb Security in the Early Dynastic Period
Reg Clark
University of Swansea

The Role and Position of Old Kingdom Royal Women in Times of Power Transition
Reinert Skumsnes
Independent Researcher

Two Steps Forward, One Step Back? Our Understanding of the Egyptian Verbal System
Rob Persson
University of Oxford

The Recorded Solar Eclipse of Nectanebo I
Rosalind Park
Independent Researcher

Kerma Culture? Regional variation in the funerary practice of Bronze Age Nubia *c.* 2500–1500BCE
Ruth Humphreys
University of Leicester

The Khopesh: a New Kingdom Saga of Trade, Interconnectivity and Adaptation of Technology
Sarah Shepherd
University of Exeter

The Role of the *Iwn-mwt.f* in the New Kingdom monuments of Thebes
Steven Gregory
University of Birmingham

Gender and Power Relations: a Revision of the Role of Queenship during the Coregency of Hatshepsut and Tuthmose III (*c.* 1479–1458BC)
Virginia Laporta
University of Buenos Aires

Poster Presentations

Nomes – their Origins, Development and Significance
Andrew Fulton
Independent Researcher

Rankin: Ship Merchant, Philanthropist and "Friend of Many"
Anna Garnett
University of Liverpool

Ancient Egypt in Tahrir Square, January 2011
Fatma Keshk and Monica Hanna
Library of Alexandria and Humboldt University Berlin

Creatures Compartmentalised: Bronze Boxes for Sacred Animal Remains in the British Museum
Jen Thum
University of Oxford

The Perception of (Real) Place in the Middle Kingdom Coffin Texts
Peter Robinson
Independent Researcher

Hidden Astronomy in the Twin-Stelae of Naukratis
Rosalind Park
Independent Researcher

Introduction

The thirteenth Current Research in Egyptology (CRE) Conference was held in March 2012 at the University of Birmingham, ten years after the Institute of Archaeology and Antiquity had previously organised the event. During one week of exceptionally warm weather and ample supplies of doughnuts, over 130 academics, students, alumni, and independent scholars congregated in Birmingham from many UK Egyptological institutions as well as fourteen international countries, covering six continents. They were greeted, during the week, with 62 presentations and six posters covering all aspects of current research in modern Egyptology; papers ranged from Predynastic iconography and architecture to an analysis of Pharaonic culture in the Arabic Middle Ages.

This year's CRE was also fortunate to have three key-note speeches. Delegates were welcomed by Dr Martin Bommas (University of Birmingham) on the first evening by a presentation of his on-going research at the Middle Egyptian site of Beni Hassan, with the mysterious title of 'Talking about the dash'. This intriguing research focuses on the lifetimes of the individuals buried at Beni Hassan, very often alluded to on modern tomb stones by a simple '~' between dates. Christopher Naunton visited the conference from The Egypt Exploration Society (EES), shortly after his promotion to director to talk about his recent travels around Egypt and how the EES is working to make Egyptology more accessible, not just to those based in the UK, but also those further afield – particularly in Egypt itself. The conference was brought to an end by Dr Tony Leahy (University of Birmingham) with a fascinating insight into his current research about a high priest of Heliopolis in the seventh century BC.

Needless to say that the theme expressed by the three key-note speakers, and also the papers in this publication is 'current research', and all of the papers presented at this year's CRE fitted well with the ethos upon which the conference is based.

This volume is therefore representative of the papers that were offered between the 27th and 30th March 2012 and it is hoped that they will continue to contribute to further current research in Egyptology.

This volume of CRE 2012 contains twelve papers from scholars studying across the UK and Europe, and it is with great thanks to Oxbow Books that it has been possible to once again publish the CRE conference proceedings.

Kelly Accetta (University of Cambridge) uses the iconographic representations of the Opet festival from Theban monuments of the Eighteenth and Nineteenth Dynasties to assess the extent to which public access to the divine differed during the period in question.

Joanne Backhouse (University of Liverpool) looks at fertility figurines from Deir el-Medina, discussing their context and form. She notes the challenges faced when relying largely on early excavation reports, comparing her own findings with those of the earlier Egyptologists, and drawing conclusions about the purpose and significance of these varied objects.

Renate Fellinger (University of Cambridge) puts forward the hypothesis that ancient Egyptian love poems represent literary landscapes which were created by the authors' own perceptions and experiences of contemporary life and aims to examine what the love poems can contribute towards the study of the role of women in society *via* phenomenology.

Rita Gautschy (University of Basel) uses chronological data from Assyrian, Babylonian and Hittite chronological data to propose a new dating scheme for the Egyptian New Kingdom. As many chronologies already circulate in Egyptological literature, Gautschy attempts to contribute some new data from astronomical events to the discussion.

Carl Graves (University of Birmingham) attempts to contribute some geoarchaeological evidence to the location of ancient Neferusi in Middle Egypt, only to succeed in clouding the discussion further.

Simon Hawkins (Swansea University) explores the nature of the marshman through their appearance in Middle Kingdom literature, in texts such as *The Pleasures of Fishing and Fowling* and *The Eloquent Peasant.* The exact role and social standing of the marshman is often thought difficult to attribute however, by studying these texts Hawkins aims to better understand the marshman's complex relationship with Egyptian society.

Joost Kramer (Universiteit Leiden) discusses a largely neglected area of Egyptological and Arabic studies by examining several Arabic scholars and studying the variety of themes within them. He uses these sources to demonstrate the extent to which the Pharonic past was incorporated and used in Islamic Egypt, arguing that medieval Egyptians had a somewhat ambiguous view of the Pharonic past.

Emily Marlow (University of Manchester) presents her preliminary results arising from data collected from adult skeletal remains housed at the Peabody Museum of Archaeology and Ethnology at Harvard University. Her analysis focuses on the accuracy of modern sex determination techniques, namely morphological or metric assessment of the skeleton, when applied to this collection of remains.

Emily Millward (University of Birmingham) examines a series of decorative images of children within funeral processions during the New Kingdom in order to establish the gestures of grief adopted by Egyptian children. The extent to which these actions were similar to the gestures adopted by adult mourners is discussed and the interaction of children with their adult companions is examined.

Sarah Musselwhite (University of Cambridge) investigates the effects of state formation and social status on the health of several early Egyptian populations, using data collected from skeletal remains. The conclusion suggests that overall health improved after the initial introduction of agriculture, however a decline in health during the later Predynastic Period may have being due to the negative effects of increasing population density caused by urbanisation.

Rune Olsen (University of Copenhagen) studies the roles and responsibilities of the Medjay leaders during the New Kingdom, to investigate whether previous assertions for them being 'policemen' are unfounded.

Daniel Soliman (Universiteit Leiden) examines the marks ostraca found in the Theban necropolis in the Eighteenth Dynasty, discussing how they can be used to enlighten scholars about the working practices of the men who built the royal tombs. He notes the importance of the content, style and presentation of the pieces in creating a fuller picture of the lives and administration of these men in the pre-Ramesside period.

This year's CRE conference could not have been possible without the hard work and support of the staff in the Institute of Archaeology and Antiquity, College of Arts and Law at the University of Birmingham; particularly for providing the necessary funding and venues required for the event. Specific thanks are made to Dr Martin Bommas and Dr Tony Leahy for their continued support, encouragement and their presentations, Mr Graham Norrie for the provision of display materials and Ms Sue Bowen for her financial guidance and advice, also to Mr Steven Gregory for his tireless efforts during both the conference and the editing for this volume. Our express gratitude goes out to The Egypt Exploration Society for their financial support, particularly to Dr Christopher Naunton for his enthralling key-note speech. Our thanks also go out to all of those publishers that donated and came to the conference: Oxbow Books, Ancient Egypt Magazine, Brepols, Oxford University Press and Archaeopress. Once again our appreciation also goes to Oxbow Books for agreeing to publish this year's Current Research in Egyptology conference and particularly to Ms Clare Litt for her instruction and direction. Finally, on behalf of the committee, we would like to thank all of those delegates who attended the conference, particularly those who presented their research, and we sincerely hope that CRE continues to grow as an international conference in future years.

Carl Graves
Birmingham, October 2012

1

Access to the Divine in New Kingdom Egypt: Royal and Public Participation in the Opet Festival

Kelly Accetta

Access to the divine is the ability for people to have direct contact with their god(s) spiritually and/or physically. In ancient Egypt, it is most often seen in relation to funerary religion, in the intimate nature between the gods and individuals, regardless of status, in their journey into the afterlife. This connection does not apply to the gods of the living, who are often depicted in art and texts as the exclusive companions of the king. It is to the benefit of the ruler to control access to the divine in order to promote themselves as the sole intermediary between the gods and mankind and substantiate their political power. In ancient Egypt, this practice resulted in a distinct divide between state religion and domestic religion. Despite this divide, state religion did not always prevent the public from access to the divine, but rather presented a structured environment in which access was allowed and encouraged.

The Opet Festival, celebrated in the New Kingdom (*c*. 1550–1069 BC), provides a unique opportunity to determine the impact of state religious rituals on public access to the divine. Officially commissioned depictions of the festival show potential occasions for direct contact with the gods, additional inscriptional and pictorial evidence seems to demand the presence of an audience for the success of a festival, and the processional route of the festival ran directly through the sacred landscape of the town of Thebes (Fig. 1.1). In this paper I will investigate how access to the divine during the Opet Festival developed over the New Kingdom by examining opportunities for public participation in the festival.

Access to the divine

It is important to note that in ancient Egypt, access to the divine includes many facets which would not fit into modern religions' interpretation of access. Egyptian religion believed that the gods were capable of physically manifesting in cult statues located at the heart of their temples, and access to temple and the god was restricted to priests, the king, and royally approved guests (Baines 1991, 183). In a theory put forward by Barry Kemp (1995, 45–6), it is suggested that the temples and shrines of the gods were not always closed off to the public: this restriction of access developed during the Old Kingdom with the establishment of formal state temples, and was enforced throughout pharaonic times. Without access to the temples, the people developed household shrines to 'domestic gods', and little evidence survives of public worship of state deities (Baines 1987, 82).

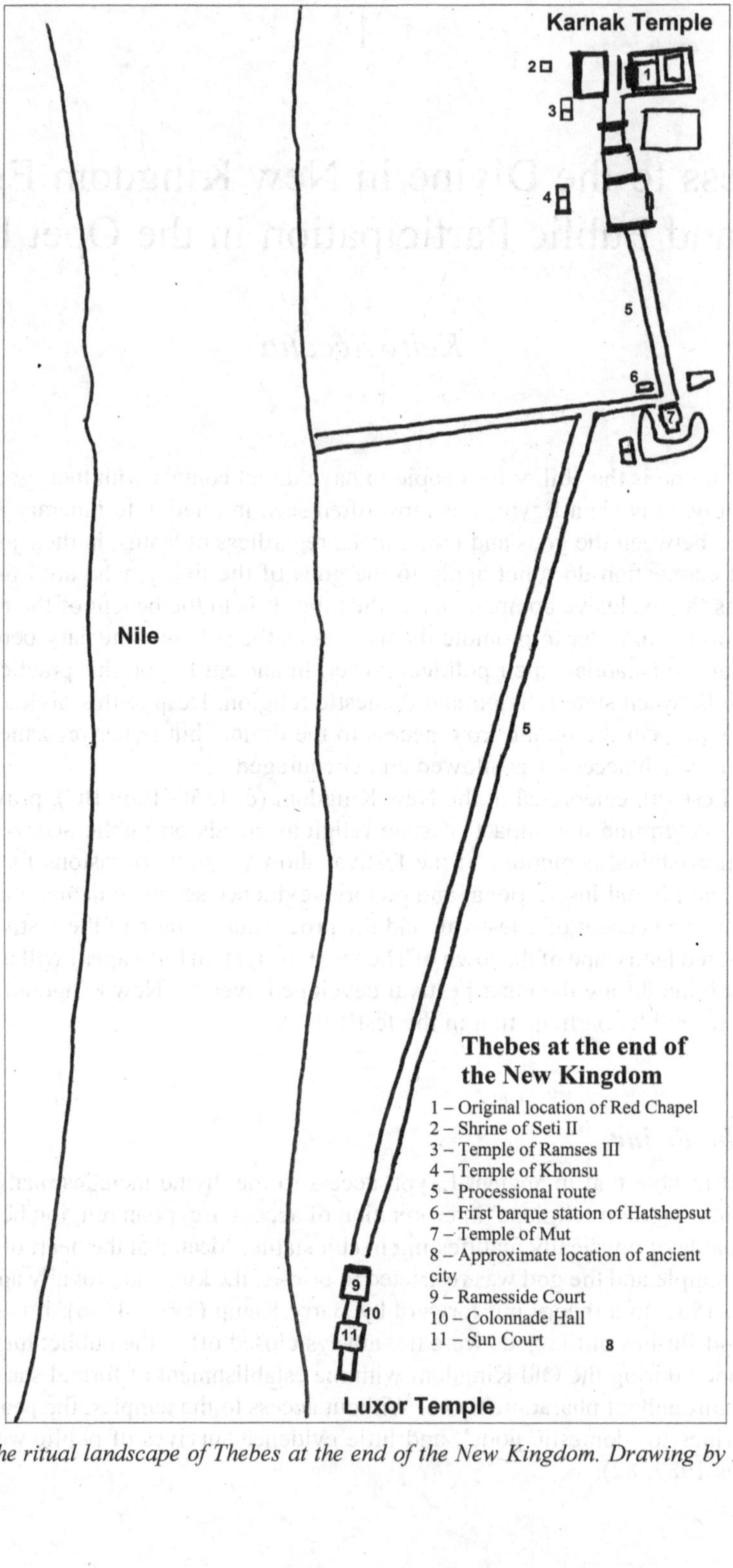

Figure 1.1: The ritual landscape of Thebes at the end of the New Kingdom. Drawing by Kelly Accetta.

A development in the New Kingdom, which scholars refer to as a 'rise in personal piety', shows a distinct change in the desire for public access to state gods (Baines 1991, 179). In the city of Amarna, objects in the form of the traditional state gods were found in both elite and workmen's residences, and chapels from the workmen's village contained stelae and painted imagery addressing state gods (Kemp 1995, 30). Small temple-shrines to Amun, Ptah, Hathor, and the deified Ramses II at the workmen's village of Deir el-Medina contained their own cult statues (Lesko 1994, 90). These were paraded through the village on feast days and consulted by the people through local oracle priests (Lesko 1994, 93).

Most significantly, at Karnak Temple – the state temple of Amun-Re and the largest in Egypt – two small temples built on the outer eastern wall of the complex may have been open to members of the public for prayer. The contra-temple of Tuthmosis III contains a statue of the king seated with Amun-Re; it is referred to as the 'chapel of the hearing ear' (Blyth 2006, 89). This title recalls New Kingdom stelae which were carved with ears and believed to persuade the gods to listen to the petition written on the stela by the worshipper (Baines 1991, 181). In the case of the chapel, the petitioner was physically present and presented his prayers to the 'ear' of the god, in this case the pharaoh was represented by his statue. Later in the Nineteenth Dynasty, Ramses II built a free-standing temple further to the east, which scholars believe served a similar purpose to the contra-temple of Tuthmosis III. In the interior was a false door, which perhaps served to link public petitioners to the sacred shrine of Amun-Re inside the temple, akin to traditional false doors in tombs (Blyth 2006, 159–60). Offerings and petitions made at the door would reach Amun-Re inside his shrine, just as offerings and prayers made by caretakers of the tomb would reach the dead in the underworld.

Returning to my initial point, access to the divine was achieved in several ways in ancient Egypt, all of which must be considered while attempting to determine the opportunities for access to the divine in the Opet Festival. This includes: proximity to the god's statue or the god's barque, either whilst at rest or in procession, public participation in the processions or aspects of religious rituals, or as witness to these rituals, oracular consultation or petitioning of the god whilst at rest or in procession, public access to locations which served as 'hearing ear' or 'false door' connections to the god, public access to the interior of state temples normally off-limits, and finally proximity to, petitioning of, or participation/witnessing of ritual activity concerning the pharaoh, who was the intermediary between the god and mankind. This final point becomes important in the New Kingdom, as the role and powers of the king conflated with those of the god.

The Opet Festival

The Opet Festival was a celebration of renewal centring on the king and Amun-Re. The god rose to prominence in the Egyptian pantheon in the Middle Kingdom, accompanied by an ever-expanding temple complex in the city of Thebes, modern-day Luxor (Wilkinson 2003, 92). As the prominence of the god increased, so did his relationship with the king: by the New Kingdom Amun-Re's temple at Karnak in Thebes was the largest non-royal landholder and was in a constant state of construction as kings strove to out-do their predecessors in honouring the god (Wilkinson 2001, 50). In return, the god granted the king life and dominion over his empire, and legitimised his reign by acknowledging the king as both an intermediary to the gods and as a god himself (Kitchen 2008, 157). This legitimisation occurred daily in private ritual, but also in public rituals – the Opet Festival was one of these.

The Opet Festival may have arisen as early as the Eleventh Dynasty, but its first surviving recorded performance was not until the Eighteenth Dynasty (Darnell 2010, 1–2). Calendrical texts show the festival occurred in the second month of Akhet, coinciding with the annual mid-summer inundation, the re-fertilization of the lands along the Nile (El-Sabban 2000, 29). Just as the Nile's flood reenergized the lands, so too did the Opet Festival renew the powers of the king. Although textual evidence discussing the purpose of the festival does not survive, texts and pictorial evidence found in temples and tombs records Amun-Re's promise to grant the king life, health, prosperity, and dominion over the enemies of Egypt in return for his faithful service, offerings, and monuments to the god (Kitchen 1993, 183; 2008, 157).

From these sources, scholars are able to piece together some of the activities which occurred during the festival. Nineteenth Dynasty reliefs in the great Hypostyle Hall at Karnak depict the king offering to Amun and censing the barque of the god inside the temple (Kitchen 1999, 391). Then the barque, accompanied by the barque of his consort Mut and their son Khonsu depart south upon the Nile headed for Luxor Temple, where additional reliefs of the festival survive in the Colonnade Hall (Epigraphic Survey 1936, pl. 84; 1994, pl. 17). In reliefs commissioned at Karnak in the Eighteenth Dynasty by Hatshepsut, this journey is made over land along a processional route lined with barque stations (Burgos and Larché 2006, 46–53). Priests carry the barque of Amun-Re while the queen follows behind, censing the barque when it is at rest in each station (Fig. 1.2).

After the barque(s) arrived in Luxor Temple, more offerings were given (Fig. 1.3) and the rituals of renewal performed. While pictorial evidence related directly to the Opet Festival does not depict these rituals, reliefs inside Luxor Temple, where the rituals were performed, indicate they may have included a re-coronation of the king (Fig. 1.4) (Bell 1985, 273; Porter and Moss 1972, 321–4). It is likely that several other rituals were performed during this part of the festival; it is known from textual evidence that the entire festival lasted between eleven days during the reign of Tuthmosis III up to twenty-seven days during the reign of Ramses III,

Figure 1.2: Hatshepsut censing the barque of Amun at rest in a barque station along the processional route. Photo by Kelly Accetta.

Figure 1.3: King censing and offering to the barques of Amun, Khonsu, and Mut at Luxor Temple. Photo by Kelly Accetta.

and the processions between the temples would not have lasted more than a day each (Sethe 1907, 824; Grandet 1994, 89).

After the completion of these rituals the barque(s) emerged from Luxor Temple and were loaded onto river barges by priests. The divine barge of Amun, the *Userhat*, was towed by the barge of the king whilst the others followed in a flotilla bound for Karnak (Epigraphic Survey 1994, pl. 68). Upon landing, further offerings were made to the gods and the king performed other renewal rituals, including the running of the bull as seen in Hatshepsut's reliefs – a ritual associated with the *sed* festival, another festival which focused on the renewal of the king's power and life force (Burgos and Larché 2006, 62–3; Gillam 2005, 29). At the completion of these rituals, the gods' statues were returned to their shrines until they again processed in other festivals, such as the Beautiful Festival of the Valley, a funerary festival whose origins reach back to the establishment of the temple of Amun-Re at Karnak in the Middle Kingdom (Gillam 2005, 78).

Figure 1.4: Coronation of Amenhotep III by Amun in Luxor Temple. Photo by Kelly Accetta.

It is relevant to note that despite the difference between the festivals, examining known participation in the Beautiful Festival of the Valley and other Middle Kingdom funerary festivals helps to target where and when public participation would be most likely to occur. Regardless of the Opet Festival being a celebration of the cult of the living king while the Beautiful Festival of the Valley celebrated the cult of the deceased king and his ancestors, they both occurred in Thebes and would have involved the same population. Inscriptional evidence from Deir el-Medina suggests that the villagers followed the procession of the barque of Amun-Re after it arrived by barge to the West Bank during the Beautiful Festival of the Valley (Lesko 1994, 91). This would have been an opportunity for oracular consultation with Amun-Re as well as other gods who participated in the festival as they were carried from their shrines in barques amongst the townspeople (Lesko 1994, 91). Some texts indicate it was the movement of the barque which indicated the god's answer to petitions (Karlshausen 2009, 296–7).

Another funerary festival at Abydos celebrated the state god Osiris, lord of the underworld (O'Connor 2009, 91). Despite his initial association with the deceased king, democratization of funerary religion in the Middle Kingdom led to the belief that all deceased became 'Osirises' after death, and the god became important for those seeking to successfully reach the afterlife (Gillam 2005, 55). Records of the actual procession and festival are fragmented, found on stelae erected on either side of the processional route, but do note non-royal participation in the festival, which was a type of re-enactment (Gillam 2005, 57–8). The stela of Ikhernofret, treasurer under pharaoh Senwosret III, boasts that he played a part in the re-creation of the myth of the death and resurrection of Osiris (Lichtheim 1975, 123–125). From these texts, we can hypothesize that privileged elites were the likely actors in a performance which would have required an audience. Whether there was a live audience is not known, but it is known that members of the public also sought participate in and benefit from the festival. Along the processional route other stelae and chapels were dedicated by individuals of varying socio-economic status as cenotaphs, empty representations of tombs, permanent attendees through which the owners might benefit from the funerary cult of Osiris in perpetuity (O'Connor 2009, 93, 96).

Public participation in these festivals, either by building chapels or following the procession, reveals that the democratization of funerary religion did not necessarily provide direct access to the gods. Attendance at these festivals may suggest people were restricted to directly accessing the divine via these public events. It makes sense then, that they would continue to seek to access the divine at state festivals in the New Kingdom.

Additionally, the king may have used the very performative festival to strengthen his political and religious role in the eyes of his subjects. In order for this legitimisation to be successful, the performance of the festival needed to be public; it required an audience as witness. This need for an audience provided opportunities for access to the divine. Despite a lack of textual or pictorial evidence explicitly testifying to public access to the divine during the Opet Festival, comparisons of depictions of the festival, inscriptions adorning the temples involved in the festival, and the archaeological evidence for the landscape of the sacred processional routes shows public access to the divine in the Opet Festival not only existed but increased over the course of the New Kingdom.

Depictions of the Opet Festival

Depictions of the Opet Festival are largely restricted to the processions between Karnak and Luxor which flanked the event – less than ten percent of the whole festival, but the best opportunity for public access to the divine. While some depictions exist in elite tombs, most are officially commissioned reliefs at Karnak or Luxor Temple. It is important to look at these depictions with a critical eye, as the purpose of officially commissioned temple artwork was to enable ritual and festival to symbolically be perfectly performed in perpetuity. They did not often depict how an event actually occurred, or even the actual people who participated in them; this is known from the ritual reliefs in every temple in Egypt depicting the king performing every daily ritual for every god – a physical impossibility. What is helpful about this 'idealized' representation of events for the Opet Festival is that the Egyptians would have attempted to perform the ritual in exactly that way in order to honour the god properly. The depiction of the order and location of the events is likely to be accurate.

In a relatively new artistic convention for the period, the reliefs depict a narrative instead of the traditional static representation of ritual or worshiping scenes (Gaballa 1976, 139). Although it is doubtful that any of the Opet scenes depict a specific festival, they are intended to represent an actual progression of events (Gaballa 1976, 89). This is achieved by what Gaballa refers to as either the 'culminating scene' or the 'multiple scenes' technique. In the 'culminating scene', the most important part of the narrative is chosen to represent the whole, usually due to a lack of space. The 'multiple scenes' technique shows episodes of the event in progression from beginning to end, and appears to be preferred over the 'culminating scene' technique when space permitted. Like traditional scenes of worship within the temples, narrative scenes often highlighted the participation of the king and the gods, while diminishing or eliminating the real-life presence of priests, spectators, and other participants (Gaballa 1976, 140).

Three reliefs embody the above narrative techniques, and present the best opportunities for interpreting opportunities for public access to the divine throughout the New Kingdom. The first relief, which was commissioned by Hatshepsut for her Red Chapel in the Eighteenth Dynasty, employed the 'multiple scenes' technique and was located in Karnak Temple (Burgos and Larché 2006). The second was commissioned by Tutankhamun during the Eighteenth Dynasty, continued by his successors Ay and Horemheb, and completed by Seti I in the Nineteenth Dynasty (Epigraphic Survey, 1994). It also employed the 'multiple scenes' technique and is located in Luxor Temple. The final relief was commissioned in the Twentieth Dynasty by Ramses III; it utilized the 'culminating scene' technique and is also located in Karnak Temple (Epigraphic Survey, 1936).

Hatshepsut's Red Chapel Reliefs

These earliest reliefs are probably the most informative pictorial source concerning the activities during the Opet Festival (Darnell 2010, 2). They are located on Hatshepsut's Red Chapel, which is currently reconstructed in the Open Air Museum at Karnak, but would have originally stood at the heart of the temple complex. It housed the barque of Amun-Re and was aligned on the central east-west axis of the temple (Blyth 2006, 53). Various depictions of the queen and her co-regent Tuthmosis III worshipping the gods decorate the interior and exterior of the chapel, but the two largest and most significant depictions are the narrative reliefs on the north and south exterior walls (Burgos and Larché 2006). The north wall depicted the Beautiful Festival of the Valley, while the south wall depicted the Opet Festival. In both reliefs, the narrative is shown through successive episodes depicted in registers. The registers are read from the bottom of the chapel to the top, although several registers at the top and bottom of each side are not a part of the festival reliefs.

A helpful aspect of narrative art is its accuracy in orientation (Gaballa 1976, 50). The direction of travel is accurate for both festivals, but in different ways. The physical orientation of the Red Chapel caused the departing vessels for the Beautiful Festival of the Valley to face west along the north wall, while the returning flotilla faces east. Physically, the departing and returning processions for the Opet Festival also face west then east, which is contrary to the actual festival routes. However, whilst the Beautiful Festival of the Valley could have been depicted on either side without issue, the Opet Festival was specifically rendered on the south exterior face of the chapel, orienting it to face Luxor and the festival route. Kate Spence's study on symbolic orientation of temples (1998, 130) found that minor temples were always subordinate to the orientation of major temples, even if cosmologically, or here simply logically, the orientation seemed incorrect. As the Red Chapel was subordinate to Karnak Temple, it physically oriented itself parallel, but during the Opet Festival it symbolically oriented itself according to Luxor Temple – south – rendering orientation of the reliefs correct.

This accuracy in orientation also helps to confirm the physical locations of several sites implied in the registers of the reliefs, as indicators of 'place' are rarely found in art at this time – narrative or otherwise (Gaballa 1976, 140). The third register begins on the right/physical east/symbolic north, which would place the king censing the barque of Amun-Re in Karnak Temple (Burgos and Larché 2006, 49). From there, the scenes depict the procession to Luxor Temple: they alternate between the barque in procession and the barque resting in the six known barque stations of Hatshepsut along the processional route (Burgos and Larché 2006, 46–53). As this depiction shows the procession occurring on land, the barque is carried by priests, who are followed by Hatshepsut and Tuthmosis III. Each shrine is flanked by Osiride statues of Hatshepsut and the barque is shown resting inside while the king(s) alone cense(s) the shrine (Fig. 1. 2). No other spectators or participants are depicted.

In the fourth register, Hatshepsut and Tuthmosis III are depicted presenting offerings to Amun-Re and his ithyphallic counterpart, Amun-Re-Kamutef (Burgos and Larché 2006, 56–58). The location of these episodes post-procession indicates that these are the rituals conducted inside Luxor Temple. It is in these episodes that the scale between the gods and the kings is most apparent (Fig. 1.5). In Egyptian art, scale is often used to show status, with equal size indicating equal status. The gods and the kings in all of these episodes are of equal scale, whilst the earlier episodes of the priests and the kings show the priests as smaller than Hatshepsut and Tuthmosis III. If Hatshepsut had herself and Tuthmosis III ideologically depicted as the equal of Amun-Re – divine – then perhaps the public also viewed the kings as gods. Their presence in the procession would have been another opportunity for access to the divine via proximity to the king.

The fifth register depicts the returning water journey to Karnak and the rituals performed there, including Hatshepsut performing the 'Running of the bull' (Burgos and Larché 2006, 60–3). This is an event associated with the *sed* Festival of the king, another festival of renewal also performed to revitalize his ruling power (Gillam 2005, 29). Finally, musicians and dancers celebrate the barque's return to Karnak. This unique scene depicts figures other than the kings, the gods, or the priests who carry the barque (Burgos and Larché 2006, 64). Although these dancers and musicians were likely employees of the temple, this one episode indicates that there were participants involved in the festival outside the kings and the priests (Epigraphic Survey 1994,

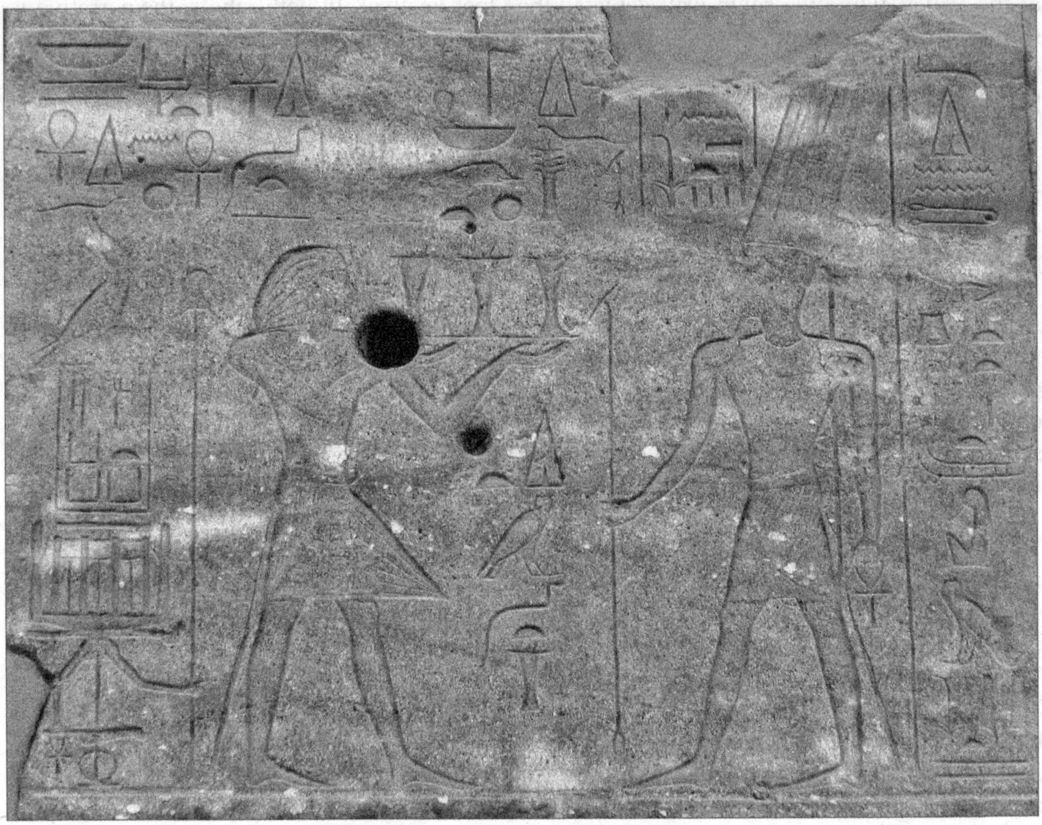

Figure 1.5: Hatshepsut offering to Amun, accompanied by her divinized ka figure. Photo by Kelly Accetta.

18–19). The sixth and final register depicts Hatshepsut and Tuthmosis III making offerings to the gods of the Theban pantheon (Burgos and Larché 2006, 68–73). Again, the register's post-processional order indicates that these rituals were performed inside Karnak Temple.

The over-land procession would provide several opportunities for access to the divine. The parade-like performance which occurred during the processions indicates the presence of an audience, the most obvious of which would be the population of Thebes, normally restricted from physical access to the king or the cult statue. During the procession, oracular petitioning of the god in his barque may have occurred, just as at Deir el-Medina. While stopping at the barque stations, the public may have had an opportunity to approach the shrine with petitions for the gods or priests as well. For many people standing along the processional route, this may have been the closest they had ever been to the god, his barque, and the king.

Luxor Temple Colonnade Opet Reliefs

Due to the larger wall space and to the artistic advancements of the Amarna Era, the reliefs commissioned by Tutankhamun for Luxor Temple are far more detailed than those of the Red Chapel. Narrative art intensified under the Amarna emphasis on realism and experience, with burgeoning detail in persons and locations involved in the events (Gaballa 1976, 139). This inclusion of non-royal, non-essential detail reveals new opportunity for public access to the divine not depicted before. The reliefs are located on the interior walls of the Colonnade Hall of Luxor Temple, which served as the main entrance to the temple from its construction by Amenhotep III until the additions of Ramses II. The reliefs themselves were commissioned and cartooned under Tutankhamun, and completed by Ay, Horemheb, and Seti I (Epigraphic Survey 1994, xvii). This shared depiction may reflect continuity in the performance of the festival from the end of the Eighteenth to the beginning of the Nineteenth Dynasties.

The reliefs are divided into ten episodes, depicted on the east and west walls of the Colonnade Hall (Fig. 1.6). They run north-south along the hall's axis, again paralleling the north-south orientation of the actual festival, as well as flanking the procession itself when it entered Luxor Temple (Epigraphic Survey 1994, xviii). The west wall contains episodes one through five progressing north to south, and the east contains episodes six through ten progressing south to north. The north and south walls include depictions of the king offering to Amun-Re and Mut inside Karnak on the north wall (Epigraphic Survey 1994, pls 3, 54) and inside Luxor on the south wall (Epigraphic Survey 1994, pls 52, 119).

Episode one depicts the pharaoh censing the barques of Amun, Mut, Khonsu, and the king inside Karnak Temple (Epigraphic Survey1994, pl. 5). In episode two, the barques are carried from the temple, which is represented by a depiction of the third pylon, to the Nile (Epigraphic Survey 1994, 7, pl. 12). Episode three depicts the barques, now loaded onto river barges, sailing and being towed upstream (Epigraphic Survey 1994, pl. 17). Here, the king's barge leads the procession, followed by the *Userhat*, the queen's barge, and the barges of Mut and Khonsu. Accompanying the barges on the riverbank are soldiers, dancers, musicians, and priests. Episode

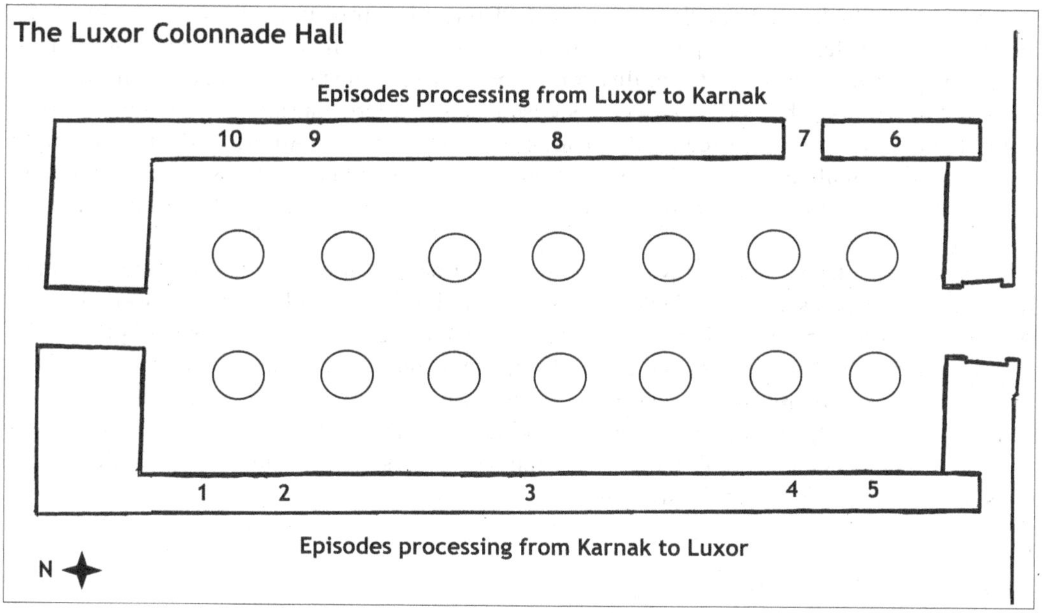

Figure 1.6: The arrangement of the scenes in the Colonnade Hall mirror the direction of the festival itself. Drawing by Kelly Accetta.

Figure 1.7: Soldiers marching, Asiatics with clapping sticks, and priests clapping in procession to Luxor Temple. Photo by Kelly Accetta.

four depicts the barques on land again, being carried from the quay into the temple of Luxor, which is represented by the portal to the Colonnade Hall (Epigraphic Survey 1994, 19, pl. 36). The fifth episode mimics the first, except that the pharaoh censes only the barques of Amun, Mut, and Khonsu, now inside Luxor Temple (Epigraphic Survey1994, pl. 43). On the east wall, the episodes are essentially identical to one through five, only they are reversed in the returning procession to Karnak (Epigraphic Survey 1994, pls 108, 101, 68, 63, 56).

The choice to depict both the departing and returning processions on the water likely indicates that the festival was performed more often on water than on the processional land route. This would cut down on the ability for people to access the procession, as the flotilla was restricted to royalty. The god's barque was ensconced in a large shrine, and the king himself would have been difficult to see on the boat, even close to shore. Additionally, people might have found it difficult to stand on the shore to watch, as the secondary procession accompanying the tow-lines would have paraded near the water's edge so that the tow ropes did not catch on any obstructions.

However, the depiction also reveals a new form of participation in the festival itself. These secondary participants were residents of Thebes – soldiers, manual labourers, rowers, bakers, butchers, dancers, foreigners (Fig. 1.7) – not all of whom were in the permanent employ of the temple with regular access to sacred areas. Their inclusion may indicate a rise in the need for audience participation for the success of the festival, and their presence may have been implicit support of the ideology of legitimisation of the king which the festival celebrated. Whatever the reason for its inclusion in the festival, this secondary procession was an increase in the access to the divine via participation in divine ritual.

Opet Relief of Ramses III

The final relief in this study is from the Twentieth Dynasty, on the west exterior wall of a small temple built by Ramses III located inside the first court at Karnak. At the time of its construction the temple actually sat outside of Karnak's walls, between the Nile and Karnak itself (Blyth 2006, 172). It has a north-south axis, as does the procession in the Opet Festival, and the relief is correctly oriented south toward Luxor. The relief itself contains one long episode in an example of the 'culminating scene' technique; it depicts the *Userhat* and the barges of the king, Mut, and Khonsu as they approach the quay at Luxor Temple (Epigraphic Survey 1936, pl. 84).

The artistic conventions of the Amarna Era have faded slightly in this Ramesside period relief. While the emphasis on realism and experience continues in the inclusion and detail of the numerous boats in the flotilla, there are no markers of location and no examples of audience members. It is simple, in the fact that it includes only the main actors and is a single scene which would have been recognizable by the viewer as a ritual flotilla. The textual accompaniment is the only indication that this is the initial procession to Luxor, and not the returning procession to Karnak (Kitchen 2008, 155). As such, it is difficult to discern any opportunities for access to the divine from the illustration itself.

The simplicity of the relief combined with its large size seems especially bizarre considering Gaballa notes that the 'multiple scenes' technique was almost always used when space allowed (1976, 140). However, other large, simple narrative reliefs found in similar locations during the Ramesside period – on the exterior walls and pylons of temples such as Karnak and Medinet Habu – may hold the reason for this artistic choice. These imposing illustrations were meant for public viewing and understanding, hence their large size and simple theme. It is possible, then, that the exterior location of the Ramses III small temple combined with its large west-facing Opet Relief indicates that this may have been a location of public gathering and viewing before the flotilla embarked.

This physical evidence is the only support the Ramses III relief gives about public access to the divine. As I mentioned above, the official commissioning of all three reliefs means that the event portrayed was the ideal performance of the festival. It almost certainly did not portray the event as it actually happened. In order to get a more comprehensive understanding, these reliefs must be compared with other textual, pictorial, and archaeological evidence of the Opet Festival.

Additional textual and pictorial evidence

Despite the fact that all Opet Festival reliefs, including the ones examined above, focus almost exclusively on the processions between Karnak and Luxor Temples, these two events made up less than ten percent of the entire festival. Additional textual and pictorial evidence in and about the events which took place at Luxor Temple must be examined in order to understand whether the public were able to access the divine during this portion of the festival as well. Lanny Bell's studies of Luxor Temple (1985; 1997) have revealed ample inscriptional evidence which points to the inclusion of an audience during some of the rituals which are depicted on reliefs within the temple. Other inscriptional evidence outside of the temple also indicates an opportunity for public access to the divine during this part of the festival.

Bell asserts that Luxor Temple may have been built specifically to celebrate the cult of the king through the revitalization of the royal *ka*, or divine spirit, during celebrations of ritual such as the Opet Festival (1985, 251–2). Reliefs inside the temple dating to the reign of Amenhotep III include the divine conception and birth of the king, the coronation of the king, and the renewal of his kingship in the *sed* Festival (Bell 1985, 255, Porter and Moss 1972, 321–4, 326–8). These reliefs all feature Amun-Re and the Theban pantheon creating, imbuing, and renewing the king's divine power and right to the throne. Re-enactments of one or all of these events may have occurred during the Opet Festival, as depicted inside the central barque shrine, as well as offering to the gods as depicted in other wall reliefs (Bell 1985, 255, 281). This pictorial evidence supports Bell's hypothesis that it was during this time that the pharaoh's divine soul, or *ka*, was renewed by Amun, re-proclaiming him the legitimate sovereign and a god on Earth (Bell 1985, 267). Of course, without a witness to this event, these renewals of legitimisation convince no-one. The need for an audience here is crucial and perhaps it is no coincidence that there is a rise in public participation in the pictorial and inscriptional records of the post-Amarna era.

The inscription in the Sun Court of Amenhotep III at Luxor describes the temple as 'the palace [...] from which he goes forth in joy at the (proper) time of his appearance (as king) [...], his transformations [...] being in every face (i.e. visible to everyone)' (Bell 1985, 254). In the building inscription of Amenhotep III, he speaks of a *maru*, or viewing platform, constructed around the same location (Helck 1957, 1651–1652). Combined with the known ritual acts of renewal which occur during the festival inside the temple, this inscription may indicate that after the successful rejuvenation of the king, he appeared to his subjects in the Sun Court (Bell 1985, 273). There is also inscriptional evidence for members of the public entering the Sun Court along the portico to the south of the Sun Court: 'All low-lying lands and all highlands are at the feet of this vigorous god [...] whom all the gods love and all the *rekhyet* adore, that they might live' (Bell 1997, 170). The term *rekhyet* can be defined as 'common people', they are depicted within the inscription as lapwings with raised human arms, and there are references to them in other portions of the temple through which the public may have entered (Bell 1997, 172).

Additional evidence of this opportunity for access to the king comes from the coronation inscription of Horemheb, who used the Opet Festival as the occasion for his coronation (Gardiner 1953, 15). After the rites had been performed he was said to be 'going forth from the King's House [...] lo, the entire people was in joy and they cried aloud to heaven' (Gardiner 1953, 15), 'when it remained only for the common folk assembled outside to acclaim their new sovereign' (Gardiner 1953, 25). Horemheb had only tenuous ties to the crown, and so assumedly would need a large audience to prove his selection by Amun and his possession of the divine royal *ka* as he emerged from the inner rooms of Luxor Temple. This would have presented the public with access to the divine via proximity to the king, witnessing of a divine ritual, and access to the interior courts of the temple.

Evidence from the Ramesside period also indicates that members of the public entered the temple during the festival to communicate with Amun-Re. Ramses II constructed the new open-air Ramesside Court, north of the Colonnade Hall at Luxor Temple. We know that the people had access to this court thanks to inscriptions on a triple barque shrine and gate inside the court. An inscription names the doorway, called the 'People's Gate', 'The Great Gateway of the King of Upper and Lower Egypt Ramses II, Whom All the *Rekhyet* Adore That They May Live' (Fig. 1.8) (Bell 1997, 166). The barque shrine depicted *rekhyet* people and *pa'et* people, who were commoners and elites, worshipping Amun-Re while an inscription reads 'Adoring Amun-Re [...] by all the *rekhyet* (or *pa'et*), that they may live' (Fig. 1.9) (Bell 1997, 164). This inscriptional evidence appears to indicate that people entered the court through the People's Gate, and worshipped Amun-Re at the barque shrine.

Kenneth Griffin argues that it is dangerous to interpret these *rekhyet* people and *pa'et* images purely as designations of public areas. He notes that these symbols are seen inside the sanctuary of several temples, on inner doorways and pillars where the public was not permitted. He therefore believes that they are a metaphysical representation of a public presence before the

Figure 1.8: The inscribed name of the 'People's Gate', with depictions of rekhyet people worshipping below. Photo by Kelly Accetta.

Figure 1.9: The Triple Barque Shrine at Luxor; converted by Ramses II from Hatshepsut's Sixth Barque Station. Photo by Kelly Accetta.

god, and in the inner sanctuaries he is no doubt correct. However, he does note that inscriptional evidence indicating *rekhyet* presence, such as in the Triple Barque Shrine and the Sun Court, does not appear accompanying the symbols inside the sacred parts of the temples (Griffin 2007, 81). As most symbols gain their significance by representing real events, at some point people may have been permitted to enter certain locations decorated with the *rekhyet* symbol. Thus I suggest that at locations where the *rekhyet* symbols can be seen accompanied by inscriptional testimony to a public presence, it is likely that actual people were allowed into the temples to witness the spectacle of the Opet Festival.

The final piece of evidence for public access to the divine during this middle part of the festival is inside the Triple Barque Shrine. In the rear of the chapel of Amun-Re is a false door (Fig. 1.10), "a kind of divinely appointed 'telephone booth'", which enables Amun-Re to hear the prayers of petitioners while he is in his shrine at Luxor (Bell 1997, 168). This false door acts similarly to the contra-temple of Tuthmosis III and almost identically to the eastern temple of Ramses II, which also contained a false door. William Murnane surmises that the Ptolemaic-era door at the rear of the barque shrine at the heart of Luxor Temple may have originally been a New Kingdom false door (1985, 141; Porter and Moss 1972, 325). The god may have used these false doors as a means to move between the areas of his temple or to be present at the supplications of petitioners in the Triple Barque Shrine even when his cult statue rested in the sanctuary (Murnane 1985, 147–8). This 'hearing-ear' type shrine would have provided direct access to Amun-Re by the public gathered in the Ramesside Court.

At the very end of the festival route, Seti II constructed a triple barque shrine for Amun, Mut, and Khonsu (Blyth 2006, 166). This shrine was located outside of the second pylon, between Karnak Temple and the quay; it opened to the south, toward the returning procession. The inscription on the shrine designates it as 'a place of honouring and praying to all the gods', which may have meant that the public were allowed to approach the shrine when the barques were inside to consult the gods before they returned to their temples (Kitchen 2003, 180).

By examining Opet Festival reliefs and supplementary inscriptional and pictorial evidence, it becomes apparent that there were many opportunities throughout the festival for various types of access to the divine. The archaeological evidence for the development of Karnak and Luxor Temples and the processional route is the final aspect which ties together the changes in public access to the divine throughout the New Kingdom.

The archaeology of the Opet Festival

By the reign of Hatshepsut, the Middle Kingdom temple at Karnak built by Senwosret I still stood, and contained the shrine housing the statue of the god (Blyth 2006, 52–3). She erected the eighth pylon along the north-south processional route, a clear marker of the growing importance of the route itself (Blyth 2006, 60). The route itself would have cut through the ancient town of Thebes, which means people could have easily stood along the route or on rooftops to observe the festival (Strudwick and Strudwick 1999, 194). Along the processional route as can be seen in the Red Chapel reliefs, Hatshepsut erected six barque stations (Darnell 2010, 2). Although only the first and sixth stations survive, it is reasonably certain that the other four existed in similar form (Cabrol 2001, 536–7). These stations would have been exposed along the processional route, as the sphinxes seen today were not erected until later in the Eighteenth Dynasty, and there is no clear evidence for a barrier wall until the Ramesside Period (Blyth 2006, 112, 117–118).

Figure 1.10: A false door at the rear of the Triple Barque Shrine. Photo by Kelly Accetta.

As the route seems accessible, the above theory that the stations may have served as locations for public oracular consultation seems to be a likely option. Without clear boundaries, the public was probably able to get quite close to the procession, and the god's barque. Once the procession exited the eighth pylon, it is possible the crowds swarmed the processional route, attempting to touch the barque of the god or the Queen herself, just as modern day crowds surround a celebrity. If this was the case, barque stations may have served as refuges from the crowd, with the oracular consultations performed en-route.

At Luxor, very little remains to prove a temple of Hatshepsut existed save for columns re-used by Amenhotep III in his building of the core of Luxor Temple, as well as her sixth barque station which resided close enough to the temple that Ramses II incorporated it into his new Ramesside Court (Bell 1997, 147–8). Of course, the Red Chapel reliefs depict the kings offering to the gods at the end of the initial procession; presumably inside a temple closed off from the public just as was Karnak Temple. After the procession re-emerged, the population could watch from the riverbank as the flotilla returned to Karnak.

By the time Tutankhamun commissioned his Opet Festival reliefs, a great amount of building had occurred in Thebes. The processional route on land had been lined with sphinxes by Amenhotep III, which proved that up until that time it was still commonly in use. However, the sphinxes may have served as a barrier to prevent people from approaching the procession, forcing them to watch from their rooftops or behind the sphinx-line. Renewal of the sphinxes under Ramses II may indicate that they had fallen into disrepair as the later Eighteenth Dynasty kings preferred the procession up the Nile depicted in the Colonnade Hall reliefs, restricting access to the members of the public participating in the procession.

However, when the barques arrived at Luxor Temple, the public were able to have more access. Amenhotep III crafted most of the temple which can be seen today, including the core temple and barque shrines, the Sun Court, and Colonnade Hall. As we know from textual evidence presented above, the king likely appeared in the Sun Court after the rituals were completed to show himself to his people. One doorway in the Sun Court faces east, toward the ancient town of Thebes, and may have been used to admit spectators into the temple (Bell 1997, 149, 159; Strudwick and Strudwick 1999, 194). This is an important advancement in access to the divine as prior to this the public only had access to Tuthmosis III's contra-temple at Karnak which was distinctly outside of the temple itself.

It was through the Ramesside period construction that access to the divine increased dramatically. Although it was Ramses II who renewed the sphinxes and expanded Luxor Temple, the significance of the Opet Festival did not diminish in the time of Ramses III. According to the Medinet Habu festival calendar, Ramses III extended the festival to twenty-seven days, the longest in the New Kingdom (Grandet 1994, 89). His construction of his temple adorned with an Opet Festival relief which was likely intended for public viewing is the possible first instance of evidence of public access to the divine at Karnak Temple during the Opet Festival.

At Luxor, the inscriptions on the People's Gate combined with its location in the eastern wall facing the ancient town of Thebes makes a clear argument that this is the public entrance to the temple during the festival (Bell 1997, 149, 159; Strudwick and Strudwick 1999, 194). The construction of the Triple Barque Shrine near the western entrance in the Ramesside Court indicates that the barques were likely unloaded from the river barges and placed directly into the shrine for some time during the festival (Bell 1997, 149, 163). Members of the public may have had the opportunity to petition at the barque shrine whilst the barques and cult statues were still in residence there.

The existence of barque shrines inside the heart of Luxor Temple indicates that at some point in the festival the barques were moved from the Triple Barque Shrine and out of public access. At this point, the false door at the rear of the Triple Barque shrine would have served as access to the divine via a 'hearing ear' intermediary. It is likely that the king still emerged after the renewal rituals to show himself to the people, perhaps also in the Ramesside Court, as the name of the People's Gate refers to the *rekhyet* adoring the king and not Amun-Re (Bell 1997, 166). At the end of the festival, the significance of the barque shrine of Seti II parallels the significance shown by Ramses III's small temple: it provides an opportunity for people to petition the god at Karnak after his return.

Public access to the divine in the Opet Festival

In this paper I have examined evidence for public access to the divine in the Opet Festival in three crucial areas: state-commissioned depictions of the festival, supplementary textual and pictorial evidence which is specifically or indirectly concerned with public access and the festival, and the archaeological evidence which provides both physical evidence and a timeline for change. All must be considered in order to give a comprehensive interpretation.

Public access to the divine was certainly not the primary purpose of the Opet Festival, but it ran obliquely to it. While the Opet Festival was for the renewal of the king's *ka*, his divine right to rule, and kingly powers, not all of this renewal and support came from Amun-Re. An important amount of it came from elites who were the king's allies and the people whom the king ruled. By including the public as a witness to his renewal, the king strengthened his political and religious status in the eyes of his subjects. An inadvertent result of this need for an audience was more access to the divine.

The results of this study confirm that access to the divine at the Opet Festival increased during the New Kingdom in quantity, quality, and variety. During the reign of Hatshepsut, access to the divine appears limited to oracular consultation, and proximity to the king and the god's barque. Although much early Eighteenth Dynasty evidence is lost, the expansion of Luxor Temple seems to correspond with the increase in public access to the divine. This new construction of sacred space provided new and unique opportunities for access to the divine, including entry into the state temples, participation in ritual – the procession, witness of ritual – the appearance of the king after his rejuvenation, and the ability to petition the god directly – in his barque or through the false door.

It is interesting to note that rise in public access to the divine in the Opet Festival corresponds with the rise in personal piety as seen in private textual and pictorial evidence throughout the New Kingdom. Why it was allowed to increase at a state festival to a state god is a matter for future research.

Acknowledgments

This paper is based on my dissertation submitted for the degree of Master of Philosophy at the University of Cambridge in 2011.

Thank you to the Division of Archaeology, my supervisor Dr Kate Spence, Professor John Ray, the Faculty of Asian and Middle Eastern Studies Library, and the Haddon Library, for all your guidance and instruction.

Additional thanks to Sarah Musselwhite, Allison Williams, Amira Kanwal, Renate Fellinger, and Dr Miriam Müller, for reading, editing, and general advice; and to Chris Crowe, Marilyn Henriksen, Kristy Accetta, Thomas Accetta, and Patricia Accetta for your love and support.

Bibliography

Baines, J. (1987) Practical Religion and Piety. *The Journal of Egyptian Archaeology* 73, 79–98.

Baines, J. (1991) Society, Morality, and Religious Practice. In B. Schafer (ed.) *Religion in Ancient Egypt: Gods, Myths, and Personal Practice*, 124–200. London, Routledge.

Bell, L. (1985) Luxor Temple and the Cult of the Royal Ka. *Journal of Near Eastern Studies* 44.4, 251–94.

Bell, L. (1997) The New Kingdom "Divine" Temple: The Example of Luxor. In B. Shafer (ed.) *Temples of Ancient Egypt*, 127–84. London, I. B. Taurus and Co. Ltd.

Blyth, E. (2006) *Karnak: Evolution of a Temple*. London, Routledge.

Burgos, F. and Larché, F. (2006) *La Chapelle Rouge: Le Sanctuaire de Barque d'Hatshepsut* 1. Paris, Culturesfrance.

Cabrol, A. (2001) *Les voies processionnelles de Thèbes*. Leuven, Peeters.

Darnell, J. (2010) Opet Festival. In J. Dieleman and W. Wendrich, ed. *UCLA Encyclopedia of Egyptology*. <http://digital2.library.ucla.edu/viewItem/do?ark=21198/zz0025n765>.

El-Sabban, S. (2000) *Temple Festival Calendars of Ancient Egypt*. Wiltshire, Liverpool University Press.

Epigraphic Survey. (1936) *Reliefs and Inscriptions at Karnak Vol. 2: Ramses III's Temple within the Great Inclosure of Amon, pt. 2, and Ramses III's Temple I the Precinct of Mut*. Chicago, Oriental Institute of the University of Chicago.

Epigraphic Survey. (1994) *The Festival Procession of Opet in the Colonnade Hall: with translations of texts, commentary, and glossary*. Chicago, Oriental Institute of the University of Chicago.

Gaballa, G. A. (1976) *Narrative in Egyptian Art*. Mainz am Rhein, von Zabern.

Gardiner, A. (1953) The Coronation of King Haremhab. *The Journal of Egyptian Archaeology* 39, 13–31.

Gillam, R. (2005) *Performance and Drama in Ancient Egypt*. London, Gerald Duckworth & Co. Ltd.

Grandet, P. (1994) *Le papyrus Harris I: Volume II*. Cairo, Institut français d'archéologie orientale du Caire.

Griffin, K. (2007) A Reinterpretation of the Use and Function of the Rekhyt Rebus in New Kingdom Temples. In Cannata, M. (ed.) *Current Research in Egyptology 2006*, 66–84. Oxford, Oxbow Books.

Helck, W. (1957) *Urkunden der 18. Dynastie: Heft 20*. Berlin, Akademie Verlag.

Karlshausen, C. (2009) *L'Iconographie de la Barque Processionnelle Divine en Égypte au Nouvel Empire*. Orientalia Lovaniensia Analecta 182. Leuven, Peeters.

Kemp, B. (1995) How Religious were the Ancient Egyptians? *Cambridge Archaeological Journal* 5.1, 25–54.

Kitchen, K. A. (1993) *Ramesside Inscriptions: Translations Volume I: Ramesses I, Sethos I and Contemporaries*. Oxford, Blackwell Publishing.

Kitchen, K. A. (1999) *Ramesside Inscriptions: Notes and Comments Volume II: Ramesses II, His Contemporaries*. Oxford, Blackwell Publishing.

Kitchen, K. A. (2003) *Ramesside Inscriptions: Translations Volume IV: Merenptah and the Late Nineteenth Dynasty*. Oxford, Blackwell Publishing.

Kitchen, K. A. (2008) *Ramesside Inscriptions: Translations Volume V: Setnakht, Ramesses III and Contemporaries.* Oxford, Blackwell Publishing.

Lesko, L. (1994) Spiritual and Intellectual Matters. In L. Lesko (ed.) *Pharaoh's Workers: The Villagers of Deir el-Medina*, 87–94. London, Cornell University Press.

Lichtheim, M. (1975) *Ancient Egyptian Literature: Volume I: The Old and Middle Kingdoms.* Berkley, University of California Press.

Murnane, W. (1985) *False Doors and Cult Practices Inside Luxor Temple.* In P. Posener-Krieger (ed.) Mélanges Gamal Eddin Mokhtar 2, 135–48. Cairo, Institut français d'archéologie orientale du Caire.

O'Connor, D. (2009) *Abydos: Egypt's First Pharaohs and the Cult of Osiris.* London, Thames and Hudson.

Porter, B. and Moss, R. (1972) *Topographical Bibliography of Ancient Egyptian Texts, Reliefs, and Paintings: Volume II. Theban Temples.* Oxford, Clarendon Press.

Sethe, K. (1907) *Urkunden der 18. Dynastie: Elftes Heft.* Leipzig, J. C. Hinrichs.

Spence, K. (1998) 'Orientation in Ancient Egyptian Royal Architecture'. Unpublished Ph.D. dissertation, University of Cambridge.

Strudwick, N. and Strudwick, H. (1999) *Thebes in Egypt: A Guide to the Tombs and Temples of Ancient Luxor.* London, British Museum Press.

Wilkinson, R. H. (2002) *The Complete Temples of Ancient Egypt.* London, Thames and Hudson.

Wilkinson, R. H. (2003) *The Complete Gods and Goddesses of Ancient Egypt.* New York, Thames and Hudson.

2

Female Figurines from Deir el-Medina: A Review of Evidence for their Iconography and Function

Joanne Backhouse

Introduction

Bruyère's report on the excavation of the village of Deir el-Medina states that hundreds of fragments of female figurines were found at the site (Bruyère 1939, 109). This includes standalone figurines, those integrated into beds, models and plaques (Bruyère 1939, pl. XLVIII, XLIV and XLV). By today's standards the material is poorly published; the exact number found is unknown, as is the current location of many published pieces. Furthermore, there is no detailed contextual information for the majority of individual figurines. This paper will re-evaluate this material, integrating Bruyère's extensive reports from the site as a whole and subsequent scholarship. It will also include an analysis of figurines that are currently in the Louvre, which represents the largest corpus of material I have studied to date. At this stage this is the only group of figurines from the site which have been located. The aim of this paper is to assess the significance of the data, examining why representations of the female form were so prevalent at the site and to discuss what purpose they served.

Source Material

Bruyère excavated at Deir el-Medina between 1922 and 1951 while working for Institut Français d'Archéologie Orientale (IFAO). The majority of evidence concerning the figurines is documented in the 1934–35 season when Bruyère excavated the village (Bruyère 1939), although some earlier reports contain references to the discovery of both figurines and model beds. The earliest record, I have found, is in the 1927 report which notes that two terracotta model beds were found in tomb 335, shaft 1099, dated to the Eighteenth Dynasty (Bruyère 1928, 13 fig. 5h). It is worth noting some tombs at Deir el-Medina were given Theban Tomb numbers but not all. Those in the eastern cemetery were simple shaft tombs; these were subsequently filled in leaving no visible remains. As such most tombs referred to in this paper follow Bruyère's numbering, only those with a TT (Theban Tomb) designation are modern tombs numbers. Bruyère's 1930 report discusses clearing piles of debris, to the east and south of the walled enclosure which had built up during the lifetime of the village (Bruyère 1933, 5). Bruyère here recalls that model beds and standalone figurines had previously been found in the tombs of the Eighteenth Dynasty, but now in the rubble of the village he finds, for the first time, figurines integrated into beds (Bruyère 1933, 13).

In the cemeteries of the east and west Bruyère recovered standalone figurines and model beds. In tomb 1375 in the eastern cemetery he records a broken 'doll' of terracotta that was found next to the foot of a bed (Bruyère 1937b, 164, fig. 86). Real beds were often included in tomb assemblages at the site, for example tomb 1377 (Bruyère 1937b, 45, fig. 19), so it is impossible to say if the association was accidental. Tiny model beds were also used as tomb goods, for example tomb 1370 contained an example only 19mm in length and 0.5mm in height (Bruyère 1937b, 132, fig. 73). In addition fragments of three standalone figurines and three model beds were also found next to a group of coffins in tomb 1352, in the western cemetery, which Bruyère dates to the end of the Eighteenth Dynasty (Bruyère 1937a, 95–97). This suggests that beds, and not just figurines, were key elements in tomb assemblages.

Bruyère's 1953 publication details his work excavating the votive chapels and temples north of the Ptolemaic temple. He records finding six fragments of figurines integrated into beds and two fragments of standalone figurines, one of which is described as being '*en état de grossesse*' (Bruyère 1953, 35–36, fig. 3.2). These were found in '*le grand puits*,' this is located behind the Ptolemaic temple and still visible today. It is believed this was dug in the Ramesside Period in an abortive attempt to reach the water table. It was a substantial undertaking, fifty metres deep and thirty-five metres wide. The abandoned pit subsequently became filled with debris (Bruyère 1953, 129). Subsequent work by Bonnet and Valbelle (1975, 445) also found half a model bed in house XX and a fragment of a figurine in house XIII. The next season they dug two sample trenches to the south of the village; here they found a fragment of a model bed, a fragment of a figurine integrated into a bed and two fragments of standalone figurines (Valbelle and Bonnet 1976, 341). The evidence suggests that figurines were endemic to the site, found in the houses, the debris of the village and tombs. It is noteworthy that no figurines integrated into beds are recorded in the tombs, but they are present in all other areas. This may reflect lack of detail in recording or it may suggest they fulfilled a different function at the site.

The Evidence

The discussion in this paper will use published material and the collection of figurines currently in the Louvre Museum, which I examined and photographed on a study visit in February 2011. For the purposes of this study I have divided the figurines into six broad groups based on iconography, each of which will be examined below. An overview of those figurines currently in the Louvre is presented in Figure 2.1. All measurements given in this paper are for current length, no estimates for fragmentary pieces are included. No individual contextual information is recorded for the majority of figurines. However, as the 1939 publication details the season of 1934–35, when Bruyère excavated the village, it is likely those published in this work were found in the debris of the houses (Bruyère 1939).

Plaques, Ostraca and Models

Bruyère's photographs (1939, pl. XLIII and XLV) show eleven plaques incorporating features of the female form, seven of which are now in the Louvre, an example is seen in Figure 2.2. The present location of the remaining plaques is unknown. An additional plaque is noted in the

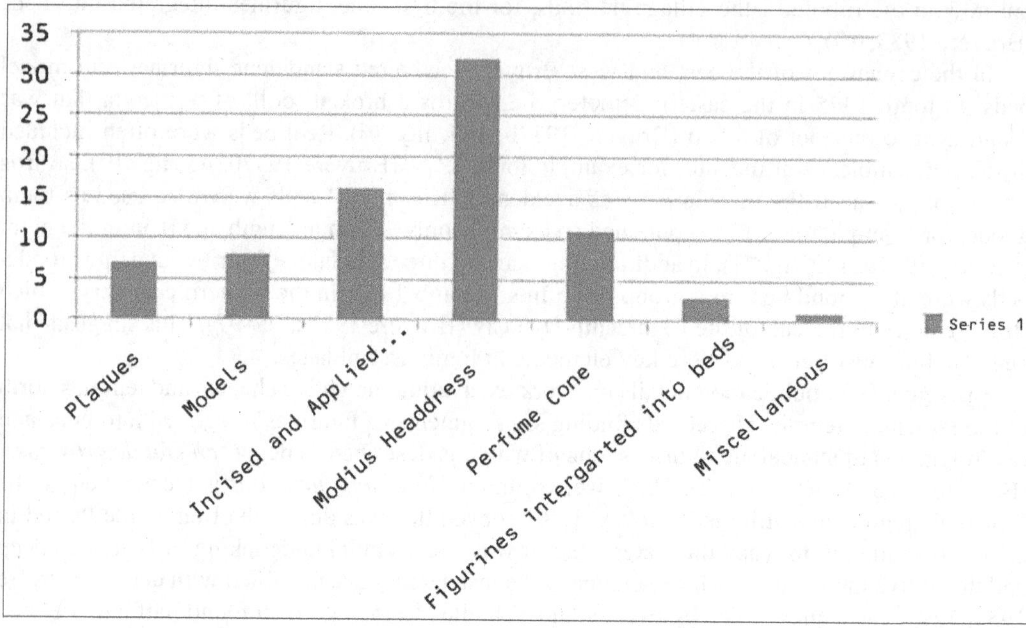

Figure 2.1: Figurines now in the Louvre.

Figure 2.2: E16503b – Plaque figurine, 8.5cm.

main body of the excavation report, found in house XXV (Bruyère 1939, 299, fig. 167). Bruyère (1939, 143) succinctly described them as polyhedrons, that is a solid object in three dimensions with flat surfaces and a flat face and edges. These plaques are hand-modelled, with incision and occasional applied decoration. The examples in the Louvre are between 3.9cm and 8.5cm in length. All complete figurines have their pubic triangle indicated, with dots or incised lines. The navel is denoted on five plaques, either by a series of dots or applied decoration. No facial features

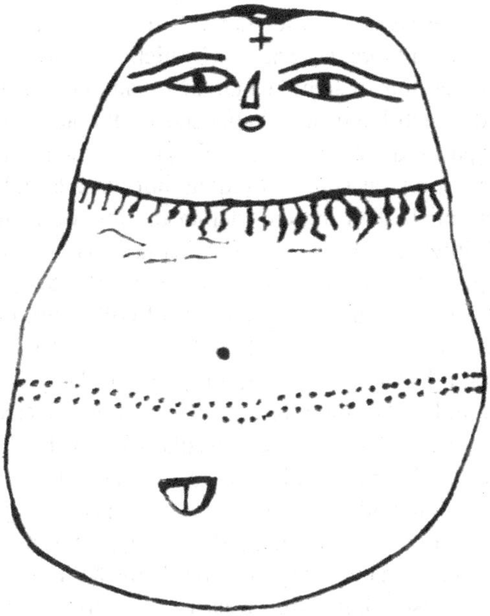

Figure 2.3: Figured ostraca – drawing based on Bruyère1939, plate XLV.

Figure 2.4: 16504a – Model, 4.7cm.

are depicted although two plaques (Louvre E16503a and Louvre E16503b) have two sets of parallel horizontal lines close to the top edge. These could indicate eyes or a hip-girdle, as seen on more realistically depicted figurines.

Bruyère (1939, pl. XLV) also records seven figured-ostraca, (current location unknown). The surface of the ostraca is used in its entirety to suggest an abstracted female form, with no limbs, although facial features are depicted. The most consistent element of iconography is the pubic triangle, appearing on all pieces and the naval is shown six times. Two of the pieces also include depictions of necklaces and hip-girdles. A cross is drawn on the forehead of four of these pieces, an example is shown in Figure 2.3. The significance of this is unknown.

Small clay, hand-crafted models representing female genitalia were also found at the site (Bruyère 1939, pl. XLV and XLIII). Bruyère (1939, pl. XLV) shows eight pieces which are now in the Louvre and Bruyère (1939, pl. LXIII) shows up to twelve additional pieces, current location unknown. The examples in the Louvre range in size from 3cm to 6cm in length, Figure 2.4 shows an example. They are decorated with a series of dots and incisions. Due to the shape of the pieces it is likely the decorative motifs are used to depict the navel (e.g. Louvre E1605b) or the pubic region (e.g. Louvre E16504a). Three examples have a deep linear incision which probably represents the vulva (for example Louvre E16504f). Two examples also exhibit a row of dots possibly suggesting a hip-girdle (e.g. Louvre E16504g). Also recorded by Bruyère (1939, pl. XLIII) were small circular pieces of modelled clay, current location unknown. They are decorated with incision and dot motifs and similar items have been recorded at Amarna (Stevens 2006, 89) and Memphis (Giddy 1999, 334). Given the similar decorative techniques and motifs, as seen on the plaques and models, I agree with Stevens (2006, 89) in her suggestion that they may represent stylised body arts.

Figure 2.5: Example of 'jeux de nature'. Drawing based on Keimer 1940–1945, plate VII.

In addition to the material published by Bruyère, Keimer (1940–45b) wrote an illuminating article on *'jeux de la nature,'* which are stones or pebbles that resemble human or animal forms and which have been enhanced by the addition of painted decoration. Keimer asserts many were found at Deir el-Medina, but were largely unpublished. A number depict the female form (Keimer 1940–45, pl. V, VI and VII). Those depicted in plate VII (Keimer 1940–45b pl. VII) wear a large wig and broad collar, with a lotus flower decorating both their head and used to symbolise the vulva, Figure 2.5 shows an example. The stones have been carefully selected as they all have a large circular groove in the centre which protrudes, suggesting an extended abdomen and possibly indicating pregnancy. Those in plate V (Keimer 1940–45b pl. V) show women with large wigs and the shape of the stone emphasises their large breasts. Bruyère (1939, 277) refers to finding *'un silex représentant un tronc de femme gross, les mains sur le ventre'* in house S.E. IX. It is likely this is what he was referring to.

Stand Alone Figurines with Incised and Applied Decoration

Over thirty figurines with incised and applied decoration were recorded by Bruyère (1939, pl. XLIII and XLV). Sixteen are now in the Louvre; all are fragmentary ranging in size from 3.6cm to 11cm. The current location of the remaining figurines is unknown. All sixteen in the Louvre have incised decoration with six also having applied decoration. The individualistic and crude style of manufacture suggests all figurines were hand-modelled, with the possible exception of one, which could have been made using a half mould, suggested by its flat back (Louvre E16505). Although individualistic in style, repeat motifs and areas of significance are identifiable. On eleven figurines the breasts are indicated, either modelled or by the use of applied and incised decoration. The dot motif is also used in extensive manner on two pieces (Figs 2.6 and 2.7); this is unparalleled in the general corpus of New Kingdom figurines. It is unlikely that this was used to suggest tattooing as it covers the whole body of the figurine. It may denote the significance and importance of the female body as a whole, illustrating the use of the female form as a vehicle for decoration and a canvas upon which to encode meaning. The navel is indicated eight times, either by a circle motif or simple incision. The pubic triangle is represented six times. Two figurines are depicted with protruding stomachs, suggesting pregnancy (Figs 2.8 and 2.9) and there is at least one other example of a figurine with a protruding stomach in Bruyère's publication (Bruyère 1939, pl. LII).

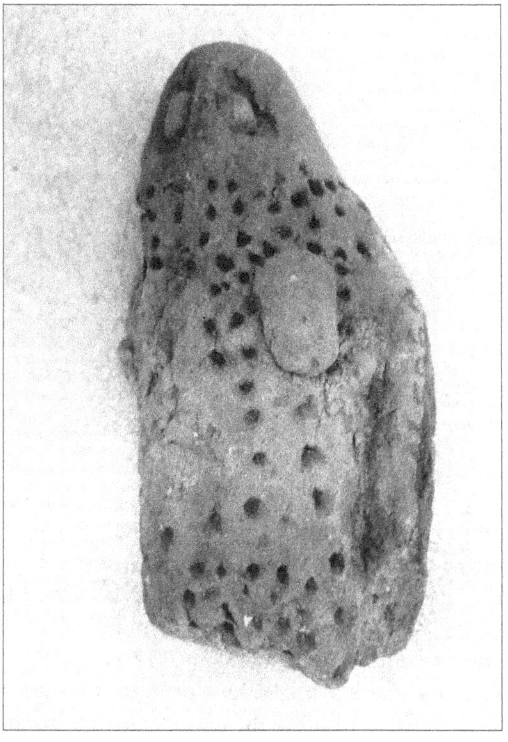

Figure 2.6: Figurine with incisions, E16506a, 7.3cm.

Figure 2.7: Figurine with incisions, E16506e, 4cm.

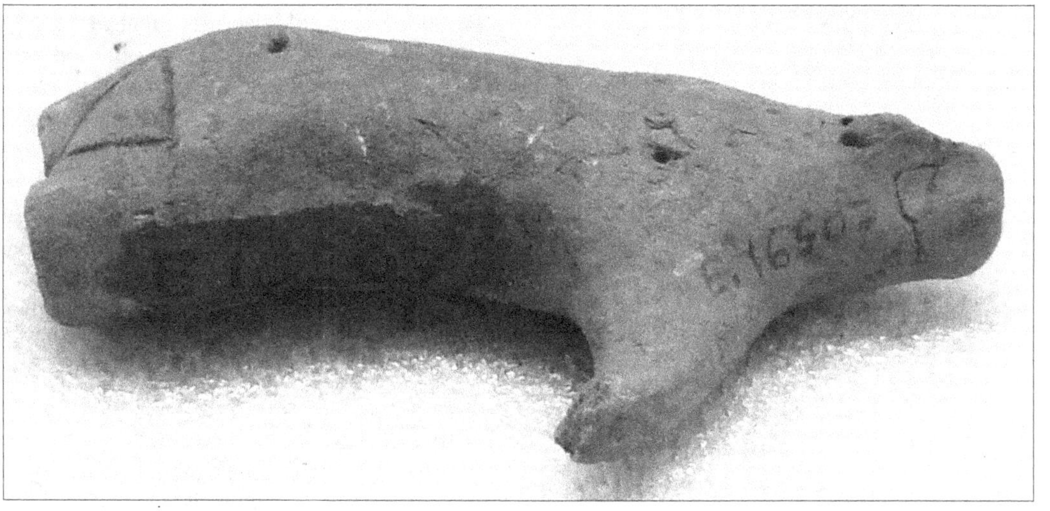

Figure 2.8: Figurine with protruding stomach, E16507, 6.9cm.

Figure 2.9: Figurine with protruding stomach, E16508, 8.3cm.

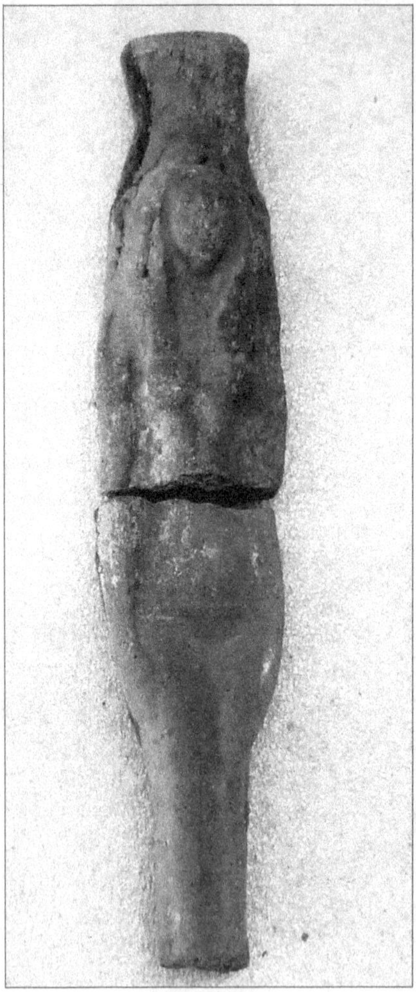

Figure 2.10: Figurine with arms elongated, E16513h, 13.5cm.

Figurines wearing a large modius headdress

Bruyère records twenty-three figurines wearing a large modius-headdress in plate XLIII, seven more are depicted in plate XLIV, with twenty-five more shown in fig. 58 (Bruyère 1939, pl. XLIII, XLIV, fig. 58) although there may be some duplication of images. Thirty-two of these figurines are now in the Louvre; all are fragmentary, ranging in size from 3.9cm to 8.2cm in length, and in twenty-eight pieces only the upper body remains. The figurines are represented in two poses. Nine have elongated arms resting at the side of their body, (e.g. Fig. 2.10). On fifteen pieces one arm is bent at the elbow and folds across the chest resting on the breast; in twelve cases it is the left arm of the figurine which bends across the chest (e.g. Fig. 2.11), on three pieces is the right arm (Fig. 2.12). The remaining pieces are too fragmentary to discern their pose. In six instances the figurines appear to be holding something, although the precise nature of the object is not distinguishable, as seen in Figure 2.11. Bruyère (1939, 141) believed the figurines held either '*menat*' necklaces or a blue lotus flowers. With regard to the figurines I have handled personally, it has not been possible to identify either of these objects. Bruyère (1939, 141) also cites one unique example which held the sceptre of Ptah, comprising of the '*was sceptre*', surmounted by an '*ankh*' and '*djed*' symbols, which I believe is depicted in the 1939

Figure 2.11: Figurine with left arm across body, E16513e, 6cm.

Figure 2.12: Figurine with right arm across body, E16513c, 8.2cm.

publication (Bruyère 1939, pl. XLIII). If so, this would be a unique piece in the general corpus of these New Kingdom figurines. Ptah was venerated at the site as the god of craftsmen and so the figurine may have been made as a votive offering to the god.

Figurines Wearing a Perfume Cone

Bruyère (1939, pl. XLIII) records six figurines with perfume cones on their heads, while a further eleven are shown in (Bruyère 1939, pl. XLIV). The latter group are now in the Louvre, and again there may be some duplication in plates. All eleven pieces in the Louvre are fragmentary, showing only the upper body of the figurines. They range in size from 4.9cm to 7.8cm in length; the perfume cones take various forms, from tapering (Fig. 2.13) to large and bulbous (Fig. 2.14). All the figurines have the remnants of painted decoration, some more pronounced than others. Red paint is commonly used for the flesh, black for the wig and white for the perfume cone. Remnants of paint are visible on the reverse of seven pieces (e.g. Fig. 2.15). This suggests the figurines were not designed to be solely displayed frontally but could be mobile, and were possibly made to be held. The figurines are carefully modelled with attention to detail, earrings or ears are seen on at least five pieces, with a lotus flower and headband shown on at least two and individual locks of hair are also represented.

Figure 2.13: Figurine with tapering perfume cone, E16512r, 5.4cm.

Figure 2.14: Figurine with bulbous perfume cone, E16512s, 4.8cm.

Figure 2.15: Figurine with paint on the reverse, E16512s, verso.

There are however, a number of hitherto unexplained iconographic traits within this dataset. In five examples the eyes are emphasised heavily with black outline (e.g. Fig. 2.13) which is undocumented in previous or subsequent scholarship. White stripes can also be seen on two figurines (e.g. Fig. 2.16). These stripes may be suggestive of a certain style of dress, as seen for example on priestesses in the Eighteenth Dynasty tomb of Ken-Amun who are vividly attired in striped robes with ribbons or beads across their chest (Davies 1930, pl. XLI). If so, the figurines may have been designed to represent priestesses and so act as votive offerings to the god they served, however only a very small number of figurines have these markings so this is not a common feature of the corpus. So called paddle dolls are often depicted with beads or ribbons diagonally crossing their chest but these are dated primarily to the Middle Kingdom, one such example being found by Winlock at Deir el-Bahri (Winlock 1942, pl.

38). Alternatively these features may be due an accident of preservation or poor workmanship. However, the latter is not in keeping with the overall degree of detail the figurines exhibit; this leads me to believe the markings were intentional.

Figure 2.16: Figurine with distinctive markings, E16512p, 7.4cm.

Figurines Integrated with Beds

Bruyère (1939, pl. XLIV) recorded eight fragments of figurines integrated into beds, three showing upper bodies and five of lower bodies. In the body of the text he also depicted two almost complete examples (Figs 2.18 and 2.19); these are now in the Louvre Museum (Bruyère 1939, 142). Bruyère (1933, 13 fig. 4) had previously included an example in his 1930 report (Fig. 2.17) which is also in the Louvre Museum. The current location of the remaining pieces is unknown. The figurines integrated into beds are substantial pieces, for example figurine E14385 (Fig. 2.17) is 19.2cm in length, 8.6cm in depth and 10.5cm in height. These artefacts, therefore, were clearly not made to be carried around as an amulet or charm. It is more likely they were created for display. They are made of clay, which has been pressed in a mould, fired in a kiln, and then painted. All three show a recumbent woman on a bed with a child. The women are all nude, yet they wear a large wig, surmounted with a perfume cone and discus earrings. Figurines E14385 and E16515 (Figs 2.17 and 2. 18) are very similar; both women lie with their heads on a pillow and with their arms resting by their side. The ochre red of their bodies, contrasts strongly with the white of the bed. Both have their wigs painted black and on one side of their body rests a child, on the other a mirror is depicted. Both beds have a foot rest and originally had four legs. Both have been broken in antiquity. Figurine E16514 (Fig. 2.19) differs from the previous two pieces, although all three are linked thematically; the woman still lies on the bed, but no pillow can be detected. Although there are traces of paint remaining, overall the piece is less vibrant, with a muted ochre tone. The child is held to the breast, and the hair of the wig tucked behind the woman's shoulder. The woman appears to be wearing a thick headband, as seen on figurine E14385 (Fig. 2.17). Similar imagery is depicted on the fragmentary pieces Bruyère records in plate XLIV (Bruyère 1939, pl. XLIV). The two poses should be seen a variation on a theme, the overriding similarity between the two groups unites them.

NB – all measurements are from top to bottom of figurines (head to toe)

Figure 2.17: Figurine integrated into a bed, E14385, 19.2cm.

Figure 2.18: Figurine integrated into a bed, E16515, 16.2cm.

Miscellaneous

There are also a number of figurines which due to their fragmentary nature and the quality of publication it is not possible to classify with any degree of accuracy (Bruyère 1939, pl. XLIII). Bruyère (1939 pl. XLIII) shows ten fragments of torsos; it is likely they belonged to the 'modius head dress' or 'perfume cone' group due to stylistic similarities. Bruyère (1939, 142) describes other standalone statutes that were produced '*la nourrice debout ou encore assise et jambs allongées.... et donnant le sein, toujours le gauche et toujours á un enfant male*.' Two such figurines are recorded in the publications (Bruyère 1937a, fig. 41; 1939, fig. 60, 142). Their present location is unknown and due to the poor quality of photographic reproduction it is not possible to make a detailed analysis of these pieces. No similar examples have been recorded in subsequent scholarship. Finally there is one example in the Louvre's collection of a standalone figurine which does not wear a perfume cone or modius headdress (Louvre E16512). This figurine has been published several times due to the high standard of workmanship and preservation (Andreu 2002, 115 fig. 56; and Musée du Louvre 1980, 93 fig. 131). Stevens (2006, 85) records a significant number of figurines which do not wear any head apparel at Amarna. She also notes the difficulty of classifying the figurines into groups due to the diverse iconography of the dataset.

Dating and Typology

Bruyère (1939, 109) believed the majority of figurines belonged to the New Kingdom; although some could be dated to the Middle Kingdom. He suggested they formed a continuum with the figurines integrated into beds being the last style developed (Bruyère 1939, 141). Bruyère (1939, 140) believed the figurines with the modius headdress preceded the figurines wearing perfume cones and both he believed were forerunners of the figurines integrated into beds. This may be due to the fact that Bruyère records finding model beds and standalone figurines in the tombs of the Eighteenth Dynasty but not figurines integrated into beds (Bruyère 1933, 12). He states he found these only in the rubble of the village, which was occupied until early/mid Twentieth Dynasty. While we have to acknowledge Bruyère's assertion on dating it must be noted that figurines integrated into beds were found in other New Kingdom cemeteries for example Edfu (Michalowski *et al.* 1939, 207–209, pl. XXV, XXVI). Also a similar diversification of evidence is found at Amarna. Stevens (2006, 85) records over two hundred fragmentary female predominantly moulded, standalone figurines. However, she also records twenty-four mud, clay and pottery plaques, and ten figurines which show signs of being joined to a bed. Also at Edfu a plaque figurine was found in a tomb which also contained a model bed, and so it is possible the two were related (Michalowski *et al.* 1938, 121; 112). This tomb is dated to the Middle Kingdom so the association of figurines and beds may be more ancient than Bruyère anticipated. Some standalone figurines were accompanied by model beds at Deir el-Medina (Bruyère 1937a, 97 fig. 41). Similar evidence is found at Sawama (Bourriau and Millard 1971, fig. 11) and Amarna (Peet and Wooley 1923, 25 pl. XII). However, at both Deir el-Medina and Amarna, the number of figurines greatly exceeds the number of beds, suggesting that not all figurines were accompanied

Figure 2.19: Figurine integrated into a bed, E16514, 17.5cm.

by a bed. The evidence suggests figurines of a diverse form were made and used concurrently at Deir el-Medina. Due to the lack of contextual information it is impossible to ascertain which figurines were accompanied by a bed, however it is clear the association of women and beds was significant, as discussed in my previous paper (Backhouse 2012, 27–30).

Production

No pottery workshops have been found at Deir el-Medina so we can only surmise if the figurines were made in the village or brought in. Many were hand-modelled and some were of a rudimentary nature. Furthermore, although the figurines incorporate common traits, many were individualistic in design (e.g. Figs 2.6 and 2.7). The lack of uniformity of the standalone figurines suggests small-scale or home production. Others were moulded suggesting that mass-production was possible and implying a workshop. The majority of moulded figurines have flat backs or show no signs of modelling, suggesting they were made in an open mould, although four figurines in Bruyère's publication (1939, pl. XLIII) and two figurines in the Louvre (E16513e and E16513i) show signs of modelling on the reverse, which suggests they were made in a double mould. The production of figurines in a mould suggests that these items were inexpensive and accessible to all. Similarly the figured-ostraca and the '*jeux de la nature*' were created from readily available source materials. They demonstrate a process of transformation, whereby disregarded materials are made into objects through a creative input. Meskell (2004, 2) describes this as the 'making of a thing from a non-thing.' They also illustrate the use of different mediums to express the same motifs. This implies that the motif, the female form, was central to the belief system of the community, given the prevalence of representations.

Iconography

Defining Characteristics

The plaques and models focus on the sexual characteristics of the female form. They are devoid of facial features and of adornment. The abstraction and physiological nature of the plaques suggests they were concerned primarily with the desire for procreation, not aesthetics; the association with fecundity is demonstrated clearly on a number of figurines (e.g. Figs 2.8 and 2.9) and the '*jeux de la nature*' pieces (e.g. Fig. 2.5) depicted with protruding stomachs, suggesting pregnancy. Depictions of pregnant women are rare in Egyptian art, although a plaque figure from Edfu also has a protruding stomach (Michalowski *et al.* 1938, 114 pl. XXVI5). At Deir el-Bahri Queen Ahmose is shown pregnant with Hatshepsut, but this is a divine conception as Ahmose was impregnated by the god Amun (Naville 1896 pl. XLIX). As birth was associated with rebirth in Egyptian culture it is likely images of pregnant woman were powerful totems in the community. This link is seen vividly in the tomb of Nefer-renpet at Deir el-Medina (TT336), where we see Meretseger breast feeding the deceased tomb owner who is depicted as a child and we are told he becomes a child again in another time (Bruyère 1929, fig. 21).

Naked but Adorned

In comparison to the lack of personification seen in the plaques and models, the remaining figurines, both standalone and those integrated into beds, are all naked but adorned with elaborate wigs and jewellery. There is some continuity with the plaques, principally the use of incision, seen on a number of examples in the modius headdress group. It is used to depict elements of personal adornment, for example hip-girdles, necklaces and to create holes for the insertion of earrings. Earrings are depicted on many of the standalone figurines and those integrated into beds, again demonstrating the iconographic continuities between the dataset. Bruyère (1939, 127) regarded the jewellery with which the figurines were decorated, as talismanic adornments which increased the power of the figurines. I believe the wearing of jewellery by naked women suggests they were adorned for a purpose, possibly for sex, with the jewellery worn to heighten their physical attraction.

Hair and Wigs

Wigs and hair are important decorative motifs within the dataset. In the collection at the Louvre there are six figurines which have holes in their head probably for the insertion of material to suggest hair. Bruyère (1933, 12) records finding crudely modelled figurines of unfired clay and figurines in terracotta with flowers or feathers attached to their head. Although he does not record any figurines with beads attached to their head, they are common at other sites for example at Gebel Zeit (Castel *et al.* 1984, fig. 4). The material is not as important as the intent, to suggest and emphasis the hair; on many of the figurines wearing perfume cones, individual braids can be differentiated (Figs 2.13 and 2.14). Two figurines in the Louvre's collection show signs of modelling on the reverse (E16513e and E16513i) and may have worn a tripartite wig. A number of pieces in Bruyère's publication (1939, pl. XLIII) are also depicted with tripartite wigs. The figurines integrated into beds all wear large wigs; there is here a juxtaposition of the naked figure, lying on a bed, yet with 'coiffured' hair. Again there must have been a reason for the adornment, possibly to entice. There are numerous reference to hair in New Kingdom Love Poetry, where hair is seen as sexually alluring for example in *Papyrus Harris 500 Collection 1* (Kitchen 1999, 357). Giddy (1999, 29) in her analysis of New Kingdom figurines from Memphis, also found hair to be one of the two most important iconographic elements in her dataset, the other being the pubic region. In all other respects the figurines at Memphis were poorly rendered with no attention to detail. The emphasis on hair and the pubic region suggests these two areas were essential to the defining characteristics of the figurines and were possibly linked.

Modius Headdress

The apparel that surmounted the hair and wigs also carried meaning and intent. I use the term modius headdress, but Bruyère (1939, 140) describes it as '*une sort de diadème ou de couronne,*' a simple cylinder more or less raised, or sometimes a reversed cone, which resembles a crown of feathers as worn by Anukis, a goddess of the cataracts. I prefer the term modius headdress as this avoids any overt associations with goddesses or royalty. Bruyère (1939, 139) also believed the headdress may have represented the hieroglyphic sign for '*neb*' which depicts a basket. Handling the figurines has confirmed many have an indentation in the middle of the headdress, giving the impression of a basket or bowl. The association may have been more etymological, based on the word '*neb,*' than the function of a bowl or basket. Linguistically this means 'lord' or 'master', with the feminine counterpart signifying mistress. The '*nb.t*' sign came to symbolise women generally and was part of the common epithet '*nb.t pr.t,*' mistress of the house. Bruyère (1939, 139), also noted the '*neb*' sign may have been used by Nephthys, as part of her distinctive headdress, which is made up of the hieroglyphic elements of her name, a tall headdress surmounted with a basket. Nephthys is most commonly shown at the head end of the coffin or sarcophagi, opposite her sister Isis, both protecting the deceased. This may reflect the ultimate funereal function Bruyère believed the figurines fulfilled. Pinch (1993, 225) also believed one of the functions of the figurines was funereal. This will be discussed in more detail later.

In the general corpus of New Kingdom figurines those wearing a modius headdress are rare. Two such figurines have been recorded by Teeter (2010, 32–33) from Medinet Habu, both dated from the late New Kingdom to the Third Intermediate Period. Another example was found in an Eighteen Dynasty tomb at Sawama, which is ninety miles north of Thebes (Bourriau and Millard 1971, fig. 11). The high modius headdress is also worn by women depicted on votive beds, which were confined to the Theban region, dated mainly from the Third Intermediate Period, as discussed by Teeter (2010, 157–159). It is possible the modius headdress was a regional trait which spanned both the New Kingdom and Third Intermediate period.

Perfume cone

Perfume cones surmounted the head of eleven of the standalone figurines, and all three of the figurines integrated into beds, in the collection of the Louvre Museum. Cherpion (1994, 80–86) demonstrates convincingly that the cones were symbolic only, used to suggest the idea of perfume and anointing. These concepts were clearly significant to the purpose and function of the figurines. Both Cherpion (1994, 87) and Manniche (1999, 96) discuss the use of word play in this symbolism, the Egyptian word '*stj*' means scent, but also engender, or beget and to pour. There are frequent references linking perfume to sex in the New Kingdom Love Poetry, one in particular '*The Cairo Love Song*' described the preparation before love making and how the body is 'sprinkled with perfume' (Tobin 2003, 318). Cherpion (1994, 79) refers to the perfume cone as '*gage de survie*.' She sees the cone as a wish for eternity, presumably through sex, birth and rebirth, although she does not fully articulate this. She makes the important point that perfume cones are rarely depicted on three-dimensional objects; instead they are shown only in two-dimensions, often on tomb scenes and engraved on stelae. However, Cherpion overlooks the inclusion of perfume cones on the three-dimensional figurines. The rarity of the depiction of a perfume cone in the round, suggests its inclusion in the morphology of the figurines was significant and purposeful.

Use

A full discussion on the function of female figurines in New Kingdom Egypt is outside the remit of this paper. The intention is to examine the possible uses of the figurines at Deir el-Medina only. Given the variations in iconography and context it is possible the figurines served different purposes. The size and the variety of textures incorporated into the design of the plaques suggest they were made to be held. Bruyère (1939, 144) noted one example with a compartment on the reverse containing chippings of nails, hair, some scraps of skin or remains of clothing. He suggested the plaques may have been used in magic (I assume he means ritual practise), possibly for bewitchment or as love charms. Waraksa (2007, ii) has suggested that New Kingdom figurines were standard ritual objects, used in magical/medical procedures. She believes they were used in conjunction with spells and a process of transference was invoked whereby the illness left the afflicted, entered the figurine, which was then snapped and disregarded, accounting for their presence in refuse zones. While the advocacy of a proactive use for the figurines has much strength, their iconography suggests that if they were used in rituals it would be relating to fertility or female aliments. Yet the textual references Waraksa (2007, 153; 170) cites call for figurines of Isis to cure snakebites and stomach aches. There is no reason to assume that the figurines represented a divinity. It is more likely, if the figurines were used in magic, that it was by women in their own personal religious/magical/medical practise, and the spells were transferred aurally, as opposed to 'official' male magical practitioners/priests, who were more likely to record the spells. In addition the figurines integrated into beds are substantial pieces and a strange choice if made to be broken. Furthermore, Bruyère did find standalone figurines and model beds in the tombs of Deir el-Medina; this is difficult to explain in light of Waraksa's theory, unless we assume they were taken to the tomb to be used as ritual objects in the afterlife. Waraksa (2007) based her theory on the work she had carried out at the temple of Mut at Karnak dating from the late New Kingdom to the Third Intermediate period. While thought provoking, her analysis demonstrates the problems of attempting to apply one theory to a whole category of objects regardless of context.

Bruyère (1939, 144) believed the figurines were used around a structure he referred to as a '*lit clos,*' in the first room of the house. He believed these were cultic installations which also served utilitarian purposes, to sleep or give birth in (Bruyère 1939, 137). These were discussed in relation to images and representations of women in my previous paper (Backhouse 2012, 32–35). The point to note is that Bruyère believed the figurines were used in the home to celebrate the daily cult of the family, which focused on ancestor cult and lineage. However, Bruyère (1933, 14) believed the figurines ultimately had a funereal function. This corresponds with the data from Deir el-Medina where we find many goods included in tomb assemblages which show signs of use in everyday life. It is quite possible the figurines were used in the home and then taken to the tomb. Bruyère (1939, 142–144) believed the figurines integrated into beds represented the final stage of evolution of this artefact, due to the inclusion of a child in many examples and saw the figurines, representing the living, symbolising the perpetuation of the family line. However, he saw their nudity as indicative of their subservience and inferiority to man (Bruyère 1939, 149). I suggest Bruyère was 'reading' the figurines as a Twentieth Century European male, not viewing them in the symbolic landscape of New Kingdom Egypt. Concerned with reproduction and rebirth the figurines represent the power of the female not her inferiority.

However, there clearly was a dichotomy in the role of women in relation to childbirth. As Roth (2000, 200) notes, women were seen as the carries of children but not the creators of life; a woman's role in ancient Egypt was to entice men to be sexual active. This is expressed in the '*Song of the Harpers*' (TT 50) which describes the life cycle, it states 'Men beget and Women Conceive' (Lichtheim 1945, 178).While in Egyptian cosmology the male is endowed with the power to give life and impregnate, at Deir el-Medina we do not see an abundance of representations of the male form celebrating their creative powers. It is the female image which predominates. It is noteworthy that many examples of wooden phalli were found in the Eighteenth Dynasty shrine of Hathor at Deir el-Bahri (Hornblower 1926, 81). Hornblower (1926, 82) suggested these could be ex-voto, but based on the principles of sympathetic magic they were more likely to be prayers for children to be born. However, no phalli are recorded from the site of Deir el-Medina, here the female organs are clearly emphasised. Perhaps at a temple, a place of organised religious practise, the emphasis was on the power of the male to produce and impregnate but domestic cult seems clearly to have centred on the female element. This may of course be linked to the unusual nature of Deir el-Medina, where the men worked away from the village, for an eight day week returning at the weekend (Janssen 1980, 132). This left a predominantly female population in the village.

It is useful to consider the work of Pinch (1993, 225) here. She believes the figurines were concerned essentially with reproduction, not simply sexuality, given the inclusion of children on many pieces. She suggested they were placed in a funerary context to ensure the fertility of the deceased in the afterlife and assist their rebirth. In addition they could be offered to or placed in the vicinity of 'higher powers' or deities associated with fertility or spirits of the dead. The multifunctional purpose of the figurines is supported by evidence from Deir el-Medina, where we find figurines in the home, tombs and in the vicinity of chapels. An interesting group has been found in a niche cut into a wall of a house at Amarna, consisting of a standalone figurine, model bed and small scale stela (Peet and Wooley 1923, 25, pl. XII). It is possible the figurines at Deir el-Medina were displayed in a similar way, as niches were cut into many of the walls opposite the '*lit clos,*' which Bruyère maintained was the focus of ancestor cult (Bruyère 1939, 60). The figurines may have served as a link between the past generations, the present and the future generations.

Conclusions

Although varied, the evidence from Deir el-Medina forms a coherent group. All depict a naked woman, with the possible exception of two miscellaneous figurines, which could be dressed. It is possible the figurines form two groups, thematically linked. The plaques and models are devoid of any personification and emphasize the sexual characteristic of the female form, as do the figurines with incised and applied decoration, the '*jeux de nature*' and the figured ostraca. These were all clearly mobile and may have been used as ritual instruments in magic or as votive offerings. The figurines wearing the modius headdress, perfume cones and those integrated into beds are richly adorned. Due to their decorative features and the more robust nature of the figurines integrated into beds, it is possible they were made for display, and some of the standalone figurines may have been displayed on models beds. These may have been used in ancestor cult and worship. Bruyère's reports suggest the figurines integrated into beds were not found in tombs but standalone figurines and model beds were. It is impossible to know the accuracy of the recording. The figurines however, form a coherent group with the emphasis on the sexual characterises of the female form, the rare depictions of pregnant women, and the inclusion of children on the figurines integrated into beds, suggesting all were concerned with reproduction. Given their presence in the debris of the village, the votive chapel area and tombs it is likely their purpose was to engender fertility in this life and rebirth in the next, through ritual magic, worship and offering.

Acknowledgements

I would like to thank Dr. Guillemette Andreu, Director of the Egyptian Department in the Louvre Museum, Paris, for allowing me to handle and photograph the objects in their collection. I would also like to thank Liverpool University Graduate School for awarding me a travel bursary, which contributed towards the cost of the trip. Finally I would like to thank Dr Steven Snape, my supervisor, for his comments, support and editorial assistance.

Bibliography

Andreu, G. (2002) *Les Artistes de Pharaon: Deir el-Médineh et la Vallée des Rois*. Paris, Réunion des Musées Nationaux.

Backhouse, J. (2012) Figured ostraca from Deir el-Medina. In H. Abd-el-Gawad *et al.* (eds) *Current Research in Egyptology 2011*, 23–39. Oxford, Oxbow Books.

Bonnet, C. and Valbelle, D. (1975) Le village de Deir el-Médineh:reprise de l'étude archéologique. *Bulletin De L'Institut Français d'Archéologie Orientale* 75, 429–446.

Bonnet, C. and Valbelle, D. (1976) Le village de Deir el-Médineh: étude archéologique. *Bulletin de L'Institut Français d'Archéologie Orientale* 76, 317–342.

Bourriau, J. and Millard, A. (1971) The excavation of Sawâma. In 1914 by G. A. Wainwright and T. Whittenmore. *The Journal of Egyptian Archaeology* 57, 28–57.

Bruyère, B. (1928) *Rapport sur les Fouilles de Deir el Médineh (1927)*. Cairo, Institut Français d'Archéologie Orientale.

Bruyère, B. (1929) *Mert Seger a de Deir el Médineh.* Cairo, Institut Français d'Archéologie Orientale.

Bruyère, B. (1933) *Rapport sur les Fouilles de Deir el Médineh (1930)*. Cairo, Institut Français d'Archéologie Orientale.

Bruyère, B. (1937a) *Rapport sur les Fouilles de Deir el Médineh (1933–1934,) The Nécropole de l'Ouest.* Cairo, Institut Français d'Archéologie Orientale.

Bruyère, B. (1937b) *Rapport sur les Fouilles de Deir el Médineh (1934–1935), The Nécropole de l'Est.* Cairo, Institut Français d'Archéologie Orientale.

Bruyère, B. (1939) *Rapport sur les Fouilles de Deir el Médineh (1934–1935).* Cairo, Institut Français d'Archéologie Orientale.

Bruyère, B. (1953) *Rapport sur les Fouilles de Deir el Médineh (1948–1951).* Cairo, Institut Français d'Archéologie Orientale.

Castel, G. *et al.* (1984) *Découverte de mines pharaoniques au bord de la Mer Rouge*. Archéologi 192–3, 44–57.

Cherpion, N. (1994) Le "Cone d'Onguent" gage de survie. *Bulletin de L'Institut Français d'Archéologie Orientale* 94, 79–106.

Davies, N. De Garis (1930) *The tomb of Ken-Amun at Thebes*, New York, Metropolitan Museum of Art.

Giddy, L. (1999) *The Survey of Memphis II: Rom Rabi'a: The New Kingdom and Post New Kingdom Objects*. London, Egypt Exploration Society.

Hornblower. G. D. (1926) Phallic Offerings to Hat-Hor. *Man* 26, 81–83.

Keimer, L. (1940–45) *Jeux de la nature: retouchés par le main de l'homme provenant de Deir el-Médineh (Thebes) et remontant du Nouvel Empire.* Études d'Égyptologie, Cairo, Imprimerie de l'Institut Français d'Archéologie Orientale.

Kitchen, K. (1999) *Poetry of Ancient Egypt*. Uppsala, Paul Aströms.

Janseen, J. (1980) Absence from work by the necropolis workmen of Thebes. *Zeitschrift fur Ägyptische Sprache und Altertumskunde*, 107, 127–151.

Lichtheim, M. (1945) The Song of the Harpers. *Journal of Near Eastern Studies* Vol 4, No 3, 178–212.

Manniche, L. (1999) *Sacred Luxuries: Fragrance, Aromatherapy, and Cosmetics in Ancient Egypt*. London, Opus.

Meskell, L. (2004) *Object Worlds in Ancient Egypt: Material Biographies Past and Present.* Oxford, Berg.

Michalowski, K. *et al.* (1938) *Fouilles Franco-Polonaises Rapports: Tell Edfou II.* Cairo, Institut Francais d'Archeologie Orientale au Caire et l'Université de Varsovie.

Michalowski, K. *et al.* (1939) *Fouilles Franco-Polonaises Rapports: Tell Edfou III.* Cairo, Institut Francais d'Archeologie Orientale au Caire et l'Université de Varsovie.

Musée du Louvre. (1978) *La Vie Quotidienne chez les Artisans de Pharaon.* Metz, Musée de Metz.

Naville, E. H. (1896) *The Temple of Deir el-Bahari: Part II.* London, Egypt Exploration Society.

Peet, T. E. and Wooley, C. L. (1923) *City of Akhenaten: Part 1.* London, Egypt Exploration Society.

Pinch, G. (1993) *Votive Offerings to Hathor*. Oxford, Griffith Institute, Ashmolean Museum.
Roth, A. M. (2000) Father earth, mother sky. In A. E. Rautman (ed.) *Reading the Body*, 187–201. Philadelphia, University of Pennsylvania Press.
Stevens, A. (2006) *Private Religion at Amarna: The Material Evidence*. England, Archaeopress.
Teeter, E. (2010) *Baked Clay Figurines and Votive Beds from Medinet Habu*. Chicago, Oriental Institute of the University of Chicago.
Tobin, V. A. (2003) The Love Songs and the Song of the Harper. In W. K. Simpson (ed.) *The Literature of Ancient Egypt*. New Haven, Yale University Press.
Waraksa, E. (2007) *Female Figurines from the Mut Precinct: Context and Ritual Function*, Unpublished thesis, Johns Hopkins University.
Winlock, H. E. (1942) *Excavations at Deir el Bahri 1911–1913*. New York, The Macmillan Company.

3

Sex Object or Equal Partner? The Role of Women as portrayed in ancient Egyptian Love Poems

Renate Fellinger

Introduction

Ancient Egyptian women are often portrayed as having a great degree of freedom and many rights (Graves-Brown 2010, 171), for example in the legal sphere (*inter alia* Johnson 1996; B. S. Lesko 1987, 22–6), in comparison with other ancient civilizations, such as Greece. As *nb.t pr* – 'Lady of the House' – represents a common title for women, it may suggest that their responsibilities focused on running the household and its economics while men fulfilled their roles in the public domain. This gender-specific division of labour has led to interpretations of women as secondary to men (e.g. Robins 1993, 191) and of Egyptian society as male-dominated (Robins 2001, 515). Does the theoretical equality and, as it seems, practical imbalance of authority as proposed by scholars derive from imposing a modern interpretation on the ancient material (as pointed out by Landgráfová and Navrátilová (2009))? Or does it reflect the perception and understanding of the ancient Egyptians themselves regarding the role of women? Literature, as a source which was drafted and copied by the members of that very society, paints an ambiguous picture. Compositions (mostly written by men for men), for example narratives or wisdom texts, create a female image incorporating a spectrum of contradictory characteristics from the trustworthy wife and mother who is regarded as a fairly equal individual to the seductive, dangerous woman. This ambiguity in the perception of the roles of women and the difficulty in determining the extent of fictionality have caused the classification of some compositions as non-representative of society or ancient practice.

Previous scholarship on the love poems has predominantly focused on establishing parallels with the *Song of Songs* by examining literary themes, motifs, and structures (Fox 1985; Hermann 1959; Mathieu 1996; White 1978). Two main conclusions have been put forward: first, women are granted an extraordinary ability to show initiative and to be assertive (Fox 1985, 289, 305–7), and second, they are occasionally described with certain passivity (Fox 1985, 291; Mathieu 1996, 172–3; White 1978, 73). The former is accepted as a justification for denying the poems' credibility in reflecting ancient practice and society (Mathieu 1996, 3; Müller 1899,

8). The latter (alongside other reasons) has been adopted as an argument for a male-dominated perspective portrayed in the poems (Mathieu 1996, 158, 173, 232, 245).

This paper intends to challenge the hypotheses that love poems do not represent a reliable source for the study of society and that they do not reflect gender roles as perceived by the ancient authors and confirmed by contemporaneous material. The concept of gender is a modern creation to describe societal phenomena. By using the terms 'gender' and 'gender roles', I do not intend to imply that the ancient Egyptians shared the same awareness of this abstract idea as modern scholars but it seems to be the best available term to apply. For this study I do not consider whether the content of the love poems and the love setting are historically correct because it is debatable whether they represent ancient practice regarding love and sexuality (Fox 1985, 297). Therefore, the gender roles are not studied in their sexual context but in a more general manner by considering the fact that the women are doing something in the poems, i.e. that they are given the opportunity by poets/scribes (these terms are used interchangeably because there is an ongoing debate on the compositional dates of the poems and their relationship to a possible oral tradition before their written form) to participate actively. The exact type of action is not taken into account because the choice of verbs may have been linked to the genre and the requirements of the literary motifs, formal devices, metrical structure, or the Egyptian language itself.

This approach is based on the interpretation of literature as a social construct influenced to a certain degree by the poets' personal experiences and perceptions of contemporaneous society and by the landscapes representing the immediate worlds of their interactions. Sweeney's research on requests in New Kingdom narratives shows that the content of the request depends on the story but the way they are phrased may occasionally derive from the authors' experience in deeming what is appropriate regarding the gender of the speaker (2008). Love poems may represent the viewpoint of ancient individuals regarding the role of women as either active agents or beautiful things and contribute to the debate as to whether modern interpretation is congruent with ancient perception.

Data set

The data set for this study comprises 41 poems as preserved on three papyri: *pHarris 500* (*pH* = *pBM 10060*), *pTurin 1966* (*pT*), and *pChester Beatty I* (*pCB* = *pBM 10681*). I focus on the papyri rather than ostraca evidence because they are less fragmentary and represent complete collections of poems. *pH* was found with other papyri in a box in the Ramesseum on the West Bank of Thebes (Budge 1923, 23; Fox 1985, 7; Gardiner 1931, 1; Schott 1950, 11), whereas *pCB* was found in the necropolis of Deir el-Medina (Černý and Posener 1978, vii; Koenig 1981, 41–2) as part of the Qen-her-khepesh-ef archive (McDowell 1999, 134). The provenance of *pT* is not attested (Pleyte and Rossi 1869–76, 2–3). The papyri date to the 19th (*pH*) and 20th Dynasties (*pT*, *pCB*) (*c.* 1295–1069 BC) of the New Kingdom (Fox 1985, 181; Hermann 1959, 138–56; Mathieu 1996, 22; Müller 1899, 13, 38; White 1978, 70–1). However, the compositional dates of the poems may differ (Mathieu 1996, 23): both the 18th Dynasty (*c.* 1550–1295 BC) (Fox 1985, 183; Hermann 1959, 138; White 1978, 75, 91, 161) and the Ramesside period (Fox 1985, 183; Hermann 1959, 149–54; Mathieu 1996, 248; Müller 1899, 38) have been suggested.

Issue of reliability

An important issue to address in order to justify the use of the love poems for the study of ancient gender roles concerns their reliability in portraying the poets' experiences and perceptions of contemporaneous society. A brief survey of the formulaic phraseology employed in the poems may determine whether they incorporate a degree of personal experience or whether they represent a fictional genre constructed on repetitive themes, phrases, and formal devices borrowed from other Egyptian literary traditions, stemming from the context of the scribal milieu.

Any type of ancient Egyptian literary or non-literary composition is based on formulaic phraseology. A variety of available themes, forming part of a verbal and pictorial repertoire occurring in both literary and artistic expressions (e.g. fowling as the artistic variant of the love-trap theme is found in tombs (Hermann 1959, 143) such as TT69 of Menna (Davies and Gardiner 1936, 106–7, plate LIV)), was incorporated into the production of these texts. Some themes, for example love-sickness, recur regularly because they constitute the genre. Some of these may be linked to one protagonist only, such as the image of the woman as trapping the man (Fox 1985, 289, 306). One could argue that women were merely included in the love poems and, to a certain extent, ascribed an active role because both men and women were important participants in the love setting, as is evident from other related documents, such as the erotic *pTurin 55001* (Omlin 1973). Even if literary themes represented the sole motivation for female involvement, the poets may not have granted them an active participation and positive image without any evidence from their own social background, especially because the scribes were very likely influenced by compositions (Brunner 1957, 88–93) such as the *Instruction of Any*, painting a rather negative picture of unmarried women (Fox ascribes unmarried status to the protagonists (1985, xii)). Motif-specific phrases (e.g. "My heart is equal to you/your heart" or "I will not be far from you/your beauty"), space fillers (e.g. *wꜥ.kw/wꜥ.ti*), and standardized incipit phrases (e.g. "I have found the brother"; for a full list, see Landgráfová and Navrátilová (2009, 231–4)) appear frequently because they belong to the linguistic repertoire of the genre. Themes, formal devices (e.g. catchword association (Fox 1985, 194; White 1978, 80), alliteration, paronomasia (Mathieu 1996, 203–4), anaphora (*ibid.* 1996, 207–9), or epiphora (*ibid.* 1996:210)), and the metric frame *(ibid.* 1996, 202), basically any feature which could create formulaic patterns through repetition, were applied as literary means. Formulaic phraseology does not provide evidence for the non-existence of the authors' own experiences of society but indicates that these were hidden by and intermingled with formulae which were characteristic of the various literary themes employed in the creation of these poems. Occasional violations of the rigid nature of the genre, for example *pH*A6 (Mathieu 1996, 187), the portrayal of personae of various characteristics, and the avoidance of creating stereotypical characters (Fox 1985, xxv, 221, 305) confirm that the poems represent the poets' experiences.

Some scholars claim an oral tradition of love poems as folk songs to have existed before they were transformed into written manifestations (e.g. tentatively Fox 1985; Landgráfová and Navrátilová 2009; Meskell 2002, 128). Even if the compositional dates of the poems lie prior to the Ramesside period, the scribes who decided to record them on papyri or ostraca would probably have amended them to fit the scribal literary conventions and milieu of that particular time (Landgráfová and Navrátilová 2009, 19) rather than noting them down verbatim. If they had noticed an aspect that opposed their world view, they may have changed it to fit the belief and understanding of their contemporaneous society. Therefore one may assume that the images of women and men, as conveyed in the poems, were fairly accurate presentations of late New Kingdom society and gender roles.

Regarding the written form of the poems, the general consensus amongst scholars accepts an elite background, portraying protagonists from the upper class (Mathieu 1996, 245; Schott 1950, 8; White 1978, 79). This interpretation is based on linguistic grounds, such as the use of sophisticated formal devices and literary themes, representing cross-genre borrowings, which poets probably would have become familiar with during their scribal education (Mathieu 1996, 217–41, 245; White 1978, 79). The poems are composed in a blend of Late and classical Middle Egyptian. The scribes experienced the former in daily life and learnt the latter during their training (Mathieu 1996, 189). If love songs originated as oral folk songs, elements from social classes other than elite may be encountered (Landgráfová and Navrátilová 2009, 76, 207). If this is the case, it may imply that certain aspects regarding gender roles as portrayed in the poems were applicable to several social classes (either through personal experience or awareness through other means) because scribes did not feel the need to amend them. Deir el-Medina, a middle-class village (Meskell 1999, 141) and the home of highly skilled craftsmen and scribes working on the royal tombs, has been suggested as the possible place of composition, or, at least, emendation of the poems (e.g. Landgráfová and Navrátilová 2009, 20, 85, 219–20; Mathieu 1996, 245). Therefore, the poems may portray gender roles as perceived at the workmen's community. This hypothesis is supported by the following: *pCB* and a large number of ostraca bearing love poems were found at Deir el-Medina (*ibid.* 1996, 22). Large amounts of textual remains may suggest a fairly high literacy rate in the workmen's community (Baines and Eyre 2007, 94; L. H. Lesko 1994, 135), which was probably a consequence of the village's extraordinary status. Additionally, White (1978, 79) pointed out that the non-textual ostraca found in Deir el-Medina depict some of the motifs as used in their literary form in the love poems.

Besides the poets' social background which would have influenced their perception of society and their experiences as operating in that landscape, the gender of the scribes is important and may have had an impact on the degree of fictionality put into the production of the poems. Regardless of whether society was male-dominated or allowed both women and men equal roles, men would have been unlikely to create fictionally active roles for women reflecting equality, if they had not perceived such a situation in their contemporaneous society. Landgráfová and Navrátilová (2009, 38, n. 58) have pointed out that male-authored literature most likely portrays what men expected from women regarding gender stereotypes. Therefore, if male scribes create an equal standing between women and men in the poems, then it may be fairly safe to assume that this actually reflects an equal position of ancient Egyptian women. The poems convey a rather positive female image, compared with some negative illustrations in other compositions, such as *The Two Brothers*, probably arising from the viewpoint of male authorship. Baines and Eyre have argued that this may imply that women were involved in the production, or, at least, the presentation thereof (2007, 87). Additionally, a large number of love poems are told from a female perspective (Landgráfová and Navrátilová 2009, 21), although this does not confirm the participation of women in the production process. Only one document (*pCBC*), entitled 'The Beginning of the Sayings of the Great Entertainer' ('*ḥ3.t-ʿ m rw nw t3 sḫmḫ.t-ib ʿ3.t*' followed by the feminine determinative), may hint at a female composer. Female poets (as a hypothetical scenario), for example songstresses (a well-known profession in the New Kingdom (Mathieu 1996, 139)), may have portrayed ancient practice but could also have used the love poems as a literary means to escape social restraints if they had faced such. However, if male scribes had recorded poems composed by women exaggerating their actual role within society, they would probably not have copied something, which contradicted their own viewpoint.

As the scribal profession was a male-dominated sphere (Parkinson 2009, 63; Schott 1950, 9), it is very likely that the majority of poems were composed by men. However, if Deir el-Medina was a place of production, then women of that very community may be considered as potential authors (*contra* Meskell 1999, 213) because of the aforementioned high rate of literacy, which may have been spread amongst women as well (Baines and Eyre 2007, 94). This may result from women being present in the home (Brunner-Traut 1987, 319; Szpakowska 2008, 107; Toivari-Viitala 2001, 189) while boys learnt or practiced writing, perhaps being taught by their fathers or future superiors (McDowell 1999, 129). Textual remains support this view: some texts sent by and addressed to women have contents deemed too trivial (e.g. laundry lists) for the employment of professional scribes, which may indicate that women themselves wrote them (Szpakowska 2008, 107; Tyldesley 1995, 119). Additionally, women either wrote or engaged with a variety of texts, including personal letters (e.g. McDowell 1999, 41), economic exchange (Toivari-Viitala 2001, 233), legal documents (such as wills (McDowell 1999, 38–40), law suits (Allam 1989, 131), and witness accounts (McDowell 1999, 186–8)), and religious-related documents (e.g. oracles (Toivari-Viitala 2001, 233)).

Evidence regarding the performance of literary compositions is scarce. As the protagonists of the poems are personae created by anonymous scribes they may have been performed by professional interpreters (Fox 1985, 256; Mathieu 1996, 139); a predominance of female performers has been suggested (*ibid.* 1996, 139). Two collections (*pH*B, *pH*C) are entitled 'Song of Entertainment' ('*ḥs.t sḫmḫ-ỉb*'), implying that the love poems may have been sung (Landgráfová and Navrátilová 2009, 16; Mathieu 1996, 134). Parkinson has reconstructed the recital of two Middle Kingdom classics in a provincial, elite setting (2009). He interpreted the performers and the audience to be predominantly male as the official elite setting was a male-focused domain and the two tales were mostly male-dominated (*ibid.* 2009, 32, 64). The audience, who may have enjoyed the love poems at various settings, for example banquets (Hughes Fowler 1994, xiv), may have been more inclusive because both women and men feature as protagonists; therefore, neither sex dominates the genre. Furthermore, the poems describe the experience of emotions which were understood across social levels and gender (White 1978, 82). Combined with the poems' possible origin as folk songs, this strongly suggests that they reflect gender roles which were accessible across society.

Analysis

The extent of freedom given to the women within the domains of speech, action and movement by the poets will provide information on how their role, in relation to men, was perceived by members of society. The analysis is based on my own translations.

Freedom of speech may be studied on several levels: principal speakers and addressees and minor addressees of the main body of the poems (including terms of endearment), and speakers and addressees of speeches within the poems. Sweeney has studied the female and male voice expressed in the love poems by examining ways of interaction within the love context, for example requests, and the grammatical constructions connected with these (2002). Her approach is based on linguistic grounds whereas this paper focuses on the contextualization of the poems and the general analysis of gender roles by examining the independence, importance and impact ascribed to the women in the poems.

As Table 3.1 illustrates, the woman is given a predominant role as principal speaker reciting more than half of the poems, for example all poems of *pH*B. She addresses the man both directly and indirectly, whereas the man only addresses the woman indirectly (Mathieu has established elaborate patterns of communication between speakers and addressees within the entire corpus of known love poems (1996, 142–6, 149)). The woman speaks to her heart, i.e. herself, as principal addressee in one poem (*pCB*C4), thereby reducing the man to the role of a minor party. Mathieu (1996:144) has argued that the absence of men directly addressing women in the poems may be due to predominantly female performers. However, one should not deny the possibility of male performers (*contra ibid.* 1996, 139). His argument may be further refuted by *O.DM 1078 Ro* in which a woman is addressed directly by a man (Landgráfová and Navrátilová 2009, 138). Regarding the terms of endearment used to address each other, the poets ascribe the woman a larger set of vocabulary. The remaining five poems (*pT*1–3, *pCB*R1–2) are spoken by third parties who address both protagonists in equal measures.

The extent of the female and male voice is determined by investigating the appearance and nature of minor addressees. This designation refers to either any third party appearing in the poems besides the principal addressee (such as the woman's heart and Pre featuring in *pH*A8) or to the principal speaker talking about him- or herself in a descriptive manner (e.g. the woman declaring: "I am with you, being alone", in *pH*B1). Third parties predominantly involve human beings but also gods and the heart of the respective protagonists which may stand for the man or the woman. Figurative images, representing the man or woman, such as the goose or the parts of the door, are considered as third parties. Although the nature of third parties may reflect the love context, they are examined to define the range of the protagonists' interactions.

Both protagonists are allowed to address approximately the same number of third parties with a slight predominance given to the man (for a full list of minor addressees, see Table 3.2). Some are addressed multiple times. The main difference between the third parties addressed by the man and the woman concerns the nature of the addressees. The woman relates third parties, who are familiar and mostly belong to the private sphere, such as hearts, family members, some deities, and animals as figurative images for the boy. Contrarily, the boy focuses on invoking a

		Man	**Woman**
Speaker of x poems (out of the total of 41 poems)		~27% (11 poems)	~61% (25 poems)
Addressee (out of the total of 41 poems)	direct	~29% (12 poems)	0%
	indirect	~10% (4 poems)	~27% (11 poems)
	mixed	~20% (8 poems)	0%
Terms of endearment (out of the total of 41 poems)		brother (~20%, 8 poems), wolf cub (~2 %, 1 poem), beloved, noble one, neglectful one, noble man, friend	sister (~ 17%, 7 poems), mistress (~2%, 1 poem)

Table 3.1: This table features the number of poems out of the total of 41, which are spoken by the man and woman in both absolute and relative numbers. Furthermore, it provides information on the number of poems in which the woman and man are addressed either directly, indirectly or changing from one to the other. Terms of endearment used by the protagonists to describe each other and the absolute and relative numbers of poems, in which they feature, are also included.

		Man	Woman
Third party		29 in main body of poems (his heart (3×), lovers, Ptah/Creator of the Arts (2×), door keeper, Sekhmet (1×), Iadetyt, Nefertem, Kind One, neighbours, Star-goddess, Unique One, men, Mehi, Golden One, Her Majesty, Lady of Heaven, Hathor, Mistress, my Goddess, chief physicians, lector priests, messengers, cattle breeder, door bolt, door, lock, jambs, key, (beautiful) girl)	24 (her heart (15×), his heart (6×), her mother (3×), Golden One, Amun (2×), people, goose, Pre (1×), swallow, another woman, heart of another, her father, neighbours, all her people, his mother, his siblings, his companions, my Goddess, messenger, general hearts, the heart of her mother, royal messenger, gazelle, royal horse); brother as minor addressee (1×)
Man/Woman	out of the total of 41 poems	~24% (10 poems)	~51% (21 poems)
	out of their respective sets of poems	~91% (10 poems out of 11)	84% (21 poems out of 25)
Terms of endearment (used by the principal speakers to describe themselves; out of the total of 41 poems)		brother (~2%, 1 poem), goose	sister (~15%, 6 poems), noblewoman (~2%, 1 poem), beloved, Lady of the House

Table 3.2: This table shows the number and nature of third parties addressed by the man or woman. It further gives the relative and absolute numbers of poems in which the protagonists describe or talk to themselves. These results are set in relation to both the total number of poems and their respective sets. The terms of endearment used by the protagonists to refer to themselves are also listed.

multitude of divine powers and refers to non-affiliated parties. The principal speakers can also talk about themselves. Out of the total of 41 poems, the woman describes herself in half of them. This predominance is linked to the overall larger set of poems in which she acts as principal speaker (25 *vs.* 11). Within their respective sets of poems, the man takes the opportunity to describe himself in almost all of his poems. The woman is given a wider range of vocabulary to refer to herself, mirroring the results as shown in Table 3.1.

Internal speeches are spoken within the main body of the poems and are introduced with "X says to Y" or other verbs implying the notion of speech, for example "I will say to [Ptah], the Lord of Truth, 'Give to me the sister tonight!'" (*pH*A5). Those open to interpretation have not been considered. Speakers and addressees of such speeches involve either one of the principal speakers or a third party. As can be seen in Table 3.3, both man and woman make almost the same number of internal speeches. The woman addresses the man in four speeches whereas the man addresses her only once, but he addresses more third parties than her. Both protagonists are almost equally often addressed by them. The woman (and some third parties) is also referred to indirectly as subject of the internal speeches. The range of third parties, with whom the protagonists communicate, is congruent with the results regarding minor addressees. The woman converses with third parties belonging to the private domain, such as her heart or her mother, whereas the man speaks with those stemming from the public sphere in addition to private ones.

In general, the poets grant the woman a more important voice than the man because she is ascribed a more dominant position as speaker. This would seem unusual if ancient Egyptian society had been predominantly male-focused. Therefore, it contradicts Mathieu's interpretation of the poems as portraying a male-dominated perspective (as mentioned above). Even if the ancient Egyptians perceived women as more associated with emotions (which is opposed by occurrences of men referring to their hearts to express their feelings), and hence love poems, than men (as in many western societies today), this does not satisfactorily explain the predominance of women as principal speakers. The woman's large verbal repertoire regarding terms of endearment is striking, and may suggest that she was perceived as a literate individual. This may be backed up by the proposed literacy rate of women in Deir el-Medina (assuming that the gender roles portrayed in the poems mirror those perceived in that community). The man is given slight predominance regarding the extent of his voice because he is allowed to relate to more third parties than the woman. This may reflect men's engagements in both private and public spheres and therefore, his wider range of interactions as experienced in society. In the poems he interacts with third parties from both domains while the woman mentions those which predominantly form part of

	Man	**Woman**	**Third party**
Speaker (out of the total of 41 poems)	~10% (4 poems)	~12 % (5 poems)	swallow (~2%, 1 poem) her mother (~2%, 1 poem) his heart (~2%, 1 poem) her heart (~2%, 1 poem) people (~2%, 1 poem) (beautiful) girl (~2%, 1 poem) anonymous (~5%, 2 poems)
Principal addressee (out of the total of 41 poems)	~10% (4 poems) woman to man	~2 % (1 poem) man to woman	~7% (3 poems) man to Ptah, Mehi and his heart
	~10% (4 poems) third parties (his heart, anonymous (2x), (beautiful) girl) to man	~7% (3 poems) third parties (swallow, mother, her heart) to woman	~2% (1 poem) woman to her heart
Minor addressee (out of the total of 41 poems)		~2% (1 poem) third party (people);	~2% (1 poem) his heart to man about Mehi;
		~2% (1 poem) man to Ptah;	~2% (1 poem) woman to man about the myrrh-anointed one (as a figurative image for man)
		~5% (2 poems) anonymous to man;	
		~2% (1 poem) man to his heart	

Table 3.3: This table gives an overview of the overall number of poems, in which the man, woman or a third party is engaged as speaker in an internal speech. These results are then compared with the total of 41 poems. The principal addressees of internal speeches are also illustrated, providing information on who addresses who in absolute and relative numbers of poems and allowing an investigation of individual interactions in more detail. Finally, the section on minor addressees shows who is mentioned indirectly.

the private setting. This may confirm the gender-specific private-public division as claimed by scholars based on other ancient material.

The freedom of action ascribed to the protagonists is identified by examining general actions (e.g. "He has found another one" (*pH*B7)) and interactivity between women and men (e.g. "She has caught my heart in her embrace" (*pCB*C1)). This investigation focuses on dynamic verbs (as opposed to stative verbs describing the state something/someone is in rather than actions proper). The analysed actions are further classified according to actions associated with negation (e.g. "I do not have mercy of my heart with your loving of me" (*pH*A4)), causation (e.g. "She will cause the necks of all the men to turn away at her sight" (*pCB*C1)), desire (e.g. "He does not know my desires to embrace him" (*pCB*C2)), commands (e.g. "Take me in your embrace" (*pCB*R1)) and internal speeches. Some of the examined grammatical constructions may correspond to more than one criterion, for example negated causation (e.g. "It does not allow me to put on the tunic" (*pCB*C4)) and negated and/or caused imperatives (e.g. "Do not let people say about me" (*pCB*C4)). I only consider phrases which are obvious in meaning and construction to avoid interpretation of the love content. Fragmentary passages with the verb missing are not included because modern additions represent scholars' interpretations of the material. The only exception to this rule concerns omitted subject suffixes which are usually easy to ascribe to a specific protagonist. Negations and imperatives are identified by the appropriate grammatical constructions while causation is marked by the verb *di*/*rdi*. I follow Mathieu regarding expressions of desire (1996, 165). The categories movement and action cannot be strictly delineated and certain verbs encompass both. Sometimes these describe actions which imply movement, for example *ms*, "to bring, present" (Faulkner 1962, 116). As it is not clear to what extent movement is involved, these verbs will be considered in this category. Actions undertaken by "your/my love" are taken into account because this has been interpreted as *inter alia* representing the man or woman (Fox 1985, 20–1, n. e). The actions of figurative images, such as certain animals or the heart representing the man or woman, are also considered because they express the range of action ascribed to the protagonists.

Although both man and woman undertake almost the same amount of general actions (as demonstrated in Table 3.4), the man's actions are included in more poems, namely ~56% out of the total of 41. It is interesting to note that the man neither causes nor desires general action nor does he act in internal speeches, whereas the woman participates in all categories. Her actions are negated substantially more often, including the negated causation stated above. She causes and desires general actions. She is ordered to do something more often than the man (two out of the four commands are given by the woman to herself, the others represent orders by third parties).

As Table 3.5 illustrates, the protagonists interact with each other in the same number of poems. However, the woman as an active agent interacts with the man three times more often than *vice versa*. The man's actions can be attributed in almost equal measures to all subcategories, i.e. two of his actions towards the woman are negated, he is causing and desiring interactive actions, and the woman commands him to interact, while she is neither ordered to interact nor does she cause any interactivity, but she is more restricted.

The actions are fairly evenly spread between men and women with a slight predominance given to women, in particular regarding interactions. As these actions portray the impact the protagonists have on each other, they can provide valuable information on gender roles. On the whole, the woman's actions are more restricted. However, she is depicted as an influential individual with the ability to cause general action and to order the man to interact. The portrayal of the woman as the one who has an impact on the man would be surprising in a society which regards women as secondary.

	Man	**Woman**
Total	~56% (23 poems out of 41)	~41% (17 poems)
	He acts 36 times in 23 poems.	She acts 37 times in 17 poems.
Negation	~6% (2 actions)	~27% (10 actions)
Causation	0%	~14% (5 actions)
Desire	0%	~3% (1 action)
Command	~ 3% (1 action)	~8% (3 actions)
Internal speech	0%	~5% (2 actions)

Table 3.4: This table illustrates the total number of general actions undertaken by the man and woman and the number of poems (both in absolute and relative figures compared with the total of 41 poems) in which these actions occur. The actions are further divided into five subcategories. Negation gives information on the extent the man and woman were restricted in their actions. Causation either shows the impact they can have by causing actions to happen or the degree to which they are allowed to do something. Desire refers to the man or woman wishing to do something. The commands given to the man or woman respectively are listed as well. Some verbs may be classified according to multiple categories. Negated causation may either show the restriction of the protagonist's actions expressed in a way which seems stronger than general negations or the restriction of the speaker's ability to have an impact on something or someone (no example available in the present data set for the latter case). Negated and/or caused imperatives emphasize the possible range of commands given by the protagonists. In all cases the absolute number of actions, which can be classified according to these criteria, and the relative number, in relation to the total number of actions ascribed to a specific protagonist, are stated.

	Man	**Woman**
Total	~39% (16 poems)	~39% (16 poems)
	He acts 25 times in 16 poems.	She acts 28 times in 16 poems.
Negation	8% (2 actions)	~14% (4 actions)
Causation	4% (1 action)	0%
Desire	4% (1 action)	~4% (1 action)
Command	% (2 actions)	0%
Internal speech	12% (3 actions)	~4% (1 action)

Table 3.5: This table is constructed on the same principles as Table 3.4, the only difference being the nature of the actions. The subcategories give an insight into how both man and woman interact with each other and the impact they may have on each other. Negations show restrictions regarding their interactions. Causation and command illustrate the way the protagonists influence each other. Desire refers to the man or woman desiring to interact with the other person.

The freedom of movement is analysed according to the same criteria as were laid out to establish the range of actions. Any verb reflecting the notion of motion is considered. The movements are further classified according to movements negated (e.g. "He cannot walk slowly" (*pCB*G2)), caused (i.e. "It does not allow me to walk like a person" (*pCB*C4)), desired (e.g. "Would that for me you may come to the sister quickly" (*pCB*G1)), and commanded (e.g. "My

	Man	Woman
Total	~29% (12 poems)	~34% (14 poems)
	He moves 18 times in 12 poems.	She moves 26 times in 14 poems.
Negation	~6% (1 movement)	~8% (2 movements)
Causation	0%	~4%(1 movement)
Desire	0%	~4% (1 movement)
Command	~6% (1 movement)	~12% (3 movements)
Internal speech	~17% (3 movements)	~8% (2 movements)

Table 3.6: This table follows Table 3.4 in layout.

	Man	Woman
Total	~24% (10 poems)	~22% (9 poems)
	He moves 12 times in 10 poems.	She moves 10 times in 9 poems.
Negation	0%	10% (1 movement)
Causation	0%	0%
Desire	The woman desires the man to come to her (25% (3 movements) out of his total of 12 movements).	
Command	~17% (2 movements)	0%
Internal speech	~8% (1 movement)	10% (1 movement)

Table 3.7: This table's layout and categories are based on Table 3.5. The principal difference between this and the preceding figures is evident in the nature of desire (rather than desiring to do something him- or herself, the protagonist desires the other party to act).

heart, and do not flee" (*pCBC*4)). They may also be part of internal speeches. Some movements may also correspond to more than one criterion (as seen in the example of caused movement).

The woman moves in ~34% out of the total of 41 poems, which represents 14 poems in absolute numbers (see Table 3.6). The man only moves in 29%. The woman is also given predominance regarding the number of actual movements. She desires to move about, whereas the man neither desires nor causes any movement, which is similar to the results regarding his general actions. The woman's movements are marginally more negated, including the above-mentioned specimen of negated causation, and she is commanded more often than the man. All commands are given by third parties except for one case in which the woman orders herself not to move. Both protagonists move fairly equally in internal speeches.

As Table 3.7 shows, both man and woman move towards or with each other (e.g. "My heart is in joy of our walking together" (*pHC*2)) in roughly the same number of poems. Within the poems, the woman moves slightly less often towards the man than *vice versa*. The woman is restricted in her interactivity, while the man is not. Neither causes any interaction. The man is subject to imperatives given by the woman and she desires him to move. They move together in one internal speech. Table 3.5 illustrates the same trend regarding the woman's involvement in the subcategories.

Both protagonists move with or towards each other in almost equal measures. However, the woman is ascribed more freedom regarding general movements. This dominance may reflect that within her areas of responsibility she was allowed to move freely to fulfil her role as *nb.t pr* and other positions, such as songstress, outside the home. However, her movements are slightly more negated than the man's. This does not necessarily suggest that she was more restricted but as the man was an active agent in the public domain in addition to being involved in household economics, he may have been ascribed less restrictions overall (as seen regarding the results for actions). Once again, she is given influential power as she orders him to come to her. These results contradict Graves-Brown's interpretation (2010, 49) that "women seem to have been expected to be passive and largely subject to male command". Scholars have pointed out that women are portrayed as more passive than men, for example by desiring physical closeness, while men hardly every reciprocate that feeling (see above). Mathieu has accepted this as an argument emphasizing the poems' reflection of a male-dominated perspective (1996, 172–3). However, I do not interpret the woman's desire for interactivity and general actions and movements to represent a sign of passivity on her part. Overall, the number of occurrences of the expression of her desire is marginal when compared with the results of some of the other subcategories, such as negation or command. As an example, the ability to command the man to come to the woman does not portray passivity at all but shows a degree of impact and independence ascribed to the woman.

Conclusion

Ancient Egyptian love poems are literary landscapes based on the poets' personal experiences and perception of contemporary society. Repetitions of themes, vocabulary, and standardized phrases interwoven with literary devices creating formulaic phraseology are part of the poets' literary language learnt during scribal training and are used for stylistic purposes. They do not affect the poems' reliability as a source for the study of society and gender roles.

The poems were probably mainly composed by male authorship. However, female involvement in the production or, at least, presentation as performers cannot be excluded (in particular, if Deir el-Medina represents a place of composition). Additionally, women probably participated passively as an audience. Therefore, the poems had to convey gender roles which were accessible and acceptable to both men and women. In connection with the results from the analysis, which emphasize an equal standing of women and men, this may contradict Mathieu's interpretation of the poems as reflecting a male-dominated perspective. The backdrop of the poems seems mostly likely to have been a middle class to elite setting as perceived in the Theban region (such as Deir el-Medina) during the Ramesside period (regional and temporal variations of gender roles may have been possible) with the possibility of some elements describing other social classes than elite to have been preserved in the poems.

Within this social setting, ancient Egyptian poets as members of that past society perceived women and men as equal partners. The poems may be classified as a more private genre (as opposed to documents relating to the public domain) because of the following: they portray a private setting centred at individuals' houses or orchards, they were probably mainly used for private enjoyment (seeing as several poems' titles emphasize this purpose), and *pCB* was kept as part of a private archive. Bearing this in mind, I conclude that the equality described in the poems may derive from ancient perceptions of women's roles and authority within the private domain. The fairly equally distributed freedom of speech, action and movement as reflected in the poems may suggest that gender roles were perceived as equal (*contra*

Graves-Brown 2010, 49). This implies that ancient individuals did not experience the private sphere as secondary to the public domain, and women as inferior to men. Ancient Egyptian society was not entirely male-dominated and women were equal partners to men. Meskell's conclusion that the invisibility of women in the material culture of Deir el-Medina is based on "sexed inequalities" in society (1999, 213) may be refuted. This is in accordance with Landgráfová and Navrátilová (2009, 38–9) who have successfully argued that this invisibility may stem from other reasons than gender discrepancies. The interpretation of gender-specific division of labour as an expression of inequality between gender roles derives from imposing modern ideas and concepts on ancient material and shows that ancient perception and modern interpretation of evidence may differ.

Acknowledgements

This paper is a condensed version of my thesis submitted for the degree of Master of Philosophy at the University of Cambridge in August 2011. Full tables with references and examples can be provided on request but had to be omitted here due to the space restriction.

I wish to express my utmost gratitude to my supervisor Professor John D. Ray for his encouragement and support during the project. Furthermore, I wish to thank Dr Kate Spence, Dr Sian Thomas, Dr Miriam Müller, Kelly Accetta, Youness Bouzinab, Amira Kanwal, Sarah Musselwhite, and Allison Williams for stimulating discussions, invaluable advice, and the immense task of proof-reading.

Bibliography

Allam, S. (1989) Women as Owners of Immovables in Pharaonic Egypt. In B. S. Lesko (ed.) *Women's earliest records from Ancient Egypt and Western Asia, Proceedings of the Conference on Women in the Ancient Near East. Brown University, Providence, Rhode Island, November 5–7, 1987*, 123–35. Atlanta, Scholars Press.

Baines, J. and Eyre, C. (2007) Four notes on literacy. In J. Baines (ed.) *Visual and Written Culture in Ancient Egypt*, 63–94. Oxford, New York etc., Oxford University Press.

Brunner, H. (1957) *Altägyptische Erziehung*. Wiesbaden, Otto Harrassowitz.

Brunner-Traut, E. (1987) Die Stellung der Frau im Alten Ägypten. *Saeculum* 38, 312–35.

Budge, E. A. W. (1923) *Facsimiles of Egyptian Hieratic Papyri in the British Museum (Second Series)*. London, Printed by Order of the Trustees; Printers: Harrison and Sons, Ltd.

Černý, J. and Posener, G. (1978) *Papyrus hiératiques de Deir el-Médineh (Documents de Fouilles 8)*. Cairo, Institut français d'archéologie orientale.

Davies, N. M. and Gardiner, A. H. (1936) *Ancient Egyptian Paintings* (3 Vols.). Chicago, The University of Chicago Press.

Faulkner, R. O. (1962) *A Concise Dictionary of Middle Egyptian*. Oxford, Printed for the Griffith Institute at the University Press by V. Ridler.

Fox, M. V. (1985) *The Song of Songs and the Ancient Egyptian Love Songs*. Madison and London, The University of Wisconsin Press.

Gardiner, A. H. (1931) *The Library of A. Chester Beatty. Description of a Hieratic Papyrus with a Mythological Story, Love-songs, and other Miscellaneous Texts. The Chester Beatty Papyri, No.* I. London, Privately printed by J. Johnson at the Oxford University Press and published by E. Walker, Limited.

Graves-Brown, C. (2010) *Dancing for Hathor. Women in Ancient Egypt*. London and New York, Continuum.

Hermann, A. (1959) *Altägyptische Liebesdichtung*. Wiesbaden, Otto Harrassowitz

Hughes Fowler, B. (1994) *Love Lyrics of Ancient Egypt*. Chapel Hill and London, University of North Carolina Press.

Johnson, J. H. (1996) The legal status of women in ancient Egypt. In A. K. Capel and G. E. Markoe (eds) *Mistress of the House, Mistress of Heaven. Women in Ancient Egypt. Catalogue of an exhibition held at Cincinnati Art Museum, Cincinnati, Ohio, Oct. 20, 1996–Jan. 5, 1997, and The Brooklyn Museum, Brooklyn, N.Y., Feb. 21–May 18, 1997, 175–86.* New York, Hudson Hills Press in association with Cincinnati Art Museum.

Koenig, Y. (1981) Notes sur la découverte des papyrus Chester Beatty. *Bulletin de l'Institut français d'archéologie orientale* 81, 41–43.

Landgráfová, R. and Navrátilová, H. (2009) *Sex and the Golden Goddess I. Ancient Egyptian Love Songs in Context*. Prague, [Czech Institute of Egyptology].

Lesko, B. S. (1987) *The Remarkable Women of Ancient Egypt*. Providence, B. C. Scribe.

Lesko, L. H. (1994) Literature, Literacy, and Literati. In L. H. Lesko (ed.) *Pharaoh's Workers. The Villagers of Deir el Medina*, 131–44. Ithaca and London, Cornell University Press.

Mathieu, B. (1996) *La poésie amoureuse de l'Égypte ancienne. Recherches sur un genre littéraire au Nouvel Empire (Bibliothèque d'étude 115)*. Cairo, Institut français d'archéologie orientale.

McDowell, A. G. (1999) *Village Life in Ancient Egypt. Laundry Lists and Love Songs*. Oxford, Clarendon.

Meskell, L. M. (1999) *Archaeologies of Social Life. Age, Sex, Class et cetera in Ancient Egypt*. Oxford and Malden, Blackwell.

Meskell, L. M. (2002) *Private Life in New Kingdom Egypt*. Princeton and Woodstock, Princeton University Press.

Müller, W. M. (1899) *Die Liebespoesie der alten Ägypter*. Leipzig, J. C. Hinrichs.

Omlin, J. A. (1973) *Der Papyrus 55001 und seine satirisch-erotischen Zeichnungen und Inschriften (Catalogo del Museo egizio di Torino. Serie 1 – Monumenti e testi 3)*. Turin, Edizioni d'arte Fratelli Pozzo.

Parkinson, R. B. (2009) *Reading Ancient Egyptian Poetry among other Histories*. Chichester, Malden and Oxford, Wiley-Blackwell.

Pleyte, W. and Rossi, F. (1869–76) *Papyrus de Turin*. Leiden, E. J. Brill.

Robins, G. (1993) *Women in Ancient Egypt*. London, British Museum Press.

Robins, G. (2001) Women. In D. B. Redford (ed.) *The Oxford Encyclopedia of Ancient Egypt. Volume 3*, 510–16. Oxford, New York etc., Oxford University Press.

Schott, S. (1950) *Altägyptische Liebeslieder. Mit Märchen und Liebesgeschichten (Die Bibliothek der alten Welt. Reihe der alte Orient)*. Zurich, Artemis-Verlag.

Sweeney, D. (2002) Gender and Language in the Ramesside Love Songs. *Bulletin of the Egyptological Seminar* 16, 27–50.

Sweeney, D. (2008) Gender and requests in New Kingdom literature. In C. Graves-Brown (ed.) *Sex and Gender in Ancient Egypt. 'Don your wig for a joyful hour*', 191–214. Swansea, The Classical Press of Wales; Oxford, Oxbow Books [distributor].

Szpakowska, K. (2008) *Daily Life in Ancient Egypt. Recreating Lahun*. Malden, Oxford, and Carlton, Blackwell.

Toivari-Viitala, J. (2001) *Women at Deir el-Medina. A study of the status and roles of the female inhabitants in the workmen's community during the Ramesside period* (Egyptologische Uitgaven 15). Leiden, Nederlands Instituut Voor Het Nabije Oosten.

Tyldesley, J. (1995) *Daughters of Isis. Women of Ancient Egypt*. London, New York, etc., Viking.

White, J. B. (1978) *A Study of the Language of Love in the Song of Songs and Ancient Egyptian Poetry (Society of Biblical Literature Dissertation Series 38)*. Missoula, Scholars Press.

4

Chronology of the Egyptian New Kingdom revisited

Rita Gautschy

Introduction

Egyptian chronology of the second millennium BC is essential not only for Egypt, but also for the Levantine, Syria, Mesopotamia and the Aegean. The local chronologies of the different regions are interwoven by documented synchronisms and archaeological finds. On first sight, the various chronologies seem to reasonably agree after about 1400 BC. On closer inspection, however, it becomes clear that many arguments concerning open questions of Assyrian, Hittite and Babylonian chronology in this period are bound to the absolute dating of Ramesses II, whose accession to power is customarily dated to 1279 BC on the basis of a single lunar date (e.g. Huber 2011, 186). Thus, when using Assyrian or Babylonian chronology as a benchmark for possible chronological scenarios in Egypt, one has to be aware that prior to 1133 BC some questions in Assyrian chronology have been solved with respect to the standard Egyptian chronology. The danger of circular arguments is self-evident, although often neglected.

Chronological Data

To derive absolute dates, records of astronomical observations are frequently used. Only few lunar and sothic dates are known from Egypt – both are not sufficient to establish a robust chronology on the basis of Egyptian astronomical data. For the period of the Egyptian New Kingdom only the last visibilities of the crescent moon and a heliacal rising of Sirius are relevant. Two lunar dates are preserved from New Kingdom Egypt in which the text explicitly states that the reported day was a first Lunar Day: one of Ramesses II and the other of Thutmose III. Alongside, there exists a couple of secondary Lunar data which can be deduced from feast data. Additionally, an account of a solar eclipse is preserved in Ḫatti. Table 4.1 summarises all available lunar data.

With only two secure lunar dates it would be useless to construct a chronological framework. Fortunately, plenty of supplementary information is available and the lunar data can then be used for fine-tuning purposes. Assyria provides information in form of the Assyrian King List

Y	Pharaoh	Date	Comments	Source
9	Amenhotep I	III Shemu 9	Papyrus Ebers date	von Beckerath (1994, 10–13)
23	Thutmose III	I Shemu 21	Date of the battle of Megiddo LD 1 exactly	URKUNDEN IV, 657.2
24	Thutmose III	II Peret 30 III Peret 1	Akhmenu foundation date	URKUNDEN IV, 835.9–836.2
20	Amenhotep II	III Shemu 10 III Shemu 9	LD 1 occurred close to III Shemu 9	von Beckerath (1968, 18–21)
21	Amenhotep III	III Shemu 1	Feast-of-the-valley date LD 1 or 2	Marciniak (1974, 92–93 no. 36)
5	Akhenaten	IIII Peret 13	King took an oath to found Akhetaten	Murnane and van Siclen (1993, 38–40 and 48)
34	Ramesses II	IIII Shemu 24	Day of the feast of Ptah-south-of-his-wall	Peden (2001, 99)
47	Ramesses II	II Peret 25	Public holiday; LD 4 or 5	Peden (2001, 99)
52	Ramesses II	II Peret 27	Piramesses; LD 1 exactly	Jansen (1961, 12 and 33)
7	Twosre	II Shemu 28	Feast-of-the-valley date LD 1 or 2	Marciniak (1974, 59–61 no. 3)
7	Ramesses III	III Shemu 9	Feast-of-the-valley date LD 1 or 2	Marciniak (1974, 69 no. 10)
3	Ramesses VI	II Shemu 20	Feast-of-the-valley date LD 1 or 2	Marciniak (1974, 88–89 no. 32)
6	Ramesses VII	III Shemu 9	Feast-of-the-valley date LD 1 or 2	Marciniak (1974, 68–69 no. 9)
22	Ramesses XI	II Shemu 22	Feast-of-the-valley date LD 1 or 2	Marciniak (1974, 87–88 no. 31)

Table 4.1: Preserved lunar data from the Egyptian New Kingdom. Abbreviations used: Y – year; LD – lunar day.

(Glassner 1993, 146–151). The Assyrian King List is accurate to within one year from 1132 BC onwards, prior to 1133 BC the uncertainty amounts to approximately 25 years starting from the beginning of the reign of Enlil-nāṣir II (1431/1406 BC). Prior to Enlil-nāṣir II the reign lengths of two kings are unknown. From Babylonia, the Babylonian King List (Grayson 1975, 171–177) and a Synchronistic King List (Weidner 1926, 66–77) are preserved. C14 data (Bronk Ramsey *et al.* 2010) from Egypt delivers further important information about the absolute dates of Pharaohs. Documented direct synchronisms, mainly from the Amarna period and from the times of Ramesses II, in combination with the above mentioned data, allows one to establish a chronological frame for Egypt and the Near East in the second half of the second millennium BC.

Synchronisms

The Amarna tablets provide the information that Amenhotep III was contemporaneous with the Assyrian king Aššur-nādin-aḫḫe II as well as with the Babylonian rulers Kurigalzu I and Kadašman-Enlil I. The Assyrian king Aššur-uballiṭ I wrote letters to Akhenaten. The long-reigning Babylonian king Burnaburiaš II was a contemporary of the Egyptian kings Amenhotep III and Akhenaten, and of the Ḫatti ruler Šuppiluliuma I. Kadašman-Turgu offered to march together with Hattušili III against Ramesses II. The Kassite king Adad-šuma-uṣur, who reigned for 30 years, provides a few further important synchronisms: he was a contemporary of the Assyrian kings Tukultī-Ninurta I, Aššur-nādin-apli, Aššur-nīrārī III, Enlil-kudurrī-uṣur and Ninurta-apil-Ekur. Table 4.2 summarises all the synchronisms which I securely categorise as direct.

C14 data

Bronk Ramsey *et al.* (2010) published new C14 data for Egypt. To narrow down the uncertainty of the C14 analysis they applied the so-called method of wiggle matching; this means that they used information about the reign lengths and the order of the Pharaohs in their modelling of the absolute dates. Such a treatment can allow the reduction of the uncertainty of the C14 determination to about 25 years for the Egyptian New Kingdom. Column 7 in Table 4.5 lists the resulting time spans for the first year of the Pharaohs. However, one has to keep in mind that incorrect assumptions about reign lengths of Pharaohs in the modelling (e.g. Horemheb) may influence the resulting absolute dates. Additionally, doubts against the applied method have arisen since the organic material was taken from museums and may have been contaminated (Bruins 2010, 1490).

Lunar data

Putting together all the available information allows for constructing different possible absolute chronologies. Between Akhenaten and Ramesses II are three kings – namely Smenkhkare, Horemheb and Seti I – for whom different values concerning their reign lengths are proposed. When referring to Smenkhkare, the total amount of regnal years of Smenkhkare and the lady Neferneferuaten are meant. The highest dates for the three mentioned kings are listed in Table 4.3. Archaeological evidence provides a strong argument against assigning more than 14 years of reign for Horemheb: in the tomb of Horemheb in the Valley of the Kings more than 200 hieratic jar dockets mentioning his year 13 or 14 have been found, but none with higher dates (Van Dijk 2008). Based on the lunar data it becomes clear that the total number of years of the kings with disputed reign lengths can amount to either 28, 42, 53, 67 or 78 years. Adopting a reign length of 14 years for Horemheb results in a reasonable sum of 28 years for all three kings,but if a reign length of 27 years for Horemheb is assumed (which is the standard value used in most chronological treatments, e.g. Kitchen 2007, Hornung 2006), the sum for all three kings amounts to 42 years.

A comparison of the lunar data with calculations (Table 4.4) shows that the astronomical data are in good agreement with a short reign length of 14 years for Horemheb as suggested by the archaeological evidence from his tomb. In respect of the lunar data, 39 years for Horemheb would fit equally well, but a total amount of 53 years for the kings with disputed reign lengths can be excluded based on the documented synchronisms with Assyria. While all possible chronological

Egypt	Ḫatti	Babylonia	Assyria	Source
		Karaindaš	Aššur-bēl-nišēšu	Syn-H
		Kurigalzu I	Aššur-nādin-aḫḫe	Chr. P
			Erība-Adad I	Chr. P
Amenhotep III		Kurigalzu I		EA 6
		Kadašman-Enlil I		EA 1–5
		Burnaburiaš II		EA 6
	Šuppiluliuma I			EA 41?
Akhenaten	Šuppiluliuma I			EA 41
		Burnaburiaš II		EA 7–11, 14
			Aššur-uballiṭ I	EA 15, 16
		Burnaburiaš II	Aššur-uballiṭ I	Syn-H
		Kara-ḫardaš		Syn-H
		Nazi-Bugaš		Syn-H, Chr. P
		Kurigalzu II		Syn-H, Chr. P
Smenkhkare	Šuppiluliuma I			EA 41
Horemheb	Muršili II			KUB 19.15 + KBo 50.24
		Kurigalzu II	Enlil-nīrārī	Syn-H
		Nazi-Maruttaš	Adad-nīrārī I	Syn-H, Chr. P
		Kadašman-Turgu I		Chr. P
Ramesses II	Muwatalli			Breyer (2010)
	Muršili III			CTH 155
	Hattušili III			CTH 155
	Hattušili III		Adad-nīrārī I?	KBo 1.14
		Kadašman-Turgu I		CTH 172
		Kadašman-Enlil II		CTH 172
	Tudḫaliya IV		Tukultī-Ninurta I?	CTH 177
		Adad-šuma-uṣur	Tukultī-Ninurta I	Chr. P
			Aššur-nādin-apli	Chr. P
			Aššur-nīrārī III	Chr. P
			Enlil-kudurrī-uṣur	Syn-H
			Ninurta-apil-Ekur	Syn-H
		Meli-Šipak	Ninurta-apil-Ekur	SKL
		Zababa-šuma-iddina	Aššur-dān I	Syn-H
		Enlil-nādin-aḫi		SKL

Table 4.2: Direct synchronisms documented in Egyptian, Hittite, Babylonian and Assyrian sources. The abbreviations stand for the following sources: EA – Amarna tablets (Moran 1992); Syn-H – Synchronistic History (Grayson 1975, 157–170); Chr. P – Chronicle P (Grayson 1975, 170–177); SKL – Synchronistic King List (Weidner 1926, 66–77); CTH – Catalogue des texts hittites (Laroche 1971); KBo – Keilschrifttexte aus Boghazköi (1916–); and KUB – Keilschrifturkunden aus Boghazköi (Berlin 1921–1990).

Pharaoh	**Secure**	**Doubtful**	**Manetho**	**Adopted**
Neferneferuaten Smenkhkare	2 1		12 6/9/29/39	3 for both together
Seti I	11	15	51/55/59	11
Horemheb	14	16, 27, 59	4	14

Table 4.3: Reign lengths of Pharaohs which are assured (Hornung 2006, 207–211), which are tentatively assigned to them (Hornung 2006, 207–211), which are given in the Manethonian sources (Josephus, Eusebius and Africanus; see von Beckerath 1997, 123–128), and which are adopted in this work.

Y	**Pharaoh**	**Date**	**P1$_{27}$**	**P2$_{27}$**	**P3$_{27}$**	**P4$_{27}$**	**P1$_{14}$**	**P2$_{14}$**	**P3$_{14}$**	**P4$_{14}$**
9	Amenhotep I	III Shemu 9	**+1**	**+1**	**+1**	**+1**	0	0	**-1**	0
23	Thutmose III	I Shemu 21	0	0	**+1**	0	0	**-1**	**-1**	0
24	Thutmose III	II Peret 30 III Peret 1	0 +1	0 +1	-1 0	0 +1	-2 -1	-1 0	-2 -1	-1 0
20	Amenhotep II	III Shemu 10 III Shemu 9	+1 0	+1 0	+1 0	+1 0	0 -1	0 -1	0 -1	0 -1
21	Amenhotep III	III Shemu 1	-1	-1	-2	**-1**	0	0	0	0
5	Akhenaten	IIII Peret 13	**-1**	**-1**	**-1**	**-1**	0	0	0	**+1**
34	Ramesses II	IIII Shemu 24	0	0	0	0	0	0	0	0
47	Ramesses II	II Peret 25	0	0	0	0	0	0	0	0
52	Ramesses II	II Peret 27	-1	-1	-1	-1	-1	-1	-1	-1
7	Twosre	II Shemu 28	0	0	0	0	0	0	0	0
7	Ramesses III	III Shemu 9	0	0	0	0	0	0	0	0
3	Ramesses VI	II Shemu 20	0	**-1**	0	0	0	**-1**	0	0
6	Ramesses VII	III Shemu 9	0	**-1**	0	0	0	**-1**	0	0
22	Ramesses XI	II Shemu 22	0	0	0	0	0	0	0	0

Table 4.4: Fits of the Lunar Data for four possible chronological solutions developed in this work - denoted as P1, P2, P3 and P4 - with a reign length of 27 years for Horemheb (grey shaded; columns 3 to 6) and with 14 years for Horemheb (columns 7 to 10). A "0" denotes a perfect fit between observations and calculations; "-1" means that the lunar crescent was not observed although theoretically it was visible; "+1" means that the lunar crescent was observed although theoretically it was not visible anymore. Abbreviation used: Y – year.

solutions with 27 years for Horemheb (shaded grey in Table 4.4) tend to show unexplainable deviations in positive direction (+1), solutions with 14 years for Horemheb regularly show deviations in negative direction (-1) with one exception only. Deviations in negative direction can easily be explained by a missed sighting of a theoretically visible lunar crescent due to unfavourable weather conditions. On the other hand, a deviation in positive direction means that the lunar crescent was observed although theoretically it was not visible anymore. Such a deviation can occasionally occur due to perfect weather conditions and a close miss of the critical value of the sighting criterion on the following day. However, in all the cases here, it was impossible to observe the lunar crescent on the following day.

To further test the hypothesis of a short reign length of Horemheb, one can take a look at Assyrian chronology and the documented synchronisms. From the ascension of Aššur-uballiṭ I, who was contemporary with Akhenaten (Table 4.2), to the death of Adad-nīrārī I, who was a contemporary of the early Ramesses II and the Hittite king Muršili III, 90 years have passed according to the Assyrian King List. A corresponding minimum distance from Aššur-uballiṭ I to Adad-nīrārī I, fulfilling all the necessary direct synchronisms, results in about 70 years. The reign lengths from Akhenaten to year 20 of Ramesses II add up to 80 years if 14 years are assumed for Horemheb. Adopting 27 years for Horemheb would result in 93 years. Both values fit within the 70 to 90 years documented in Assyria when taking into account that year 20 of Ramesses II is a *terminus ante quem* for the accession of Hattušili III; it is very likely that he came to power a few years earlier. Nevertheless, a short reign length of Horemheb can be accommodated easier within the given Assyrian time frame. In all events, a reign length of 39 years of Horemheb – which results in comparable fittings of the lunar data to the solution with 14 years – can be excluded. Thus, I will consider in the following only chronological solutions with 14 years of reign for Horemheb.

Chronological frame

The beginning of the Egyptian New Kingdom is usually dated to years 18 to 22 of Ahmose (e.g. Schneider 1996, 62), but Ryholt (1997, 188) opts for year 11 based on the text of the reverse of Papyrus Rhind whose year indication he relates to Ahmose. The chronological solutions presented in Table 4.5 start with year 1 of Ahmose, thus slightly earlier than the beginning of the New Kingdom.

Within a generous time frame, four different chronological solutions can be proposed, two of them are feasible with the assumption that the Egyptian day began at dawn (P1 and P3 in Table 4.5), the other two with the assumption that the day began with sunrise (P2 and P4). Since the fit is of comparable quality in each case, the lunar data cannot be used to select the correct chronology. Instead, one should turn to Hittite chronology.

Synchronisms with Ḫatti

Unfortunately, the exact reign lengths of the Hittite kings can only be estimated. For a comparison with Hittite chronology, years 5 to 21 of Ramesses II are crucial. Muwatalli II was the antagonist of Ramesses II in the battle of Qadeš (Breyer 2010, 214–215). Between the battle of Qadeš in year 5 of Ramesses II and the peace treaty in his year 21 which he signed together with Hattušili III, 16 years are left to accommodate for several events in Hittite history: the occurrence of the

Y	Pharaoh	P1	P2	P3	P4	C14	Reign Length
1	Ahmose	1539	1550	1564	1575		25y 4m (*)
1	Amenhotep I	1514	1525	1539	1550		20y 7m (*)
1	Thutmose I	1494	1505	1519	1530		12y 9m (*)
1	Thutmose II	1481	1492	1506	1517		13y (*)
1	Thutmose III	1468	1479	1493	1504	1498 – 1474	54y (*)
1	Amenhotep II	1414	1425	1439	1450	1445 – 1423	25y 10m (*)
1	Thutmose IV	1388	1399	1413	1424		9y 8m (*)
1	Amenhotep III	1378	1389	1403	1414	1408 – 1386	38y 7m (*)
1	Akhenaten	1339	1350	1364	1375	1370 – 1348	17y (*)
1	Smenkhkare	1322	1333	1347	1358		3y (see Table 3)
1	Tutankhamun	1319	1330	1344	1355	1353 – 1331	10y (+)
1	Ay	1309	1320	1334	1345		4y (+)
1	Horemheb	1305	1316	1330	1341		14y (see Table 3)
1	Ramesses I	1291	1302	1316	1327		1y 4m (*)
1	Seti I	1290	1301	1315	1326		11y (see Table 3)
1	Ramesses II	1279	1290	1304	1315	1297 – 1273	66y 2m (*)
1	Merneptah	1213	1224	1238	1249		9y 6m (*)
1	Seti II	1203	1214	1228	1239		5y 10m (+)
1	Siptah	1197	1208	1222	1233		5y 9m (+)
1	Twosre	1192	1203	1217	1228		2y (+)
1	Sethnakhte	1190	1201	1215	1226		3y (*)
1	Ramesses III	1187	1198	1212	1223		31y 2m (*)
1	Ramesses IV	1156	1167	1181	1192		6y 9m (+)
1	Ramesses V	1149	1160	1174	1185		3y 10m (*)
1	Ramesses VI	1145	1156	1170	1181		9y (#)
1	Ramesses VII	1136	1147	1161	1172		7y (+)
1	Ramesses VIII	1129	1140	1154	1165		2y (*)
1	Ramesses IX	1127	1138	1152	1163	1143 – 1117	18y 3m (*)
1	Ramesses X	1109	1120	1134	1145		3y (*)
1	Ramesses XI	1106	1117	1131	1142		28y (*)
	End of NK	1078	1089	1103	1114		

Table 4.5: Four possible chronological frames of the Egyptian New Kingdom (P1 to P4) based on the Lunar Data (all dates are BC) developed in this work. Column 7 gives the C14 data of Bronk Ramsey (2010), column 8 the adopted reign lengths of the Pharaohs. Hatshepsut's years are included in the year count of Thutmose III. The adopted reign lengths have been taken from the following sources: (*): Schneider (2010, 402–403); (+): Shaw (2000, 481); (#) based on the Lunar Data 9 instead of 8 years (Schneider 2010, 403). Abbreviation used: Y – year.

death of Muwatalli, 7 years for Muršili III, the taking-over of the throne in Ḫatti by Hattušili III, Muršili III's escape to Egypt, Ramesses' refusal to extradite Muršili III, and a change of mind on both sides with negotiations of a peace treaty.

Muwatalli II is assumed to have reigned between 18 and 23 years (Breyer 2010, 59; Bryce 2005, xv). His immediate predecessor was Muršili II who reigned for about 25 to 28 years (Bryce 2005, xv; Breyer 2010, 59). A fragmentary text of a prayer of Muršili II contains an allusion to a solar eclipse. Muršili II talks about intrigues by his stepmother Malnigal, the old queen. Huber (2001, 644) interpreted the text such that when Muršili was marching toward the land of Azzi, the old queen tried to make use of a solar omen to depose him (KUB 14.4, Col. IV, 24):

[When] I was marching [toward the land A]zzi – now the Sun-god made an omen.

From his Annals, it can be deduced that this should have happened during the early part of Muršili's campaign to Azzi in his ninth or tenth regnal year. His stepmother insisted that the solar omen did not concern any other person, but the king himself. The omen is not explicitly described as an eclipse and therefore some scholars render moot that an eclipse is meant (e.g. Cornelius 1954–1956, 306–307 and references therein). But eclipses were the only omens having severe consequences for the reigning king. It has to be stressed, however, that no solar eclipse is mentioned in Muršili's Annals where he describes the events of his campaign to Azzi. This may suggest that Muršili himself did not see an eclipse. It is conceivable that an eclipse was recognised in Hattuša, but not by Muršili on his march. Thus, counting backwards in time, starting from year 5 of Ramesses II for the four proposed chronological options, one obtains the time slots listed in Table 4.6 for a solar eclipse with large magnitude, visible in Hattuša.

Six serious candidates remain: three of them, 1312 BC, 1328 BC and 1355 BC, are not compatible with the interpretation of the text that Muršili II started campaigning around the time of the eclipse. Nevertheless, they won't be excluded as possible identifications at once. For each combination of solar eclipse and chronological option, there exist two fixed points: year 5 of Ramesses II given by the chronological option, and the year of the solar eclipse in year 9 or 10 of Muršili II. These fixed points are determined by different kinds of astronomical data and thus are *independent* of each other. Establishing Hittite chronology starting from year 9/10 of Muršili II down to the death of Hattušili III and comparing it with the chronological options of Egypt does not have a conclusive result. Instead, each combination can be harmonised with the following basic key facts: Muwatalli alive in year 5 Ramesses II, Hattušili III king before year 21 Ramesses II, Hattušili III still alive after year 34 Ramesses II when Ramesses II marries the Hittite princess Maathorneferure and exchanges letters with Hattušili III and his wife (Edel 1994, 95–99 and 214–223). Thus, although an account of a solar eclipse is preserved, the uncertainty

Option	**Time-span**	**Possible solar eclipse identifications**		
P1	1319–1299	13/04/1308	24/06/1312	
P2	1330–1310	24/06/1312	17/10/1328	13/03/1335
P3	1344–1324	17/10/1328	13/03/1335	08/01/1340
P4	1355–1335	13/03/1335	08/01/1340	27/10/1355

Table 4.6: Possible solar eclipse identifications for the four chronological options developed in this work. All dates are BC.

in the reign lengths of the Hittite kings makes it impossible to eliminate immediately any of the four proposed possible chronologies for Egypt based on these data.

Recently, the synchronism between year 8 or 9 of Muršili II and year 1 of Horemheb has been derived from a fragmentary Hittite text (KUB 19.15 + KBo 50.24; Miller 2007, 252–53) where a person named ‘Arma’a is mentioned in connection with events which can be dated to years 7 to 9 of Muršili II. The key question is whether ‘Arma’a can be equated with Horemheb. However, since he is called Armais, Harmais, Armesis or Armaios in the later Manethonian textual tradition (see Waddell 1964, 103–117; 243), this seems likely. Horemheb would be referred to with his personal name in the text, which suggests that his function must have been that of a viceroy and commander in Asia, *i.e.* before taking the throne. Since at the beginning of the next text column an accession to the throne is mentioned, it may be that in the first column Ay was the king in Egypt during year 7 of Muršili II (Miller 2007, 253–255). In the whole text, however, the person in question is called ʾArma’a, even after the passage mentioning an accession to the throne. Thus it seems possible that this is a reference to the accession of Ay. In that case, the proposed synchronism would have to be changed to year 8 or 9 of Muršili II equal to year 1 of Ay. Indeed, Devecchi and Miller (2011, 157) showed that the remaining traces on the tablet would be compatible with the restoration of the throne name of Ay, nevertheless other restorations are equally possible. Groddek (2007) derived a different synchronism from the same fragmentary Hittite text; he concludes that year 12 or 13 of Horemheb equals year 10 of Muršili II.

Without abandoning any of the interpretations of the text *a priori*, three different hypotheses are to be tested with the possible chronological options based on the astronomical data. Table 4. 7. summarises the results. Groddek’s (2007) proposed synchronism is not supported by the astronomical data. Three possible chronologies remain: one low chronology with the synchronism year 1 of Ay equal to year 9 of Muršili II in 1309 BC ($P1_1$), and two high chronologies fulfilling the synchronism year 1 of Horemheb equal to year 8 or 9 of Muršili II (1330 BC and 1341 BC; $P3_1$ and $P4_2$). Thus, the synchronism between Muršili II and Ay/Horemheb led to the exclusion of the chronological option P2 for Egypt with year 1 of Ramesses II in 1290 BC.

Option	1 Ay	1 Horemheb	8/9 Muršili II	12/13 Horemheb	10 Muršili II
$P1_1$	1309	1305	1310/09	1294/93	1308
$P1_2$	1309	1305	1314/13	1294/93	1312
$P2_1$	1320	1316	1314/13	1305/04	1312
$P2_2$	1320	1316	1330/29	1305/04	1328
$P3_1$	1334	1330	1330/29	1319/18	1328
$P3_2$	1334	1330	1337/36	1319/18	1335
$P3_3$	1334	1330	1342/41	1319/18	1340
$P4_1$	1345	1341	1337/36	1330/29	1335
$P4_2$	1345	1341	1342/41	1330/29	1340
$P4_3$	1345	1341	1357/56	1330/29	1355

Table 4.7: The possible chronological options developed in this work, based on the Egyptian Lunar Data and on the Hittite solar eclipse, tested against the different proposed synchronisms between Horemheb or Ay and Muršili II. The grey shaded areas designate matches.

After having narrowed down the possibilities, the solar eclipses can be looked at in more detail (see Gautschy 2012, online material for maps of the eclipse paths). The exact location of the land of Azzi is unclear, but it is usually thought to be situated in the north-east of Anatolia, somewhere around the lake of Van. For the solar eclipse of 1308 BC ($P1_1$) the maximum magnitude of about 0.7 in Hattuša occurred before sunrise (Gautschy 2012, online material). It was probably recognised only because the sun was eclipsed at the moment of sunrise. Further to the east, the eclipse was presumably not recognised because there the magnitude at the moment of sunrise was already too small. A date in April also agrees well with the interpretation of the text of Muršili II starting to campaign in Azzi. In the case of the eclipse of 1340 BC ($P4_2$) it is barely understandable why Muršili did not mention it in his Annals since it was total or almost total. However, the real drawback of identification with this solar eclipse is the fact that it is highly unlikely that Muršili II was on a campaign around the beginning of January (Pruzsinszky 2009, 76). In the case of the eclipse of 1328 BC ($P3_1$) the problem is that it occurred late in the year. In this case Muršili should have been already on his way back from Azzi to Hattuša – if still campaigning at all.

Synchronisms with Assyria

To select the most probable chronology for Egypt, a comparison with Assyrian chronology can be sought once more. The reign lengths of the Assyrian kings during the requested period are well preserved in the Assyrian King List (Glassner 1993, 146–151). Prior to 1133 BC, from Aššur-nādin-aḫḫe II onwards, only the exact reign lengths of Aššur-nādin-apli (3 or 4 years), Ninurta-apil-Ekur (3 or 13 years) and Aššur-dān I (36 or 46 years) vary in different copies of the Assyrian King List. Additionally, the exact meaning of the term *ṭuppišu* can be questioned. Thus, taking into account these uncertainties, absolute dates can be reckoned with an uncertainty of about 22 years. Calculating the distances of the Assyrian kings based on the Assyrian King List, Table 4. 2. and Table 4. 5. results in that the reign of Aššur-nādin-aḫḫe II (contemporary with Amenhotep III) started between 1401 BC and 1379 BC, the one of Aššur-uballiṭ I (contemporary with Akhenaten) between 1364 BC and 1342 BC. Additionally, not every year in the given time spans can be the accession year. A comparison with the absolute dates of Amenhotep III, Akhenaten and Tutankhamun for options P1, P3, and P4 (Table 4.5) shows that only options $P1_1$ and $P3_1$ seem to be in accordance with the traditional translation of the Akkadian term *ṭuppišu* to mean a short reign length of a few months. In order to fulfil all direct synchronisms in Table 4.2, option $P4_2$ would require about 10 years for the two Assyrian kings with *ṭuppišu* reign lengths, which seems unlikely. Thus, adopting a reign length of 14 years of Horemheb eliminates the long chronology with year 1 of Ramesses II in 1315 BC and an identification of the solar eclipse of Muršili II with the one of 1340 BC.

Daḫamunzu-affair

When checking the remaining two chronological options against the so-called Daḫamunzu-affair (e.g. Bryce 1990) – in which the widow of an Egyptian Pharaoh claims that she had no sons and asked the Hittite king Šuppiluliuma I for one of his numerous sons to become her husband and the king of Egypt – it becomes apparent that only Akhenaten, and for the earlier option also Smenkhkare, are candidates to be the deceased Egyptian Pharaoh in question. This is against the common opinion according to which the Pharaoh in question is usually thought to be Tutankhamun. Firstly, the name of the Pharaoh in the Hittite text (Güterbock 1956, 94–98 and 107–108), once denoted as Bibḫururiya and once as Nibḫururiya, seems to match better the throne-name of Tutankhamun (Nb-ḫpr.w-Rʿ) than that of Akhenaten (Nfr-ḫpr.w-Rʿ-wʿ-n-Rʿ) or Smenkhkare (ʿnḫ-ḫpr.w-Rʿ). Secondly, the described situation – widow of a deceased king without children, who does not want to get married to a servant of hers – suits well the known historical situation after Tutankhamun when finally Ay ascended the throne (Bryce 1990, 102). Akhenaten and his wife Nefertiti certainly had children, six daughters of this couple are known. But they had no male heir. Smenkhkare, on the other hand, had no living children together with his wife Meritaten, a daughter of Akhenaten and Nefertiti. The exact relation between Akhenaten, Smenkhkare and Tutankhamun is not known. Genetic tests (Hawass *et al.* 2010) have shown that the mummy found buried in tomb KV 55 was the father of Tutankhamun and a son of Amenhotep III and queen Tiye. Nevertheless, it is not clear whether the mummy has to be identified with Akhenaten or with Smenkhkare. Besides, considerable caveats have been expressed against the methodology of this study (e.g. Lorenzen 2010, 2471).

However, with a 2-year reign of the lady Neferneferuaten – occurring in between Akhenaten and Smenkhkare or between Smenkhkare and Tutankhamun – it seems obvious that no smooth transition took place, thus leaving open a time-slot for a possible temporal placement of the Daḫamunzu-affair also in times before the death of Tutankhamun.

Evidence from the Amarna correspondence and Hittite sources

The cuneiform tablets of the so-called Amarna letters cast some light on Egyptian relations with Babylonia, Assyria, Mitanni, Amurru, Ḫatti, Syria, Canaan, and Alašiya. For additional hints on which Pharaoh is most probably the Pharaoh in question concerning the Daḫamunzu-affair, the letters from Mitanni, Amurru and Byblos are particularly helpful. Unfortunately, only few letters from Ḫatti itself are preserved. In letter 41 (Moran 1992, 114) Šuppiluliuma talks about the Pharaoh "Ḫuriya's" recent ascension to the throne and expresses his wish for exchanging further presents as Šuppiluliuma did with "Ḫuriya's" father. Letter 42 (Moran 1992, 115–16) is less polite, asking the Pharaoh whether he wrote to Šuppiluliuma with peace in mind. Either Šuppiluliuma was on good terms with Amenhotep III, congratulated Akhenaten to his ascension and in the following correspondence their relation cooled considerably, or the kings in question were Akhenaten and Smenkhkare, respectively. In Mitanni, at the time of the beginning of the Amarna archive around year 30 of Amenhotep III (Moran 1992, xxxiv), Šuwardata was king. But soon Tušratta followed as king; in year 36 of Amenhotep III he wedded a daughter to the Egyptian Pharaoh. At some point during the reign of Akhenaten Tušratta was murdered by his own son. In Amurru, Abdi-Aširta ruled approximately until the end of Amenhotep III's reign. Afterwards, Abdi-Aširta's sons seem to have ruled together for a while until Aziru took the leading position. The Pharaoh ordered Aziru to come to Egypt and Aziru repeatedly delayed his departure to Egypt with the allusion to Šuppiluliuma's presence in the land of Nuḫašše which constituted a threat to Aziru's territory. Tušratta's death and the presence of Šuppiluliuma in Nuḫašše are mentioned in Hittite texts too (e.g. Deeds of Šuppiluliuma (Güterbock 1956, 85), Šuppiluliuma-Šattiwaza treaty (Beckman 1996, 38–48)). Another important event documented in an Amarna letter (no. 170) as well as in Hittite sources (fragment 28 of the Deeds of Šuppiluliuma) is a raid of Amqu, shortly before the occurrence of the Daḫamunzu-affair. Putting together all these pieces of evidence, I come to the conclusion that it is very likely that Akhenaten is the deceased Pharaoh mentioned in the texts concerning the Daḫamunzu-affair, although Smenkhkare cannot be entirely excluded due to his very short reign length. Cordani (2011, 113) – arriving at the same main conclusion – remarked that an identification of the deceased Pharaoh with Smenkhkare would imply a relatively long stay of Aziru in Egypt, which seemed implausible to her.

Discussion

The chronological options proposed in this work were constructed based on the following data and basic assumptions:

1. Lunar data from the period of the Egyptian New Kingdom
2. Horemheb reigned 14 years, Smenkhkare 3 years and Seti I 11 years
3. Occurrence of a solar eclipse in Muršili II's tenth year (i.e. the solar omen reported is indeed an eclipse account)
4. Synchronism between Muršili II and Horemheb (*i.e.* Arma'a can be equated with Horemheb)
5. Direct synchronisms listed in Table 4.2 of this paper
6. The Assyrian King List

Table 4.8 summarises some key data of the second half of the second millennium BC for the remaining two chronological options $P1_1$ and $P3_1$.

The most serious drawback of option $P1_1$ may be the fact that Šuppiluliuma I would have died only 3 to 4 years after the Daḫamunzu-affair, namely in the year when Smenkhkare died and Tutankhamun ascended the throne. This is in contradiction to the common reconstruction of the various fragments of the "Deeds of Šuppiluliuma" which would require some 5 to 6 years (e.g. Bryce 2005, 188). Option $P3_1$ adds up to 8 or 9 more years for Šuppiluliuma I after the death of Akhenaten, which on the other hand seems too long. But if the deceased Pharaoh in question is Smenkhkare, then option $P3_1$ provides a perfect fit with its 6 years between the death

	$P1_1$	**Remarks to $P1_1$**	**$P3_1$**	**Remarks to $P3_1$**
Year 1 Thutmose III	1468		1493	
Year 1 Amenhotep III	1378		1403	
Year 1 Akhenaten	1339		1364	
Year 1 Smenkhkare	1322		1347	
Last year Šuppiluliuma I	1319		1339	
Year 1 Tutankhamun	1319		1344	
Daḫamunzu-Pharaoh		Akhenaten		Smenkhkare Akhenaten
Year 1 Ramesses II	1279		1304	
Year 1 Hattušili III	1264	Šuppiluliuma I: 25 years Muršili II: 25 years Muwatalli: 18 years Muršili III: 7 years	1287	Šuppiluliuma I: 25 years Muršili II: 25 years Muwatalli: 18 years Muršili III: 7 years

Table 4.8: Key data of the two possible chronologies of the Egyptian New Kingdom during the Amarna period and Ramesses II developed in this work.

of Smenkhkare and the death of Šuppiluliuma I. While option $P1_1$ accords to a Low Assyrian Chronology (36 years of Aššur-dān I, 3 years of Ninurta-apil-Ekur), option $P3_1$ requires a High Assyrian Chronology (46 years of Aššur-dān I, 13 years of Ninurta-apil-Ekur). In both options the direct synchronisms summarised in Table 4. 2. are fulfilled. Concerning the match of the lunar dates, option $P1_1$ fits slightly better, but not in a statistically decisive manner. Unfortunately, in both options deviations occur especially in those cases, where the texts state explicitly that the mentioned day is a first lunar day. It should be noted, that the supposed sothic date from the Papyrus Ebers Calendar – III Shemu 9 in year 9 of Amenhotep I (e.g. Gautschy 2011, 125 or von Beckerath 1997, 45–46) – is in agreement with a place of observation in Thebes for option $P3_1$ while no match can be obtained for option $P1_1$. Concerning the C14 data (see Table 4.5), they are in full agreement with option $P3_1$ prior to Ramesses II and deviate not more than 5 to 12 years after Ramesses II. Since the C14 data were modelled assuming a higher reign length of Horemheb, such a deviation is well within the limits of this dating method. For option $P1_1$ the opposite applies: dates prior to Ramesses II deviate by approximately 10 years.

Krauss (2009, 133–139) proposes chronological option $P1_1$ as the correct chronology of the Egyptian New Kingdom using a selection of the lunar dates in Table 4.1. The unexplainable sothic date in the calendar of Papyrus Ebers he interprets as wrongly attributed to Amenhotep I. Instead, he suggests that it should be assigned to the last Hyksos ruler Khamudi (Krauss 2009, 137–139) which is, however, pure speculation. Chronological option $P3_1$ he dismisses with regard to an unexplainable divergence of 25 years to the standard chronology of the Third Intermediate Period. But the chronology of the Third Intermediate Period is far from settled (e.g. Kitchen (2009, 202), Aston (2009, 26–27), Payraudeau (2009, 295–297), Jansen-Winkeln (2006, 234–264) for recent different reconstructions).

Conclusions

Collecting all pieces of evidence, the best fitting chronology of the Egyptian New Kingdom – based on lunar and sothic data, one solar eclipse, C14 data, known synchronisms, textual witnesses and archaeological finds from Horemheb's tomb – seems to be the one that puts year 1 of Ramesses II in 1304 BC, year 1 of Thutmose III in 1493 BC and year 1 of Ahmose in 1564 BC (option $P3_1$). This chronological solution comprises reign lengths of 14 years for Horemheb, 11 years for Seti I and 3 years for both Neferneferuaten and Smenkhkare. This chronology is in good agreement with Assyrian, Babylonian and Hittite chronology. Accepting the considerably lower reign length of Horemheb, which is suggested by the archaeological facts from his tomb and supported by the lunar data, means that one has to accept that the Pharaoh of the Daḫamunzu-affair is definitely not Tutankhamun but very likely Smenkhkare. Nonetheless, the lower Egyptian chronology with year 1 of Ramesses II in 1279 BC and year 1 of Ahmose in 1539 BC cannot be excluded (option $P1_1$). In that case the Daḫamunzu-Pharaoh would be Akhenaten. My preference of the higher chronology is based on two facts only: firstly the supposed sothic date of Amenhotep I, which is not in accordance with any reference point in Egypt for option $P1_1$, while for option $P3_1$ it fits well with an observation point in the surrounding of Thebes. And secondly, the contradiction to the common reconstruction of the various fragments of the "Deeds of Šuppiluliuma" for option $P1_1$. But it is probably a thorough investigation of the Third Intermediate Period which will finally allow choosing the correct New Kingdom Chronology among the two possible ones. However, accepting a reign length of

14 years for Horemheb excludes the high chronology with year 1 of Ramesses II in 1315 BC which has recently been discussed by Huber (2011, 211), since it would require about 10 years of reign for the two kings with *ṭuppišu* reign length in the Assyrian King List. Otherwise the synchronism between Amenhotep III and Burnaburiaš cannot be maintained.

Acknowledgements

This work was supported by grant R-134/10 of the cogito foundation. I thank Daniel Arpagaus and Oskar Kälin who commented on a draft of this manuscript. I am grateful to the referees for the constructive and improving comments and suggestions, and to the editors for eliminating language problems.

Bibliography

Aston, D. A. (2009) Takeloth II, A King of the Herakleopolitan/Theban Twenty-Third Dynasty Revisited: The Chronology of Dynasties 22 and 23. In G. P. F. Broekman, R. J. Demarée and O. E. Kaper (eds) *The Libyan Period in Egypt*, 1–28. Leuven, Peeters.

Beckman, G. (1996) *Hittite diplomatic texts*. Atlanta, Scholars Press.

Breyer, F. (2010) Ägypten und Anatolien. *Politische, kulturelle und sprachliche Kontakte zwischen dem Niltal und Kleinasien im 2. Jahrtausend v. Chr.*. Vienna, Österreichische Akademie der Wissenschaften.

Bronk Ramsey, Ch. *et al.* (2010) Radiocarbon-Based Chronology for Dynastic Egypt. *Science* 328, 1554–1557.

Bruins, H. J. (2010) Dating Pharaonic Egypt. *Science* 328, 1489–1490.

Bryce, T. (1990) The Death of Niphururiya and its Aftermath. *Journal of Egyptian Archaeology* 76, 97–105.

Bryce, T. (2005) *The Kingdom of the Hittites*. Oxford, Oxford University Press.

Cordani, V. (2011) Aziru's Journey to Egypt and its Chronological Value. In J. Mynářová (ed.) *Egypt and the Near East – the Crossroads*, 103–113. Prague, Faculty of Arts Charles University in Prague.

Cornelius, F. (1954–1956) Die Chronologie des Vorderen Orients im 2. Jahrtausend v. Chr. *Archiv für Orientforschung* 17, 294–309.

Devecchi, E. and Miller, J. L. (2011) Hittite-Egyptian Synchronisms and their Consequences for Ancient Near Eastern Chronology. In J. Mynářová (ed.) *Egypt and the Near East – the Crossroads*, 139–176. Prague, Faculty of Arts Charles University in Prague.

Edel, E. (1994) *Die ägyptisch-hethitische Korrespondenz aus Boghazköi in babylonischer und hethitischer Sprache*. Opladen, Westdeutscher Verlag.

Gautschy, R. (2011) Sirius im Alten Ägypten. *Zeitschrift für Ägyptische Sprache und Altertumskunde* 138, Vol. 2, 116–131.

Gautschy, R. (2012) Sonnenfinsternisse und ihre chronologische Bedeutung: Ein neuer Sonnenfinsterniskanon für Altertumswissenschaftler. *Klio* 94, Vol. 1, 7–17. Online maps: http://www.gautschy.ch/~rita/archast/solec/solec.html.

Glassner, J. – J. (1993) *Chroniques Mésopotamiennes*. Paris, Les Belles Lettres.

Grayson, A. K. (1975) *Assyrian and Babylonian Chronicles*. Locust Valley (N. Y.), Augustin.

Groddek, D. (2007) Zu den neuen ägyptisch-hethitischen Synchronismen der Nach-Amarna-Zeit. *Göttinger Miszellen* 215, 95–107.

Güterbock, H. G. (1956) The Deeds of Suppiluliuma as Told by His Son, Mursili II. *Journal of Cuneiform Studies* 10, 41–68, 75–98, 107–130.

Hawass, Z. *et al.* (2010) Ancestry and Pathology in King Tutankhamun's Family. *The Journal of the American Medical Association 303,* 638–647.

Hornung, E. (2006) The New Kingdom. In E. Hornung, R. Krauss and D. Warburton (eds) *Ancient Egyptian Chronology*, 197–217. Leiden, Brill.

Huber, P. J. (2001) The Solar Omen of Muršili II. *Journal of the American Oriental Society* 121, Vol. 4, 640–644.

Huber, P. J. (2011) The Astronomical Basis of Egyptian Chronology of the Second Millennium BC. *Journal of Egyptian History* 4, 172–227.

Jansen, J. J. (1961) *Two Ancient Egyptian Ship's Logs*. Leiden, Brill.

Jansen-Winkeln, K. (2006) The Chronology of the Third Intermediate Period: Dyns. 22–24. In E. Hornung, R. Krauss and D. Warburton (eds) *Ancient Egyptian Chronology*, 233–264. Leiden, Brill.

KBo (1916–) *Keilschrifttexte aus Boghazköi*. Leipzig, Berlin, Wissenschaftliche Veröffentlichungen der Deutschen Orient-Gesellschaft.

Kitchen, K. A. (2007) Egyptian and Related Chronologies – Look, no Sciences, no Pots!. In M. Bietak (ed.) *The Synchronisation of Civilisations in the Eastern Mediterranean in the Second Millennium B. C. III*, 163–172. Vienna, Österreichische Akademie der Wissenschaften.

Kitchen, K. A. (2009) The Third Intermediate Period in Egypt: An Overview of Fact & Fiction. In G. P. F. Broekman, R. J. Demarée and O. E. Kaper (eds) *The Libyan Period in Egypt*, 161–202. Leuven, Peeters.

Krauss, R. and Warburton, D. A. (2009) The basis for the Egyptian dates. In D. A. Warburton (ed.) *Time's Up! Dating the Minoan eruption of Santorini*, 125–144. Athens, Danish Institute at Athens.

KUB (1921–1990) *Keilschrifturkunden aus Boghazköi*. Berlin, Akademie-Verlag.

Laroche, E. (1971) *Catalogue des textes hittites*. Paris, Klincksieck.

Lorenzen, E. D. (2010) Letter to the Editor. *The Journal of the American Medical Association* 303, 2471.

Marciniak, M. (1974) *Les inscriptions hiératiques du temple de Thoutmosis III*. Warsaw, Éditions scientifiques de Pologne.

Miller, J. L. (2007) Amarna Age Chronology and the Identity of Nibḫururiya in the Light of a Newly Reconstructed Hittite Text. *Altorientalische Forschungen* 34, 252–293.

Moran, W. L. (1992) *The Amarna Letters*. Baltimore, Johns Hopkins University Press.

Murnane, W. J. and van Siclen, C. C. (1993) *The boundary stelae of Akhenaten*. London, Kegan.

Payraudeau, F. (2009) Takeloth III: Considerations on Old and New Documents. In G. P. F. Broekman, R. J. Demarée and O. E. Kaper (eds) *The Libyan Period in Egypt*, 291–301. Leuven, Peeters.

Peden, A. J. (2001) *The Graffiti of Pharaonic Egypt*. Leiden, Brill.

Pruzsinszky, R. (2009) *Mesopotamian Chronology of the second millennium BC*. Vienna, Österreichische Akademie der Wissenschaften.

Ryholt, K. (1997) *The Political Situation in Egypt during the Second Intermediate Period c. 1800 – 1550 B.C.* Copenhagen, Museum Tusculanum Press.

Schneider, Th. (1996) *Lexikon der Pharaonen*. Munich, Deutscher Taschenbuchverlag.

Schneider, Th. (2010) Contributions to the chronology of the New Kingdom and the Third Intermediate Period. *Egypt & Levant* 20, 373–403.

Shaw, I. (2000) *The Oxford History of Ancient Egypt*. Oxford, Oxford University Press.

URKUNDEN IV (1984) *Urkunden des ägyptischen Altertums*. Berlin, Akademie-Verlag.

Van Dijk, J. (2008) New evidence on the length of the reign of Horemheb. *Journal of the American Research Center in Egypt* 44, 193–200.

von Beckerath, J. (1968) Ein neues Monddatum der ägyptischen Geschichte?. *Zeitschrift der Deutschen Morgenländischen Gesellschaft* 118, 18–21.

von Beckerath, J. (1994) *Chronologie des ägyptischen Neuen Reiches*. Hildesheim, Gerstenberg.

von Beckerath, J. (1997) *Chronologie des Pharaonischen Ägypten*. Mainz, Philipp von Zabern.

Waddell, W. G. (1964) *Manetho*. London, Heinemann.

Weidner, E. (1926) Die grosse Königsliste aus Assur. *Archiv für Orientforschung* 3, 66–77.

5

The Problem with Neferusi: A Geoarchaeological Approach

Carl Graves

What is the Problem?

For a long time Egyptology has suffered from a lack of understanding regarding the geographic nature of the river Nile and its surrounding alluvial plain, which may account for the apparent difficulty in locating the ancient site of Neferusi, a town thought to be situated inside the boundaries of the 16th Upper Egyptian nome. The aim of this brief paper is to contribute some geoarchaeological considerations to both the solving of this 'problem' and further studies regarding the urban geography of ancient Egypt.

It has only been in the last decade that an increased use of geoarchaeological evidence has allowed a better appreciation of the geographic context of ancient sites and subsequently their social history. Recent work at the sites of ancient Thebes (Bunbury *et al.* 2008), Memphis (Bunbury and Jeffreys 2011), Hermopolis and Antinoopolis (Bunbury and Malouta 2012), has contributed greatly to the present understanding of these significant places and how the ancient populace interacted with them, or in some cases planned them. It therefore seems that the correlation of similar geoarchaeological methods with studies of relevant textual evidence can assist in positing a more confident conclusion regarding the location of Neferusi within the Egyptian Nile floodplain. This paper does not therefore aim to provide a solid solution to this problem but instead hopes to discount some theories and assist in proving others.

Through a discussion regarding the geographic context of Neferusi's location, it is hoped that the social landscape of the Oryx nome can be better understood and the various known monuments and sites of the area be placed within their correct ancient geographic landscape.

Geographical Context: The Oryx nome

The 16th Upper Egyptian nome, known to the ancient Egyptians as *Mꜣ-ḥḏ* or The (White) Oryx nome, lies somewhere within the modern region of Middle Egypt and is usually located between the towns of Tihna in the north and el-Ashmunein in the south (Fig. 5.1). The area is first attested in sources from the 3rd Dynasty Step Pyramid enclosure (Helck 1974, 109) and

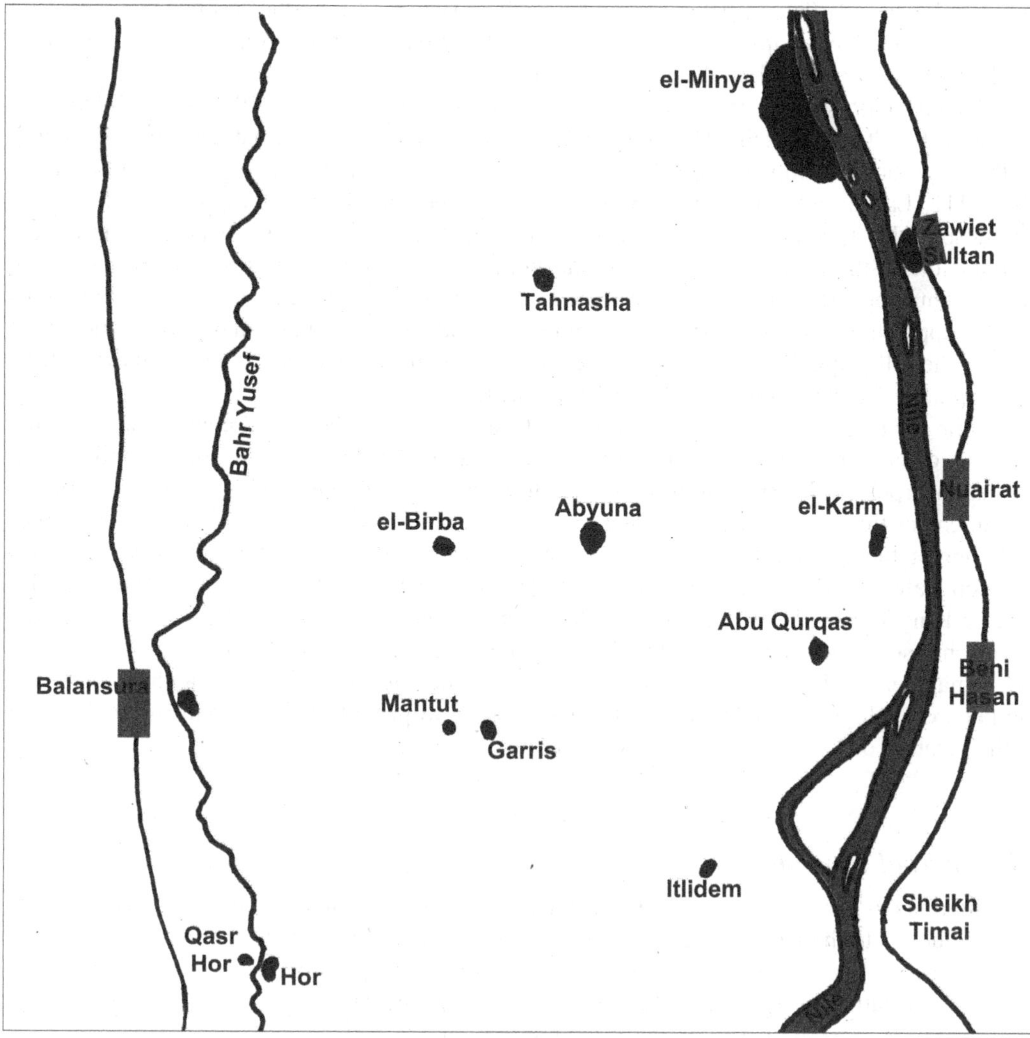

Figure 5.1: The region of modern day el-Minya around the modern town of Abu Qurqas. Sites discussed in this paper are highlighted, including some of the larger settlement mounds in the area. Cemeteries are indicated by the grey rectangles on the desert edges.

became a prosperous province during the late First Intermediate Period – as is evinced by the appearance of finely constructed tombs for the Nomarchs, Overseers of the Eastern Desert, and officials on the east bank at Beni Hasan (Newberry 1893–1900; Garstang 1907). The 39 rock-cut tombs of the upper necropolis at Beni Hasan are by far the most imposing monuments of the region while the 888 tombs of the lower necropolis constitute the largest excavated cemetery of the late First Intermediate Period and Middle Kingdom within the Oryx nome itself. Another cemetery, that of Balansura, is located on the west bank low desert area roughly opposite Beni Hasan and dates to the later Middle Kingdom and continued in use until the New Kingdom

(Kessler 1981, 168). The decision to switch use from Beni Hasan on the east bank to Balansura in the west may have implications regarding the changing landscape of the Oryx nome during the 13th Dynasty and will be discussed later in this paper.

While the east-west extent of the nome is therefore established, its north-south measurement is more difficult to ascertain. The White Chapel of Senwosret I at Karnak provides the length of the Oryx nome along the river Nile as 4*iteru* and 7*kha*, approximately 45.661km (Helck 1974, 111; Lacau and Chevrier 1956, pl. 3). It will be seen however throughout this paper that despite this specific measurement of the nome's length the White Chapel data is largely inapplicable to the modern river due to substantial geographic changes over time. Therefore any current geographic analysis of the ancient Nile valley should take account of the limitations that are apparent in the task of simply defining the Middle Kingdom boundaries of the nomes of Egypt. The following discussion will consequently only make conclusions based on the textual, geographic and archaeological information presented here.

While the focus of this paper is to contribute some geoarchaeological considerations to the problem of Neferusi's location, the presence of textual evidence should not be ignored, but instead incorporated into the discussion. Together with Her-wer, Neferusi is the most mentioned settlement in the texts of the Beni Hasan rock-cut tombs (Kamrin 1992, 43). Later sources including statues found at Balansura, the Kamose stela and the Pi(ankh)y Victory Stela also mention Neferusi. All of these indicate that Neferusi was a regional centre from at least the mid-Middle Kingdom until the Late Period. However, despite the number of texts mentioning the town it has so far not been equated with any archaeological site or town mound with certainty. The remainder of this paper will briefly draw together these texts with past research, theories and the geoarchaeological considerations discussed above to provide a more confident conclusion to the location of Neferusi within the Oryx nome.

The Textual Evidence

Past attempts to locate Neferusi have relied heavily on textual information. These texts provide ample clues as to the nature of the settlement and its role within historical episodes of Egypt's past. However, this section will demonstrate that these texts provide only limited information to assist in locating Neferusi, and that to rely on these alone can result in a number of possible theories that will be discussed in the following section.

The earliest mention of Neferusi itself comes from the tomb of *Ḫwns* at Zawiet Sultan (13.5km north of Beni Hasan). The caption to a relief depicting a flotilla of ships states that they are 'sailing upstream to the festival of Hathor, Mistress of Neferusi' (Champollion 1889, 448). Three things can be gleaned from this brief mention; the local deity of the town, Hathor, and more importantly to this discussion, the notion that Neferusi must have had access to a river and perhaps a quay or harbour – either within the town or certainly within a short distance. Thirdly, this quay must also have been located to the south of Zawiet Sultan, or of the town in which *Ḫwns* resided, due to the flotilla 'sailing upstream' in the depiction. As Zawiet Sultan is also thought to be the site of the ancient town of Hebnu, where *Ḫwns* lived, we can postulate that Neferusi should be situated south of this locality. It is important to note however that the equation of Hebnu with Zawiet Sultan is not certain and has not undergone a similar assessment as this paper aims to complete for Neferusi – this issue is outside the scope of this paper but has potential for future research.

Despite the number of mentions of Neferusi in the Beni Hasan tombs, none of them allude to its geographic setting. Most of these references relate the deceased and their families to the cult of Hathor located in the town; information which may indicate that Neferusi was the residence of these individuals (Newberry 1893, 14; 43). However, the close proximity of Neferusi to Beni Hasan could be tentatively assumed based on the volume of references in the tombs. Should Beni Hasan be seen as the regional necropolis of the town, which I believe can be inferred for the evidence discussed below, this proximity becomes more probable. In this light, the decision to begin using Balansura as this regional cemetery during the 13th Dynasty becomes an issue more worthy of further consideration, as will be seen later in this paper.

Texts dated to the post-Middle Kingdom provide further implications of Neferusi's location, although caution should be taken when using texts not dated to the period of study. The stela of Kamose from the late Second Intermediate Period narrates the siege of Neferusi by the Theban ruler during his campaign northwards to Avaris, the Hyksos stronghold in the Delta (Smith and Smith 1976, 60). As Neferusi is mentioned closely in the text after the city of Hermopolis (el-Ashmunein), it is perhaps at this time that a close administrative relationship developed between the two sites that can also be seen in later texts. This connection may also be implicit of a geographic proximity between the two settlements indicating a location close to the border between both the Oryx nome and Hare nome (the latter of which Hermopolis was the regional centre). Kamose's reference to spending the night in his boat prior to the attack, followed by records of the women 'descending to the shore' (Smith and Smith 1976, 69) again reiterate the location of Neferusi alongside a river, or perhaps water channel.

A similar relationship can also be seen to emerge between Neferusi and Her-wer, another frequently mentioned town in the tombs of Beni Hasan and therefore also likely located in the Oryx nome. The two towns are frequently mentioned close to each other and in the Onomasticon of Amenemope, discussed below, appear consecutively (Gardiner 1947, 83–87). The early 18th Dynasty stela of Inena mentions the 'divine boat of Khnum, Lord of Her-wer in Neferusi' (Glanville 1932, 40) which implies that the local God Khnum of Her-wer visited Neferusi, or indeed that the name of 'Neferusi' had come to denote the region around both towns as well as the specific administrative settlement of concern in this paper (Glanville 1932, 41). Dated to this same dynasty are two statues, discovered at the Balansura necropolis, depicting the Mayor of Neferusi, Ani, and his wife, Mut-nefer (Daressy 1919). The presence of these sculptures allows the tentative conclusion, mentioned above, that Neferusi should also be located within a close proximity to Balansura. The use of Balansura as a burial ground increased during the 13th Dynasty at the expense of Beni Hasan, from which it could be assumed that the inhabitants of Neferusi found it more convenient to travel to the western desert edge (Balansura) rather than the eastern (Beni Hasan). This could be due to a number of factors; the appropriateness of burial in the west, lack of space at Beni Hasan, or geographic proximity. Clearly, burial in the east had not concerned the Oryx nome administration previously as can be seen by the locations of the older cemeteries of Zawiet Sultan, Nuairat and Beni Hasan in Fig. 5.1. The presence of Roman period burials in the lower necropolis of Beni Hasan discounts a theory relating to a lack of space for interment. Therefore if, as we may assume, the town of Neferusi remained located in the same place (with allowance for urban expansion and contraction) we may then approach a theory related to geographic proximity whereby changes in the landscape of the region resulted in changes of attitude to the environment and subsequent changes in land use, particularly during the late Middle Kingdom.

As already stated above, Neferusi immediately precedes Her-wer in the Onomasticon of Amenemope (Gardiner 1947, 83–87) – due to the arrangement of the Onomasticon this would indicate that Neferusi was located east and south of Her-wer, although distances between locations are not recorded in the evidence. However the relationship between the two towns, as discussed earlier in this section, continues to be seen throughout much of Pharaonic history, such as in the 25th Dynasty Victory Stela of Pi(ankh)y (Lichtheim 1980, 68). This text records the incident whereby 'Namart, ruler of Hermopolis, mayor in Hutweret (Her-wer)… demolished the wall of Neferusi', again alluding to a connection, developed since the Late Middle Kingdom, between Neferusi, Her-wer and Hermopolis. As the ruler of Hermopolis is also now the mayor of Her-wer and has jurisdiction over the town of Neferusi we can once again conclude that all three towns should be located within a short distance of one another. This also implies that the border between the 15th and 16th Upper Egyptian nomes had clearly changed nature or position since the Middle Kingdom, although an analysis of this change is beyond the scope of this paper, other than understanding that Neferusi should be located near to the Middle Kingdom northern border of the Hare nome.

Locating Neferusi: The Historiographical Perspective

Past scholars have attempted to locate Neferusi by basing much of their evidence on the texts discussed above and this section provides a select summary and review of these attempts.

The first attempt to locate Neferusi within the modern landscape was by Maspero in 1891 (517), who equated the town with the settlement of Itlidem, where he felt the southern border of the Oryx nome was located. Currently this town is situated 3km from the Nile on the west bank opposite Sheikh Timai. Itlidem's location, within walking distance to the river, would have allowed it the harbour access that is mentioned twice in the texts already discussed. Maspero also reported finding granite columns and a 'large temple' within the ruins of the modern town, which he linked to the temple of Hathor, Mistress of Neferusi. However, it can be said that the presence of columns does not necessarily denote the presence of a temple, and certainly not that of Neferusi.

During Daressy's analysis of the two statues discovered at Balansura he recognised that a close connection between the towns of Neferusi and Her-wer had developed before the New Kingdom. Daressy therefore chose to situate Neferusi at the modern town of Balansura, close to the cemetery of the same name (Daressy 1919, 56–57), on the basis of Maspero's equation of Her-wer with Qasr-Hur, slightly further south. However, this decision does not concur with the arrangement of the Onomasticon of Amenemope, which places Neferusi to the south and/or east of Her-wer. Daressy also failed to explain the reasons and logic behind Beni Hasan being used as a regional necropolis earlier than Balansura. This omission of other textual and archaeological evidence in Daressy's theory makes his suggested location of Neferusi highly implausible, even without the addition of geoarchaeological considerations.

In 1961 Montet proposed that, due to the frequent mentions of Neferusi in connection with Hermopolis and the 15th Upper Egyptian nome, it should be located at Sheikh 'Abada (Montet 1961, 152). This site is most famous as the later Roman settlement of Antinoopolis, located on the east bank desert edge. This would place Neferusi far away from both the Beni Hasan and Balansura necropoleis, as well as locating it within the traditional Middle Kingdom boundary of the Hare nome. It would therefore be incongruous as to why the town featured so prominently in the tombs of the officials of the Oryx nome during the Middle Kingdom.

Finally, the most recent and thorough study of the region and its settlements is the topographical study by Dieter Kessler (1981). Kessler not only relied on texts but also used geographic and archaeological data to compile his research and, by using this data, he equated the modern town of Garris, in the middle of the west bank flood plain between Balansura and Beni Hasan, as the site of Neferusi. While the location of Garris fits well with most data, the environmental situation of the town does not currently allow for the river access discussed in the texts above. Kessler's solution to that problem was to suggest the use of canals over 10km long connecting the settlement to both the river Nile and the Bahr Yusef (1981, 74–75). Kessler saw the modern Gizr el-Azraq canal as the successor of these early water channels. While Kessler's study is certainly the most inclusive of data available until 1981, more recent studies regarding the geographic nature of the Nile Valley could allow greater confidence in identifying Garris as the modern location for ancient Neferusi.

Geoarchaeological considerations

Land use in Egypt has changed much since the Pharaonic Period: long canals seen in the modern landscape in many instances reflect ancient water courses and Nile branches which have since been drained, diverted, narrowed and straightened by human activity. Even more recently, over the last century, the use of land and water in the Egyptian Nile valley has changed considerably, particularly so due to the hydrological changes brought about by the construction of dams in the region of Aswan. Such changes appear to have created some misconceptions about life in the valley in earlier times; therefore the remainder of this paper will focus on the geographic evidence that can contribute to a greater understanding of settlement archaeology in Egypt.

The river Nile is a complex feature of the African landscape stretching 6825km from equatorial Africa northwards until it spreads into a delta before entering the Mediterranean Sea (Said 1993, 9). The major tributaries that contribute to the main Nile river are the White Nile from the Equatorial Lakes Plateau in Central Africa, as well as the Blue Nile and the Atbara both from the Ethiopian highlands (Said 1993, 7). These tributaries converge north of Khartoum in Sudan to form the main Nile which flows through Egypt into the Mediterranean. The White Nile's input into the main Nile contributes a constant flow of water encouraging the perennial nature of the river (Stanley *et al.* 2003, 400), while the Blue Nile and Atbara contribute most water to the Nile but within a short period of time, which produces the annual inundation from July to September (Woodward *et al.* 2007, 278, fig. 13.11a.). At various points in Egypt's history the climate over Africa has fluctuated between wet and dry phases; with the wet phases creating large wadis across the Egyptian eastern desert (Said 1993, 32–56). During the most recent dry phase (2450BC to present (Said 1993, 55)) the people of Egypt were dependant on annual floods of an adequate discharge to allow the irrigation of the fields in the floodplain to encourage the emergence of agriculture and a sedentary lifestyle – hence the development of urbanism. This annual inundation took minimal management, usually in the form of cutting natural dykes, but over time human action became more and more necessary in managing the river, due to an increasing population that was both sedentary and reliant on crop surplus to provide for specialised personnel. This culminated in the 1960's with the construction of the High Dam at Aswan in southern Egypt, which has since managed the annual flooding of Egypt according to regulations relating to the amount of discharge to release and the height of the reservoir behind the dam (Saad 2002; Attia and Sadek 2010). Before the High and Low Aswan dams were constructed the population in Egypt had to live in relative congruence with the Nile, allowing it a degree of freedom in the landscape which will become apparent in the following discussion.

The Inundation

The annual inundation in Egypt came in late summer and allowed the cultivation of most of the floodplain. Whilst the population was reliant on the inundation for crop production, too much flood water could also cause damage to urban areas. Due to their dependence on the inundation, the Egyptians often recorded Nile flood levels, and through these it is possible to plot periods of destructively high or low floods. These two extremes could cause chaotic events in Egypt if unmanaged and may have contributed towards the downfall of ruling dynasties and the start of political upheaval. Due to the extensive flooding of the valley, the early population of Egypt developed modes of urbanism that allowed for a degree of flexibility and harmony with the unreliable nature of the riverine setting in which they had chosen to live. For example, all settlements were built on high ground, such as turtle-backs and levees, or alternatively on the edges of the desert where they would have had access to water and yet remain protected from average inundation heights, as can be seen in Figure 5.2. The highest levees in the Nile valley are those formed on the nearest banks of the river and can stand up to 3m higher than the rest of the floodplain providing ideal locations for settlement foundation. Although the process of inundation helps little with regards to locating Neferusi, it is possible to take account of these town planning considerations which makes selecting an opportune site for ancient settlements easier to be found.

While it is difficult today to imagine inundations flooding the entire width of the valley due to the construction of the High Dam and rapid population growth and settlement of flood prone areas (Attia and Sadek 2010, 79), it would have been much more important to the Egyptians to fully understand the consequences of the inundation and other alluvial processes, good or bad.

Nile Migration

As mentioned above the River Nile is a very complex and dynamic system. While flooding was the most immediate concern of the local inhabitants many other processes occur at a slower pace – yet can prove to be just as alarming over time, such as Nile migration. It was recognized

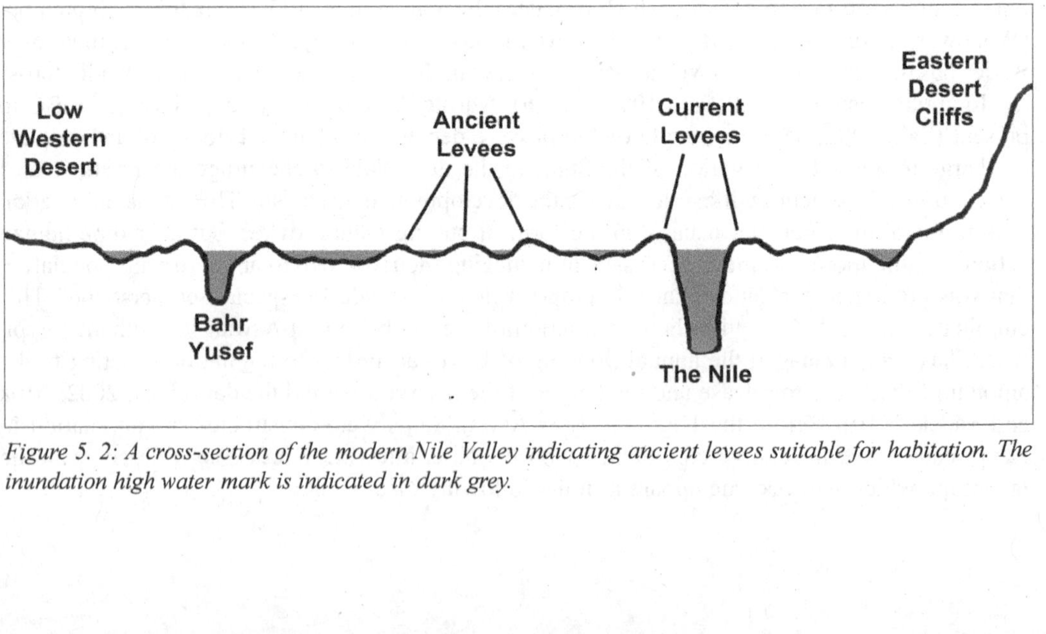

Figure 5. 2: A cross-section of the modern Nile Valley indicating ancient levees suitable for habitation. The inundation high water mark is indicated in dark grey.

in 1976 by Karl Butzer (35) that the Nile in antiquity was once located much further west in Middle Egypt than its current position. This was based on the perception that many of the ancient settlements known from this region lie in the centre of the modern western flood plain, such as Hermopolis for example (modern el-Ashmunein). Butzer then analysed the terrain of this area and realised that various ancient levees are preserved within the floodplain which would once have been located directly alongside the river Nile and would have provided high ground for urban development. It was these levees which would have been breached to allow the Nile flood waters into the basins beyond during the annual inundation (1976, 16–17). The ruins of Hermopolis are currently situated approximately 8km west of the modern Nile channel, indicating a migration east of around 56.25m per century (although this ignores complexities of migration patterns and meander change over time). Rates of migration also differ by region, an average is recognized as 2km per thousand years (Bunbury and Malouta 2012, 120).

At various areas of the valley the Nile has also migrated in different directions. Hillier *et al.* (2007) found that the river had drifted west in the Karnak region while it travelled eastwards in the Memphite area. Similarly Bunbury and Jeffreys (2011) at Memphis have found that the Nile has developed from two branches surrounding the city to one eastern branch before migrating further east across the floodplain. It is also recognised that bends in meanders move outwards (east or west) and downstream over time (Lutley and Bunbury 2008, 3). With an understanding of these processes it is possible to draw a tentative plan (Fig. 5.3) of where the Nile could have been located in ancient times within certain areas of the valley.

Changes in the river course can be seen by studying satellite imagery, aerial photographs and detailed topographic maps. Field boundaries are often located perpendicular to water courses, monuments, settlements and settlement mounds (Hillier *et al.* 2006, 4). These features can assist in constructing the past movements of meander bends in particular as the field boundaries preserve these ancient river channel borders in the landscape. These are found throughout the Nile river valley and further analysis of these features will provide a greater understanding of how the river has migrated, although not necessarily how far and in which direction the movement occurred.

Occasionally islands in the river gradually merge with the adjacent river bank as the river migrates in the opposite direction. Similarly in areas of high deposition (often on the inner bends of meanders), islands may form and become stable enough for cultivation and subsequently settlement. This process of migration meant these islands provided very suitable settlement sites as they rose higher than the low water level and could be stabilised by cultivation and succeeding habitation (Graham 2010, 139). As the island grows it would allow the expansion of urban areas, until it joined the river bank and allowed for even greater expansion. During the early times the island location would also provide a defensive position and ample river access. Therefore the process of island formation and subsequent inclusion in the floodplain indicates both direction of river migration, as well as some ancient Egyptian attitudes toward town planning and location.

Nile branching and avulsion

At points in the course of the river, particularly in the White Nile, the high sediment load of the river causes it to become braided. Further downstream this can result in multiple river channels (known as anastomosing rivers) which can connect to each other across the floodplain, shown in Figure 5.4. Movements in the positions of these branches could occur easily over the period of inundation, especially if sediment deposition resulted in the silting up of channels and subsequent erosion of others. As mentioned previously, two branches were found to have existed at ancient

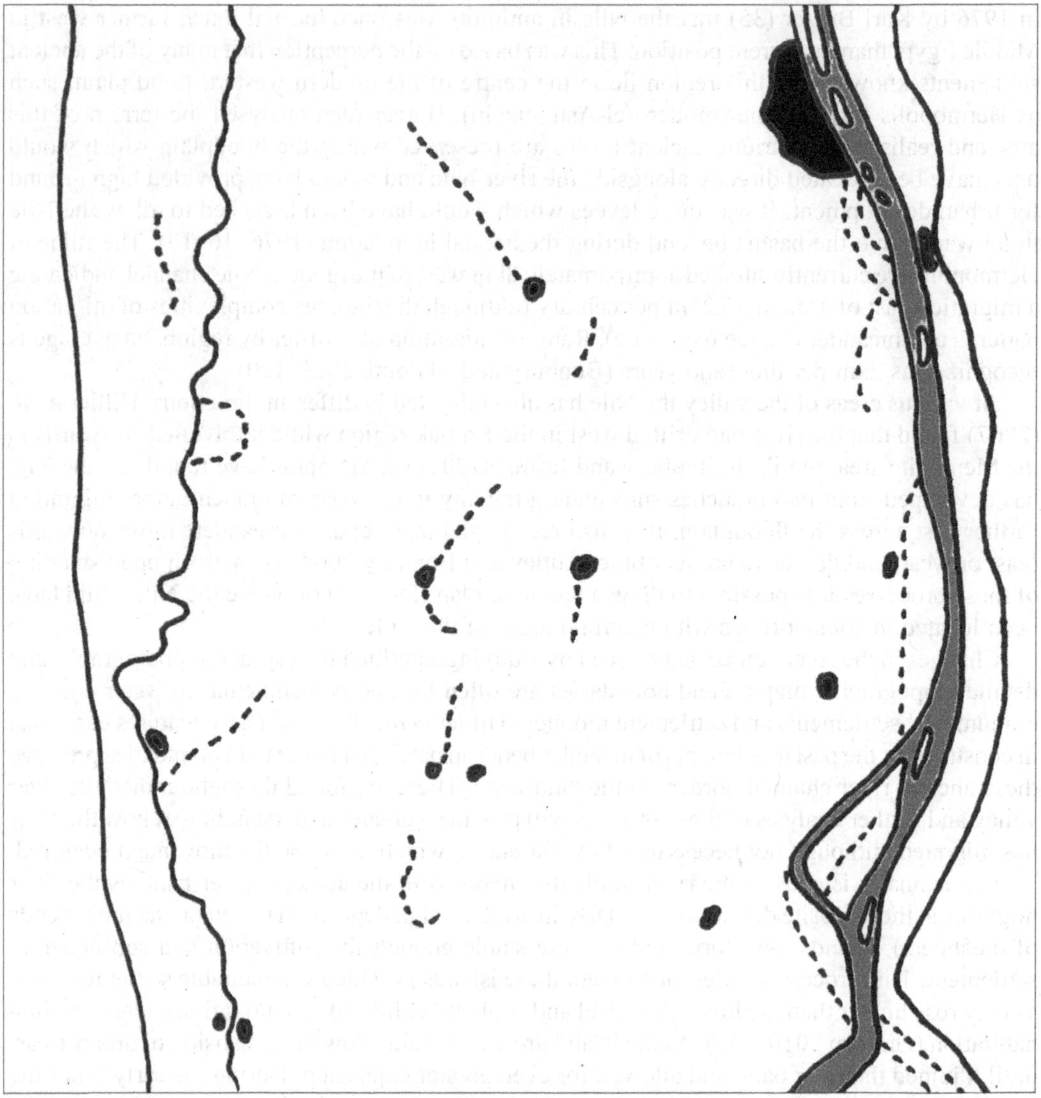

Figure 5. 3: Indications in the Oryx Nome of past Nile migrations through analysis of field boundaries. The significant city of Hermopolis is located 8km south of the area depicted in this map in the centre of the floodplain, but was located alongside the river Nile during its foundation in the Old Kingdom.

Memphis and this may be the case for other areas further upstream, such as around Hermopolis or also Neferusi (Butzer 1976, 17; Bunbury and Jeffreys 2011). Multiple branches would allow for greater transport and river access to many settlements in the valley, which would otherwise have been landlocked. Changes in these branches could result in drastic changes of land use in the floodplain and surrounding areas – for example, by making some areas more difficult to reach by boat. Butzer noticed a narrowing of the river and a general straightening of its course

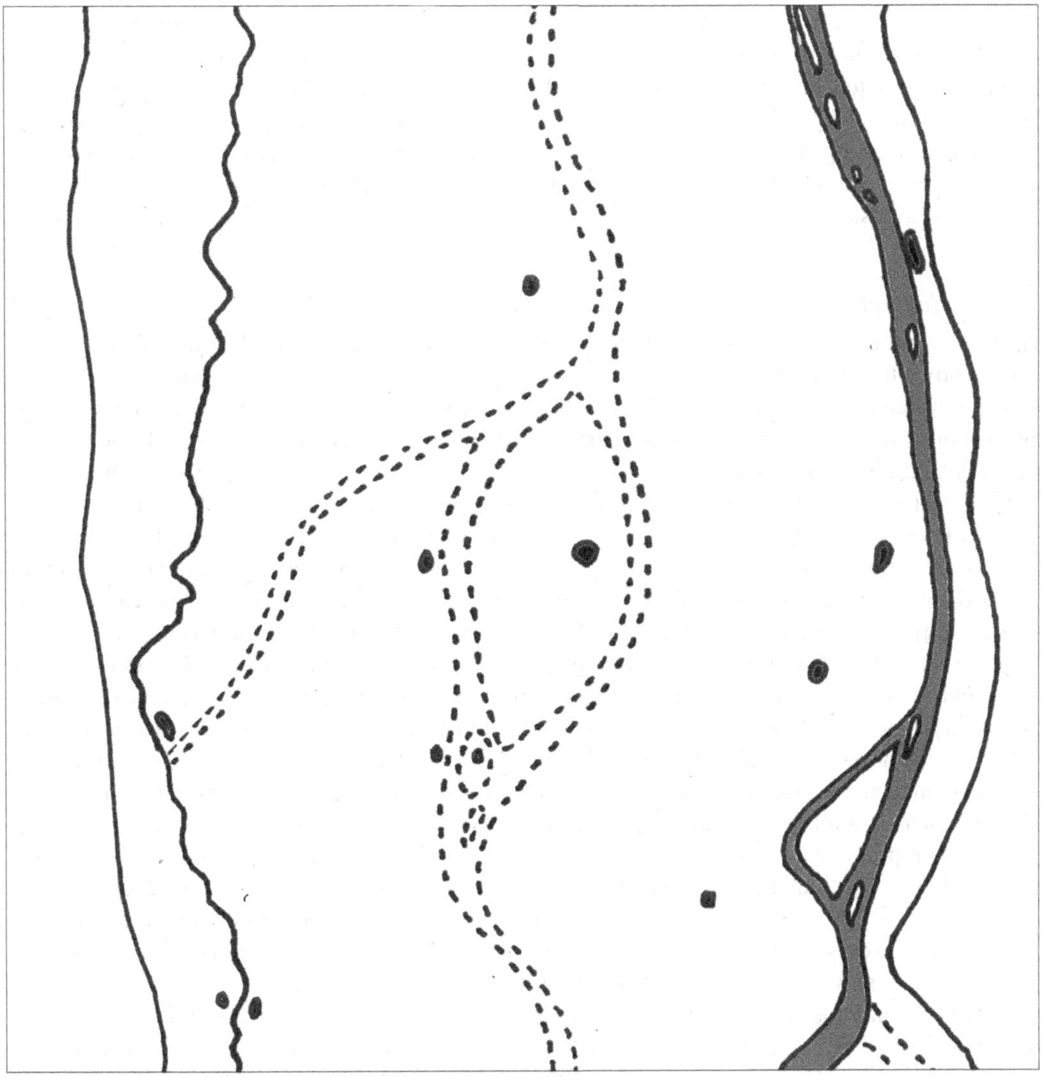

Figure 5. 4: Possible implications of Nile branching in the el-Minya area. Multiple branches would have allowed for greater transport possibilities in the region and may have once connected the settlement mounds preserved in the region. The modern Nile is still indicated to the left (east) of the image – while a possible example of the ancient river is indicated by hashed lines.

through time, which could imply that during the Pharaonic Period multiple branches did in fact exist in the Upper Egyptian portion of the Nile valley (Butzer 1976, 35; Graham 2010, 125).

The presence of multiple river branches can result in the main channel of the river alternating its course through the process of avulsion and it is well documented that rivers can avulse during periods of high flood and high sediment deposition. As waters recede following a flood the river will attempt to locate the most efficient and lowest accessible course to reach the outlet (the Mediterranean). This could result in a dramatic change in water channel over a very short period of time (the period of the inundation), as was shown in Morozova's analysis of the impact of avulsion in the Tigris and Euphrates valleys which could be correlated with that of the Nile (2005, 407). Avulsion can also result in settlements losing their access to the river – in some cases causing abandonment. Within Middle Egypt the lower areas of land between the ancient levees investigated by Butzer would have suited the redirection of Nile waters by the process of avulsion.

Human Impact

Increasing human impact on the river and the floodplain over time has resulted in both advantages and disadvantages. During the Pharaonic Period settlements were defended from flood waters by being elevated onto higher ground through the deposition of waste products onto the river bank, or the construction of dams and flood barriers. This would have reduced the risk of flooding and also allowed for greater expansion of towns. Flood defences found at Qasr el-Sagha for example were constructed to protect the site from the rising waters of the Faiyum Lake during the late Middle Kingdom (Sliwa 1988, 200), while damming sections of river allowed for the connection between the east and west islands of Elephantine and subsequent expansion of the island's urban areas (Kaiser 1998, 12). Small dams (in comparison to modern examples) and breakwaters in ancient Egypt have been found but their efficiency was probably low, acting as a first barrier of defence against rushing flood waters but also assisting in the encouraged deposition of alluvial sediment in front of settlements to protect them from migrating water courses and facilitating future expansion (Bommas 1995, 141–143). By building up the river banks of settlements human impact could have marginally added to the processes of river migration, thus urban expansion into this reclaimed area to remain alongside the water course could be labelled settlement migration. Settlement migration was likely a prominent aspect of Egyptian urbanism, allowing urban areas to compromise with the movements of the river. For example, if the river moved steadily eastwards, the quayside of the settlement likely moved alongside it, as has been seen at Karnak (Bunbury *et al.* 2008, 368). Over time this process of settlement migration would result in east-west expansion of urban areas towards the river bank. However, the continued movement became obsolete and a new settlement was founded on the river front, abandoning large tell sites in the central floodplain (as can be deduced at Memphis and Cairo, or Hermopolis and Antinoopolis). The use of mudbrick as a building material is also a result of river processes on Egyptian town planning and urban development, due to its affordability and accessibility following the flood. By using Nile mud to build meant that the rebuilding of structures and redevelopment of areas was easily achievable in short periods of time. While attempts to control water channels are evident, it can be seen that the compromising nature of ancient Egyptian urbanism allowed for a relatively harmonious relationship with the river during its annual flooding.

Application of Georarchaeological data

When the information above is considered it becomes much more complicated to assign identities to settlements within the Nile floodplain. The region of the Oryx nome is almost 20km wide and at present has two water courses running from south to north, the main Nile and the Bahr Yusef, making it possible to assume, with little imagination, that more than two Nile branches crossed this area during the Egyptian Middle Kingdom; particularly in the late 12th Dynasty and early 13th Dynasty during a period of higher Nile floods. This period of higher floods was recorded at the Middle Kindgom fortresses of Semna and Kumma: the recordings were on average 7m higher than the 19th Century high flood levels (see Seidlmayer 2001, 73–74 for a full discussion of these, and other, Nile flood records). This period of high floods also coincides with the change in necropolis from Beni Hasan to Balansura and it may be deduced that a rapid change in position of the Nile (perhaps through avulsion) resulted in greater desirability to bury the local deceased at a location to the west of the floodplain. Various town mounds can still be seen in the street plans of the modern settlements of the el-Minya region, and Garris is one of the largest and most pronounced. It is located atop an ancient levee and is surrounded on its eastern and western sides by depressions which have been noted to hold standing water by Kessler who also attributed the identity of Her-wer to Mantut, a settlement 1km west of Garris (1981, 333). If this is the case then the two settlements must have been separated by a narrow water channel which silted up, perhaps through the use of dams and breakwaters, allowing them to each expand towards each other. Through careful management of the flood water both towns would have been able to maintain water access throughout dynastic history, perhaps with the assistance of canals at later dates which connected them to a river still much further west than it is today.

Problem solved?

In the beginning of this paper I outlined the limitations of what I hoped to achieve, and in these final remarks it is clear that no clear conclusion to Neferusi's location within Middle Egypt can be confidently reached. However, it is possible through the information presented to give further evidence to a hypothesis already promoted, or indeed to draw an alternative theory altogether. The geographic information explored above has therefore added a new depth of knowledge to the ideas put forward by Kessler and in many ways assists in promoting his proposal that Garris was the location of ancient Neferusi. It would, however, also be plausible to draw similar conclusions about many of the other settlement mounds within the Nile valley around Garris. It is also possible to discount other theories based on geoarchaeological information.

The theory of Itlidem being the site of Neferusi for example is unfounded in my current research. If the river has migrated to the east since the Middle Kingdom then the site of Itlidem would most likely have being located on the east bank rather than the west during that period. An analysis of recent water channel migration around the towns of Mischat Dabes and Zaafraneh opposite Beni Hasan has shown that migration around/over a town does not necessarily imply its imminent destruction. This allows greater potential than previously thought towards mapping the landscape of ancient Egypt, particularly for other towns in this area mentioned in the Beni Hasan tombs such as Menat-Khufu, Hebnu and Her-wer.

The idea of settlement migration in response to changes in river position provokes the theory that older areas of settlement mounds should be sought further from the direction of the water movement. This theory alone can provide some degree of certainty on choices for dig sites in the future and it is the aim of future research to revisit assessments of other towns mentioned in the Beni Hasan tombs to better understand the landscape of the Oryx nome using geoarchaeological evidence to aid further archaeological investigation in the area. Future fieldwork in the region would, of course, be more capable of proving or disproving these theories with certainty. Moreover, until settlement archaeology becomes a primary concern of Egyptology, theories based on such evidence can assist in providing the confidence to geographically contextualise Egyptological social studies.

Acknowledgements

This research is funded by the University of Birmingham, College of Arts and Law. I would like to thank Mr Steven Gregory for proof reading my work and helping it 'flow' more appropriately and iron out grammatical issues. I would also like to express my gratitude to Dr Andrew Howard and Dr Martin Bommas of the Institute of Archaeology and Antiquity, University of Birmingham for their kind advice and support with regards to the content of this paper.

Bibliography

Attia, K. and Sadek, N. (2010) Innundation by High Releases Downstream High Aswan Dam. *Nile Basin Water Science & Engineering Journal* 3, 79–87.

Bommas, M. (1995) Nordoststadt: Siedlungsbebauung der 1. Zwischenzeit und des Mittleren Reiches nordwestlich des Inselmuseums. *Mitteilungen des Deutschen Archäologischen Instituts Abteilung Kairo* 51, 141–147.

Bunbury, J., Graham, A. and Hunter, M. A. (2008) Stratigraphic Landscape Analysis: Charting the Holocene Movements of the Nile at Karnak through Ancient Egyptian Time. *Geoarchaeology: An International Journal* 23, 351–378.

Bunbury, J. and Jeffreys, D. (2011) Real and Literary Landscapes in Ancient Egypt. *Cambridge Archaeological Journal* 21, 65–75.

Bunbury, J. and Malouta, M. (2012) The Geology and Papyrology of Hermopolis and Antinoopolis. *eTopoi: Journal for Ancient Studies* 1 (special volume 3), 119–122.

Butzer, K. (1976) *Early Hydraulic Civilization in Egypt: A Study in Cultural Ecology*. Chicago and London, University of Chicago Press.

Champollion, J. F. (1889) *Monuments de l'Égypte et de la Nubie: Notices descriptives II*. Paris, Chez Firmin Didot frères.

Daressy, G. (1919) Deux statues de Balansourah. *Annales du service des antiquities de l'Égypte* 18, 53–57.

Gardiner, A. (1947) *Ancient Egyptian Onomastica: Vol. II*. London, Oxford University Press.

Garstang, J. (1907) *The Burial Customs of Ancient Egypt as Illustrated by the Tombs of the Middle Kingdom: Being a report of excavations made in the necropolis of Beni Hasan during 1902–3–4*. London, Constable.

Glanville, S. R. K. (1932) Records of a Royal Dockyard of the Time of Tuthmosis III: Papyrus British Museum 10056 (Part II). *Zeitschrift fürÄgyptische Sprache und Altertumskunde* 68, 7–41.

Graham, A. (2010) Islands in the Nile: A Geoarchaeological Approach to Settlement Location in the Egyptian Nile Valley and the Case of Karnak. In M. Bietak, E. Czerny and I. Forstner-Müller (eds) *Cities and Urbanism in Ancient Egypt*, 125–143. Vienna, Verlag der Österreichischen Akademie der Wissenschaften.

Helck, W. (1974) *Die altägyptischen Gaue*. Wiesbaden, Dr. Ludwig Reichert Verlag.

Hillier, J., Bunbury, J. and Graham, A. (2007) Monuments on a Migrating Nile. *Journal of Archaeological Science* 34, 1011–1015.

Kaiser, W. (1998) *Elephantine: The Ancient Town*. Cairo, German Institute of Archaeology Cairo.

Kamrin, J. (1992) *Monument and Microcosm: The 12th Dynasty Tomb Chapel of Khnumhotep II at Beni Hasan*. Unpublished thesis, University of Pennsylvania.

Kessler, D. (1981) *Historische Topographie der Region zwischen Mallawi und Samalut*. Wiesbaden, Dr. Ludwig Reichert Verlag.

Lacau, P. and Chevrier, H. (1956) *Une chapelle de Sésostris Ier a Karnak*. Cairo, Imprimerie de l'Institut français d'archéologie orientale.

Lichtheim, M. (1980) *Ancient Egyptian Literature: The Late Period*. Berkeley and Los Angeles, University of California Press.

Lutley, K. and Bunbury, J. (2008) The Nile on the Move. *Egyptian Archaeology* 32, 3–5.

Maspero, G. (1891) Notes au jour le jour. *Proceedings of the Society of Biblical Archaeology* 13, 496–525.

Moeller, N. (2005) An Old Kingdom Town at Zawiet Sultan (Zawiet Meitin) in Middle Egypt: A Preliminary Report. In A. Cooke and F. Simpson (eds) *Current Research in Egyptology II*, 29–38. Oxford, Archaeopress.

Montet, P. (1961) *Géographie de l'Égypte ancienne: deuxiéme partie, la haute Égypte*. Paris, Libraire C. Klincksieck.

Morozova, G. (2005) A Review of Holocene Avulsions of the Tigris and Euphrates Rivers and Possible Effects on the Evolution of Civilizations in Lower Mesopotamia. *Geoarchaeology: An International Journal* 20, 401–423.

Newberry, P. (1893) *Beni Hasan: Part I*. London, Egypt Exploration Fund.

Newberry, P. (1913) Notes on the Carnarvon Tablet no. 1. *Proceedings of the Society of Biblical Archaeology* 35, 117–122.

Parcak, S. (2008) Site Survey in Egyptology. In R. Wilkinson (ed.) *Egyptology Today*, 57–76. Cambridge, Cambridge University Press.

Saad, M. B. A. (2002) *Nile River Morphology Changes due to the Construction of the High Aswan Dam in Egypt*. Report for the Ministry of Water Resources and Irrigation, Egypt.

Said, R. (1993) *The River Nile: Geology, Hydrology and Utilization*. Oxford, Pergamon Press.

Seidlmayer, S. (2001) *Historische und modern Nilstände: Untersuchungen zu den Pegelablesungen des Nils von der Frühzeit bis in die Gegenwart*. Berlin, Achet Verlag.

Sliwa, J. (1988) Qasr el-Sagha: Studies on the Middle Kingdom and Second Intermediate Period Settlements in 1979–1985. *Fontes Archaeologici Posnanienses* 36, 189–215.

Smith, H. and Smith, A. (1976) A Reconsideration of the Kamose Texts. *Zeitschrift für Ägyptische Sprache und Altertumskunde* 103, 48–76.

Stanley, J., Krom, M., Cliff, R. and Woodward, J. (2003) Short Contribution: Nile Flow Failure at the End of the Old Kingdom, Egypt: Strontium Isotopic and Petrologic Evidence. *Geoarchaeology: An International Journal* 18, 395–402.

Waterfield, R. (2008) *Herodotus: The Histories*. Oxford, Oxford University Press.

Woodward, J., Macklin, M., Krom, M. and Williams, M. (2007) The Nile: Evolution, Quaternary River Environments and Material Fluxes. In A. Gupta (ed.) *Large Rivers: Geomorphology and Management*, 261–292. Chichester, John Wiley.

6

'If only I could accompany him, this excellent marshman!': An analysis of the Marshman (*sḫty*) in ancient Egyptian literature

Simon Hawkins

In a number of Middle Egyptian texts, the *sḫty* will be mentioned, often in passing, but on occasion as an integral part of the narrative. Despite their familiarity, it is still difficult to ascertain the exact role which this class of people played in ancient Egyptian society. The purpose of this paper is to examine how the *sḫty* is portrayed by the literature of ancient Egypt and to identify their importance to the functioning of ancient Egyptian society. This shall be achieved by firstly examining the most famous occurrences of the word in ancient Egyptian literature, chiefly from *The Tale of the Eloquent Peasant*, and then working towards identifying exactly who the *sḫty* was and what their role was. This will be achieved by analysing their activities and contrasting the different views of the *sḫty*, both positive and negative, in order to paint a more accurate picture of this enigmatic group of people. All of the following literary quotes are the author's own translations.

Grammatically, the word *sḫty* is derived from the noun *sḫt*, which refers to the marshland environment. *Wb.* lists the word as 'das Feld, Gefilde' (IV, 229), while Faulkner (1962, 239) translates the word as both 'marshland' and 'field'. Therefore, it is clear that the word *sḫty* literally means 'man of the marshland' or something similar, and as a result I prefer the translation of marshman or marshdweller, following Quirke (2004a, 151). The commonly accepted translation of peasant, as employed by Parkinson (1998, 54–88) and many before him, is unacceptable for reasons which will become clear. It is important at this point to define exactly what is implied by the term 'Peasant'. The Oxford Dictionary of English (2005, 1295) defines the word 'Peasant' as 'a poor smallholder or agricultural labourer of low social status (chiefly in historical use of with reference to subsistence farming in poorer countries)' and it is from this definition that comparisons with the ancient Egyptian *sḫty* shall be based. The marshman (*sḫty*) should also be viewed as distinct from the terms for fishermen and fowlers, such as *wḥꜥ* which can be translated as either 'fisherman' or 'fowler' depending on its determinatives (Faulkner 1962, 66), though I prefer 'huntsman' based on the duel nature of the word as found in *The Pleasures of Fishing and Fowling*, B2, 18. The chief difference is that a *wḥꜥ* is a person fulfilling a job or role, whereas as *sḫty* is a more encompassing statement of the person's identity. An example of this could be that referring to a person as a builder is a statement of that person's role, at that point in time. Referring to a person as an Englishman however, is a label which is laden with far more cultural information and imparts a sense of permanence.

The Tale of the Eloquent 'Peasant'

By far the most famous occurrence of the marshman in a Middle Egyptian text is in the Twelfth Dynasty (Parkinson 1991b, 171–181) composition *The Tale of the Eloquent Peasant*, the main character of which is referred to as a 'marshman from the *sḫt ḥm3t'* (usually translated as Wadi Natrun, cf. Devauchelle (1995, 34) for an alternative view of the *sḫt ḥm3t* being located near Oxyrhynchos). The plot of the tale is generally concerned with the abuse of authority and the quest for justice (for a more detailed appraisal of the text's plot, see Loprieno 2000, 183–198), but it also tells us a great deal about what type of people the marshmen were. The tale opens with the marshman at home with his family. While the scale of the dwelling is not clear, it was at least big enough to feature a storehouse for grain. This, coupled with the fact that the marshman owned multiple donkeys, would seem to indicate that the marshman was not poor enough to be labelled a peasant. This fact is underlined when you consider the goods which the marshman was taking to the town to trade. While there are many items on the list which defy translation, there are enough known items to indicate that the produce was likely to be of reasonably fine quality. Items such as natron, animal skins, as well as various birds, herbs, stones and 'all good produce of the Wadi Natrun' would indicate that, while perhaps not the finest goods available, they were above what you would expect a mere peasant to be able to trade. As the entire plot of the tale hinges on someone of higher station coveting the goods of the marshman, they therefore must be of reasonable quality in order to be desirable. It is also a point of conjecture as to how isolated the home of the marshman was from any potential neighbours, given the rural and self-sufficient nature of their existence (see Quirke 2004a, 151). Gnirs (2000, 151) raises an interesting point in her paper on the language used in *The Tale of the Eloquent Peasant*, that the 'ten loaves of bread and two jugs of beer daily', which were sent to aid the marshman's family would not have aroused the marshman's suspicion because it was an amount which could realistically be expected to have been given in assistance from the marshman's wider community, given that similar quantities occur in Middle Kingdom labour supply lists (see Müller 1975, 249–263). Gnirs sees this as implying an act of neighbourhood solidarity which would have been commonplace in times of hardship. In this way it can be imagined that marshmen would have inhabited loose rural communities, rather than totally solitary existences. Indeed, given that many of the fishing and fowling techniques that would have been utilised by the marshmen would have required teams of a few people to successfully employ (see Brewer and Friedman 1989, 31–46), this seems more than likely. While we know from artistic and literary sources such as non-royal tomb scenes and *The Pleasures of Fishing and Fowling*, that the immediate family (i.e. the wife and children) of the marshman would have been involved in hunting expeditions (see Caminos 1956, 10), these same sources also make it clear that the employment of large nets and traps would have required teams of marshmen working together. An example of this is the large seine nets and bird traps used in the Tomb of Baqt (BH 15) (Newberry 1893, pl. IV; VII).

While it is clear that the marshman of *The Tale of the Eloquent Peasant* was not of the lowest rung of society, the text also makes it clear that such marshmen were not of society's elite. The opening dialogue of the marshman demonstrates the colloquial dialect used by him, with the demonstrative *p3* employed in direct violation of the rules of 'proper' Middle Egyptian grammar.

šm swt ḫ3 n=i n3 n it
nty m p3 mḫr m wḏ3t n sf

But go and measure for me that grain
which is in the granary as remains of yesterday. (*Peasant* R 1.3–1.4)

Though the form became standardised in Late Egyptian grammar (see Junge 2005, 51–57), at this point it was still considered colloquial and 'low brow', as identified by Allen (2000, 53–54). If you imagine the marshman to have the equivalent of a thick accent you would start to understand the implied sense. In having such a dialect, the eloquence of the marshman's later petitions is all the more significant and surprising, as would be the author's intent (see Parkinson 2000, 29–30). The petitions often include archaic and 'high' grammatical forms, and as such the contrast could not be clearer. The use of excellent speech by an unlikely source was not a new idea in Egyptian literature however, and *The Instructions of Ptahotep*, which date from the later Old Kingdom to early Middle Kingdom (Vernus 1990, 185) state that:

dg3 mdt nfrt r w3ḏ
iw gm st m-ꜥ ḥmwt ḥr bnwt

Good speech is more hidden than greenstone,
Yet it may be found among the women at the grindstone. (*Ptahhotep*, P. Prisse 58–59)

This indicates that this was an ingrained literary idea. The marshman as a lower class of people is also prevalent when you consider how the marshman of this tale is described by the officials:

smwn sḫty=f pw iw n ky r gs=f
mk irt=sn pw r sḫtyw=sn iww n kt-ḫt r-gs=sn

Surely it's only a marshman of his who's run off to someone else.
Look, this is what people do to their marshmen who run off to others. (*Peasant*, B1 75–77)

This statement seems to be incompatible with the idea of the marshman as something other than the traditional peasant figure, but is contrary to the wealth of evidence which will be examined throughout this paper. It stands alone as the only piece of evidence to support the 'peasant' hypothesis in the entire text, and given the vagueness of the identifications found in these lines it is debatable how much credence should be given to it. I would suggest that the marshman could be working not just for himself, but also for a person or family to whom they are loosely bound to in some way, it being their role to provide food from the marshlands and perhaps to assist in hunting trips. These arrangements would seem to be binding, and breaking the terms of the arrangements was clearly punishable. What the marshmen obtained in return for these services is not recorded, but it seems that they were also free to pursue their own trade.

Identifying the Marshman

While marshmen were certainly not the poor peasant figures often depicted, they did inhabit the outskirts of Egyptian society. They are clearly distant from the Egyptian towns, living in areas traditionally viewed as borderlands, not just of the physical Egypt but of the spiritual. Most texts which deal with these marshland areas make clear the magical elements of the environment, from the closeness to the local deities as described in *The Pleasures of Fishing and Fowling*, to the fantastical creatures found there, such as in *The Tale of the Herdsman*. Given the common representation of the marshland in non-royal tombs, it is clear that such areas were viewed with reverence. This distance from the rest of Egyptian society has led some scholars to argue that as a result marshmen were strangers and outsiders to the Egyptian system, in many ways no different from foreigners (Gnirs 2000,143, labelling the marshman as a *rwty* or outsider, even though they are never explicitly labelled as such). This representation of the marshman is intrinsically flawed: Poo (2005, 31) argues that, given the relative stability of the Egyptian language and its resistance to change from outside elements, the ability to speak Egyptian was likely one of the most important aspects of being culturally Egyptian.

The Tale of The Eloquent Peasant also gives us a good representation of the legal rights of a marshman. From the text, it is clear that a marshman had the right to report and petition against a wrong done to him, as well as the right to appeal against an unjust decision (see Bontty 2000, 93–107. Note that the point I stress is not that the marshman has equal rights to his oppressor, but just that he has *some* rights). I find it unlikely that an outsider or stranger would be granted such legal rights, especially against a higher status individual as occurs in the text. It is also clear that the Egyptian bureaucratic system viewed the marshmen as belonging to the system, as shown through the use of titles. Throughout the Middle Kingdom there were references to *imy-r sḫtyw*, who were Overseers of the Marshmen (Ward 1982, 45). This title is known into the New Kingdom (Ayedi 2006, 113), and seemed to gain more prestige as time went on. Quirke (2004b, 70–71) believes that this may be indicative of increasing affluence and/or population density in regions east of the east Nile delta branch, around Tell el-Daba. Far from being poor outsiders to Egyptian society, there were elite individuals bearing the responsibility of overseeing the marshman population in Egypt. Berlev (1974, 110) refers to an individual called Sonabnay, from the Second Intermediate Period, who held a number of titles including Overseer of the Marshmen and sees him as being tasked with delivery of goods from the marshes to the palace. An individual who also held the title of Overseer of the Marshmen of the Royal Household is found in *The Tale of Sinuhe*:

> *rdi.in ḥm=f iwt imy-r sḫtyw mnḫ nt pr-nsw*
> *ʿḥʿw 3tpw m-ḫt=f*
>
> Then, his majesty caused the worthy Overseer of Marshmen of the Royal Household to come,
> laden ships accompanying him… (*Sinuhe*, B 243–244)

This individual is tasked by the Pharaoh to meet Sinuhe and his companions and accompany them back to Egypt and the residence. Parkinson sees this to be fitting due the marginal and outside nature of Sinuhe likened to that of the 'peasants' (1998, 51 n.67). However, I think that this individual must have been of reasonably high standing to have been entrusted with this task and referred to as *mnḫ*, and the fact that the title is featured here is likely a statement of its importance. The presence of these overseers would also seem to agree with the earlier statement found in *The Tale of the Eloquent Peasant* B1 75–77, that marshmen were required to provide for those they were bound to, either the pharaoh or other members of the ancient Egyptian elite. Ultimately, far from being a loose group of outsiders eking an existence from the marshland, the marshman was a recognised member of Egyptian society, and governed as such, with the legal rights and privileges of any other mid status Egyptian. There is however the point, discussed by Poo (2005, 105–112) and others, that foreign peoples were easily assimilated into the fabric of

Egyptian society and could be found in a multitude of roles, from the military and household servants to high ranking officials. It is theoretically possible that at least some marshmen were outside immigrants, although given the lack of hard evidence for this group, it is impossible to affirm a separate ethnicity or cultural identity. Suffice to say that the marshman of *The Tale of the Eloquent Peasant* was most likely culturally Egyptian.

While we have ascertained that the marshman was probably culturally Egyptian, spoke Egyptian (albeit with a colloquial twang), was overseen by the state and was far from the poor and wretched individual often imagined by scholars, we have yet to identify exactly what a marshman did and what his role in society was. The marshman, as might be expected, was an individual who lived and worked in the marshlands of Egypt. Generally this work seems to have entailed the hunting of birds and fish, which were plentiful in such environments, as well as the gathering of certain plants. *The Pleasures of Fishing and Fowling*, a Middle Egyptian text concerned with a non-royal hunting expedition to the marshes, mentions the marshmen in a reverential light. The main character states that:

> *šḫtyw tpw-ʿw* [.........] *nb ḥr*
> *ḥꜣ wi m-ḫt=f sḫty pn iḳr*
>
> The marshmen of former times and every [........] is (saying):
> "If only I could accompany him, this excellent marshman!" (*Fishing and Fowling*, B.2 12–13)

In stating that the marshmen of the past wish to accompany him, he is likening himself to the great marshmen of the past and showing his desire to be like a marshman. This is, in many ways, similar to a proud amateur comparing themselves to an expert in the field. The marshmen were considered hunters *par excellence* by the characters in this literary text.

It was not just the mortal characters of literary texts who wished to be associated with the marshmen, but also the gods themselves. The *Edfu Dramatic Text*, which is recorded in scenes inscribed on the temple at Edfu, concerns the triumph of Horus over his enemies by symbolically harpooning a hippopotamus in what could be interpreted as a religious drama to be acted out on particular festival days (Blackman and Fairman 1942, 33). In this text, Horus is at various times associated with the marshman, such as here in Scene 4 where the chorus are to proclaim:

> *imny n ḥr m msw sḫtyw*
>
> The right arm of Horus is as (those of) the children of marshmen (*Edfu*, 73, 8)

This attestation is very interesting, as the arm of Horus is not being compared with those of the marshmen, but those of the children of marshmen. This is a telling statement on how the ancient Egyptians viewed the health and strength of the marshmen, for their children are equitable with Horus' arm here. Perhaps there was a cultural convention in ancient Egypt which equated the children of marshmen with strength and vitality. A later line similarly states, this time as direct speech of Horus:

> *ḫꜣʿ.n=i m imny=i sš.n=i m iꜣby*
> *mi ir.n sḫty ḳnw*
>
> I have thrown with my right hand and drawn with my left hand,
> like a brave marshman would have done. (*Edfu*, 83, 13–14)

Horus compares himself directly to a marshman in his actions. The importance here is that, if a deity can be directly compared to a group of people, then those people must be highly regarded. There may have been a more direct relationship between marshmen and Horus in this later period of Egyptian pharaonic history, as the text also states, again by the chorus:

> *ỉnḏ ḥr=k ḥr mr sḫtyw*
>
> Hail to you, Horus! Beloved of Marshmen! (*Edfu*, 74, 7)

By this point in time, Horus may have been venerated as a hunting deity along with Sobek and Sekhet, who seem to have been established as the most important marshland deities by the Middle Kingdom, as indicated by the many references to them in *The Pleasures of Fishing and Fowling* (Caminos 1956, 1–21).

Throughout this paper, the marshman has been identified as a hunter of the wildlife of the marshlands of ancient Egypt. *The Tale of the Eloquent Peasant* however, outlines another important aspect of the marshman, that of a trader. The entire plot of the tale hinges on the marshman taking goods to the town to trade, and such a trip must have been a relatively common occurrence in order to trade his wares for those things which cannot be acquired from the marshlands, such as grain. A far more telling point however, is referred to in the goods list of the marshman which details the items which he was taking to trade. This goods list is longer in the R version of the tale than the others, a section of which version is referred to below:

> *m ỉ33 rdmt ḥsmn ḥm3t ḫt* [...]*tyw* ꜥ*wnt nt t3-ỉḥw*
> *ḫnwt nt b3w ḫ3wt nt wnšw nš3w* ꜥ*nw tnmw ḫpr wr*
>
> ...of reeds, herbs, natron, salt, wood of [...]-land, sticks of Farafra Oasis,
> skins of animals, jackal furs, *nš3* plants, ꜥ*nw* stones, *tnmw* plants, *ḫpr wr* plants...
> (*Peasant*, R 2.1–3.5)

Alongside the type of goods you would expect to be produced by a marshland area, such as reeds, herbs, and plants, there are also more exotic goods in this list. Most notable of these are the 'sticks of Farafra Oasis' which the marshman is taking to town. Farafra Oasis is usually associated with an oasis area to the west of the Nile Valley. If we take the marshman's home of the *sḫt ḥm3t* to be the Wadi Natrun, then we find that there is some distance between the two places. This raises the question of how the marshman came to be in possession of these sticks to trade, given that it is unlikely that he would have been able to make the journey to Farafra Oasis himself as the hunter-gatherer lifestyle of the marshman would have precluded any lengthy time away from the marshland and the family. The simplest explanation would be that the marshman obtained these sticks as part of trade with the oasis inhabitants as they came east towards the Nile. Given its location, the Wadi Natrun would be a convenient stop off point for eastward bound traders, and it is likely that they too would be interested in the wares of the marsh. The scenario would then be that a trading party from Farafra Oasis visited the Wadi Natrun and traded goods such as these sticks, which are then being traded again by the marshman in the towns of Egypt proper. This sees the marshmen as links in a trade network, selling goods, not just from their own marshes but from places further afield and acting as middle men to incoming trade. This adds to the character of the marshman, and while other interpretations are possible, it would seem that marshmen are far from simple hunter-gatherers.

As people who lived in the marshlands and worked them to survive, it is natural that even the most affluent amateur huntsman would perhaps be envious of the marshman's skills and lifestyle, at least superficially. However, just as today's anglers would perhaps admire much about the skills of their professional mid-atlantic trawlermen compatriots, few would be willing to trade places with them due to the arduous nature of the job, so it was in ancient Egypt. Indeed, *The Pleasures of Fishing and Fowling* also makes this clear in places, such as the main character's admission that:

> *n ḫnm.n wỉ wgꜣsw sšmw=ỉ šꜣbw*
>
> The gutting does not please me, my concern is the food. (*Fishing and Fowling*, B.2 9)

In such amateur hunting trips, it seems that these unpleasant tasks were given to subordinates because the wealthy did not want to be associated with fish smell and arduous gutting (visual examples of this are to be found in the fish gutting scenes of the tomb of Niankhamun and Khnumhotep (Moussa and Altenmüller 1977, pl. 13)). The marshman, his wife or his children however, would have no option but to complete such tasks. As a result the marshman would also acquire some negative characteristics in the eyes of the main Egyptian populace.

The Middle Egyptian didactic text commonly known as the *Satire of the Trades* does not explicitly mention marshmen in its list of trades, but does refer to fowlers and fishermen as the last two, and therefore the worst, jobs which an Egyptian could do. These people are referred to as being full of lamentation and discontented, dangerously labouring with crocodiles in the river. While the *Satire of the Trades* is most likely intended to be a humorous appraisal of Egyptian work options in comparison with the work of the scribal profession (see Parkinson, 2002, 273–277, cf. Helck (1970, 161–162) who reads the text as serious propaganda), as with all good satire, there is a degree of truth to the statements. It is easy to see why the majority of Egyptians would look down on any work where the danger of the marshes is mixed with the uncertainty of the catch; where failure to catch enough to eat could be the difference between life and death for the whole family. The hunter-gatherer lifestyle may even have been seen as more primitive by the town dwelling Egyptian populace. In other texts it is the more physical elements of the marshman's trade which provoke scorn. *The Dialogue between a Man and his Soul* for example, explicitly highlights the reek of fishermen and the marshland environment where they work, as well as the reek of ducks and reeds full of waterfowl. The impression is that the marshland and, by extension the marshmen, smells unpleasant.

> *mk bꜥḥ rn=ỉ*
> *mk šsp sbnw m hrw rsfw pt tꜣt*
> *mk bꜥḥ rn=ỉ*
> *mk r st ꜣpsw r bwꜣt nt trỉw ẖr msyt*
> *mk bꜥḥ rn=ỉ*
> *mk r st ḥꜣmw r ḫꜣsw nw sšw ḥꜣm.n=sn*
> Look my name reeks!
> Look, <more than> a haul of *sbnw* fish on a hot day!
> Look, my name reeks!
> Look, more than the smell of vultures, more than reed shelters full of waterfowl!
> Look, my name reeks!
> Look, more than the smell of fishermen, more than the waterways of the pools which they had fished (*Man and Soul*, 88–95)

It is possible that the practice shown in many tomb scenes involving the females of the scene holding flowers to their noses is an attempt to combat this smell, though this cannot be proven.

In any case, in *The Pleasures of Fishing and Fowling* the main characters take steps to reduce their contact with elements which may smell bad, such as their refusal to gut their catch. Clearly, in the literature there was a commonly held wisdom among most Egyptians that fishermen and fowlers, and by extension marshmen, while being skilled individuals were grumbling, smelly individuals doing a frustrating and dangerous job. This may also be underlined by the fragmentary Middle Kingdom composition *The Discourse of the Fowler*; preserved in two separate manuscripts which Parkinson (2002, 306–307) believes comprises two parts of the same composition. This discourse concerns a fowler lamenting the worsening state of his profession, and the use of a fowler may indicate an underlying comment on the complaining nature of such professions. Of course, this did not stop the elite from heading to the marshes for civilised sporting pursuits. This is recorded in another scribal training text from the New Kingdom. Papyrus Lansing is a text which attempts to persuade a scribal student to ignore distractions and concentrate on his studies. Here, the teacher implores his student:

> *m rdit ib=k n tꜣ bw-wꜣt*
> *mkḥꜣ ḳꜣmw šꜣpw*
>
> Do not long for the place of sporting!
> Turn your back on throwing (the stick) and chasing (?)! (*Papyrus Lansing*, 10–11)

This seems to indicate that days spent in marshland sporting pursuits were desirable. The text also includes a list of undesirable professions, similar to the *Satire of the Trades*, but notably here fishing and fowling are absent. This could represent a change of attitude towards the marshman and his role into the New Kingdom.

Conclusions

As discussed throughout this paper, the marshman is a particularly fascinating and enigmatic character, which has almost been lost to us from ancient Egyptian history. Most of the references we have to these people are literary, and this has led to much misinterpretation. This paper has argued that, far from the lowly peasantry often imagined by scholars, the marshmen were skilled hunters, admired and respected by all. Though they were not wealthy or powerful, they could afford a reasonable standard of living, and had clear legal rights of petition. While aspects of their work may have been maligned by more urbanised groups of Egyptian society, the marshman was respected, blending a hunter-gatherer lifestyle with that of a merchant trader. As time progressed, and the Middle Kingdom gave way to the New Kingdom, the marshman seemed to become ever more admired. Comparisons between marshmen and gods have been discussed and to be compared with a god is perhaps the highest form of praise.

The view of the marshman which comes to us from ancient Egypt is fragmentary, contradictory in places, and difficult to reconcile with our own cultural examples. However, if we compare the evidence we do have for the marshman with the definition of the word 'Peasant', given earlier in this paper, we can instantly see that 'peasant' is not an adequate word to describe the *sḫty*. The marshmen were clearly not agricultural labourers and while their exact social status is unclear, to describe them as having the low status implied by the word 'Peasant' would be incompatible with most evidence. As scholars, we have to accept that there are some aspects of ancient Egyptian culture which cannot be easily reconciled with a European example .While this could be accepted as occurring in the infancy of Egyptology as a discipline, for it to still persist on a widely accepted level from modern scholarship is something which needs to be addressed and I hope to have made a start here.

Bibliography

al-Ayedi, A. (2006) *Index of Egyptian Administrative, Religious and Military Titles of the New Kingdom.* Ismailia, Obelisk Publications.

Allen, J. P. (2000) *Middle Egyptian: An Introduction to the Language and Culture of Hieroglyphs.* Cambridge: Cambridge University Press.

Berlev, O. (1974) A Contemporary of King Sewaḥ-en-rêʿ. *Journal of Egyptian Archaeology* 60, 106–113.

Blackman, A. M. and Fairman, H. W. (1942) The Myth of Horus at Edfu – II. *The Journal of Egyptian Archaeology* 28, 32–38.

Bontty, M. (2000) Images of Law and the Disputing Process in The Tale of the Eloquent Peasant. In A. M. Gnirs (ed.) *Reading the Eloquent Peasant: Proceedings of the International Conference on The Tale of the Eloquent Peasant at the University of California, Los Angeles, March 27–30, 1997. Lingua Aegyptia 8*, 93–107.

Brewer, D. J. and Friedman, R. F. (1989) *Fish and Fishing in Ancient Egypt.* The Natural History of Egypt: Volume II. Warminster, Aris and Phillips.

Caminos, R. A. (1956) *Literary Fragments in the Hieratic Script.* Oxford, Oxford University Press.

Devauchelle, D. (1995) Le Paysan déraciné. *Chronique d'Égypte* 70, 34–40.

Drioton, É. (1948) *Le Texte Dramatique D'Edfou.* Cairo, Imprimere de l'Institut Français d'Archéologie Orientale.

Faulkner, R. O. (1956) The Man Who was Tired of Life. *Journal of Egyptian Archaeology* 42, 21–40.

Faulkner, R. O. (1962) *A Concise Dictionary of Middle Egyptian.* Oxford, Griffith Institute.

Gardiner, A. H. (1937) *Late-Egyptian Miscellanies.* Bibliotheca Aegyptiaca 7. Brussels, Fondation égyptologique Reine Élisabeth .

Gnirs, A. M. (2000) The Language of Corruption: On Rich and Poor in The Eloquent Peasant. In A. M. Gnirs (ed.) *Reading the Eloquent Peasant: Proceedings of the International Conference on The Tale of the Eloquent Peasant at the University of California, Los Angeles, March 27–30, 1997. Lingua Aegyptia 8*, 125–155.

Helck, W. (1970) *Die Lehre des Dwꜣ-Ḫtjj.* 2 Vols. Kleine Ägyptische Texte. Wiesbaden, Harrassowitz.

Junge, F. (2005) *Late Egyptian Grammar: An Introduction.* Second English Edition. Oxford, Griffith Institute.

Koch, R. (1990) *Die Erzählung des Sinuhe.* Bibliotheca Aegyptiaca XVII. Brussels, Éditions de la Fondation Égyptologique.

Loprieno, A. (2000) Literature as Mirror of Social Institutions: The Case of The Eloquent Peasant. In A. M. Gnirs (ed.) *Reading the Eloquent Peasant: Proceedings of the International Conference on The Tale of the Eloquent Peasant at the University of California, Los Angeles, March 27–30, 1997. Lingua Aegyptia 8*, 183–198.

Moussa, A. M. and Altenmüller, H. (1977) *Das Grab des Nianchchnum und Chnumhotep.* Mainz and Rhein, Verlag Philipp Von Zabern.

Müller, D. (1975) Some Remarks on Wage Rates in the Middle Kingdom. *Journal of Near Eastern Studies* 34.4, 249–263.

Newberry, P. R. (1893) *Beni Hasan, Part II.* London, Kegan Paul, Trench, Trübner and Co.

Oxford Dictionary of English (2005) Revised Second Edition. Oxford, Oxford University Press.

Parkinson, R. B. (1991a) *The Tale of the Eloquent Peasant.* Oxford, Griffith Institute.

Parkinson, R. B. (1991b) The Date of the Tale of the Eloquent Peasant. *Revue d'Égyptologie* 42, 171–18.

Parkinson, R. B. (1998) *The Tale of Sinuhe and Other Ancient Egyptian Poems 1940–1640 BC*. Oxford, Oxford University Press.

Parkinson, R. B. (2000) Imposing Words: The Entrapment of Language in the Tale of the Eloquent Peasant. In A. M. Gnirs (ed.) *Reading the Eloquent Peasant: Proceedings of the International Conference on The Tale of the Eloquent Peasant at the University of California, Los Angeles, March 27–30, 1997. Lingua Aegyptia 8*, 27–51.

Parkinson, R. B. (2002) *Poetry and Culture in Middle Kingdom Egypt: A Dark Side to Perfection.* London: Continuum.

Poo, M. (2005) *Enemies of Civilization: Attitudes towards Foreigners in Ancient Mesopotamia, Egypt, and China.* Albany, State University of New York Press.

Quirke, S. (2004a) *Egyptian Literature 1800 BC: Questions and Readings*. London, Golden House Publications.

Quirke, S. (2004b) *Titles and Bureaux of Egypt 1850–1700 BC*. London, Golden House Publications.

Vernus, P. (1990) *Future at Issue. Tense, Mood and Aspect in Middle Egyptian: Studies in Syntax and Semantics*. Yale Egyptological Studies 4. New Haven, Yale University.

Ward, W. (1982) *Index of Egyptian Administrative and Religious Titles of the Middle Kingdom*. Beirut, American University of Beirut.

Wb – Erman, A. and Grapow, H. (eds) (1925–1963) *Wörterbuch der ägyptischen Sprache* (12 volumes). Berlin, Akademie Verlag.

7

Wrestling with the past: the origins of pharaonic history in the Islamic Middle Ages

Joost Kramer

Introduction

When we open a random introduction to ancient Egyptian history it seems that there was an active interest in this era in the Hellenistic period, which was then revived in the European Renaissance. That leaves us with a gap of more than a thousand years, almost as if medieval scholars and travellers neither wrote about, nor wondered at the sight of these monuments. On the contrary ever since the ninth century AD Islamic scholars have included pharaonic history in their works, presenting its chronology and describing its monuments. Thus, from the ninth to the fifteenth century, a corpus of historical narratives on ancient Egypt was compiled. This paper will discuss several of those narratives and will subsequently shed new light on the following question: what are the origins of medieval narratives on ancient Egypt and are these narratives continued from earlier traditions? In answering this question we will be able to say more about what is historical fact – as seen in modern day Egyptology – and what was invented, added, or corrupted by Islamic historians.

The narrative of Shaddād b. ᶜĀd

The first narrative, which will be discussed, is that of Shaddād b. ᶜĀd. The earliest preserved source we have is the *Futūḥ Miṣr wa akhbāruhā* (*The Conquest of Egypt and its Reports*) by Ibn ᶜAbd al-Ḥakam (*d.* 871), but since one of his sources was Ibn Lahīᶜa (*d.* 790), a fellow Egyptian scholar, this story was at least a century older. King Shaddād allegedly built the pyramids of Giza (Ibn ᶜAbd al-Ḥakam 1922, 43; Yāqūt 1984, V, 401; Abū Jaᶜfar al-Idrīsī 1991, 23; 93; 110; Maqrīzī 2002, I, 318; Suyūṭī 1967, I, 70; 77) and the city of Alexandria (Ibn ᶜAbd al-Ḥakam 1922, 43). According to later authors he ordered the construction of the pyramids because he had seen a vision of an eschatological flood (Abū Jaᶜfar al-Idrīsī 1991, 104; Maqrīzī 2002, I, 322).

Throughout the Quran there are passages concerning an Arabian tribe called ᶜĀd (primarily Q7:69–72). Here the tribe of ᶜĀd, originating from the area that makes up Yemen today, was visited by the prophet Hūd, who was sent by God to preach to them. They did not heed the call of the prophet and were thereupon destroyed by God. Quranic exegetes add that the wrath of God was caused by the fact that their king Shaddād built his capital Iram to rival with paradise (Cobb 2002, 559). Islamic historians also incorporated Shaddād and the ᶜĀdites into their histories on the pre-Islamic Arab kings. According to them ᶜĀd was the first ruler to form a kingdom after Noah and the Flood (Masᶜūdī 1864, III, 79–80). His son Shaddād ruled for 900 years (Masᶜūdī 1864, III, 81) and conquered Syria, Iraq, India, and Egypt (Qalqashandī 1914, V, 18).

This narrative presents a distinctively Islamic story in which the hero Shaddād is an Arab king who conquers many lands and who builds amazing structures. In this latter aspect, he was well suited as the creator of the pyramids. However, most importantly this narrative places the pyramids within the context of Islam.

The granaries of Joseph

The second narrative was based on the well known Biblical and Quranic story of Joseph (Gen. 41–47 and Q12). When Joseph was released from prison by the pharaoh, he was appointed as overseer to store food surplus for the seven meagre years he predicted. The pyramids of Giza were identified as these granaries of Joseph.

This identification was already forged in late antique Byzantium. The eighth century patriarch of Antioch Dionysius of Tell Maḥrē (*d.* after 775) refers to the Byzantine archbishop Gregory of Nazianzus (*d.* 389 or 390), also known as Gregory the Theologian, as follows:

> *'In Egypt we have seen these pyramids about which the Theologian spoke in his chants. They are not the granaries of Joseph, as some think them to be, but admirable constructions, built over the tombs of ancient kings'* (translated from Chabot: Dionysius of Tell Maḥrē 1895, IV, XXV).

Although Dionysius himself refutes the notion that the pyramids were built by Joseph, this was apparently a view in late antiquity (cf. Silvestre de Sacy 1905, 225). This view was repeated by Michael the Syrian (*d.* 1199), patriarch of the Syrian church (Michael the Syrian 1905, III, 82), and by the Syrian church father and historian Bar Hebraeus (*d.* 1286) (Baghdādī 1810, 504). In a different context the Spanish Jew Benjamin of Tudela (*act.* second half of the twelfth century) wrote in his travelogue *Sefer ha-massaᶜot* (*The Book of Travels*) that either the pyramids of Giza or the ruins of Memphis were built by Joseph (Benjamin of Tudela 1907, 73). According to the French Franciscan priest André Thevet (*d.* 1590) in his travelogue *Cosmographie du Levant* many Jewish chroniclers identified the pyramids of Giza with the granaries of Joseph (Thevet 1985, 154). Thevet himself did not think it was credible but rather said that the pyramids were sepulchres.

In the Arabic tradition, the identification of the pyramids of Giza with the granaries of Joseph is rarely attested. According to al-Masᶜūdī, Joseph built the pyramids, but he does not mention that the prophet used them as storage facilities (Masᶜūdī 1863, II, 365). Both al-Muqaddasī (*d.* 990) and Abū Manṣūr al-Thaᶜālibī (*d.* 1038) claim that Joseph indeed built the pyramids as granaries (Muqaddasī 1903, 210; Abū Manṣūr al-Thaᶜālibī 1908, 414). Ibn Ḥawqal (*d.* after 973) goes a bit further in stating that 'some pretend that the pyramids are tombs. That is utterly wrong ... some more recent kings made these two pyramids [of Kheops and Khefren] into their granaries and stored grain in them' (Ibn Ḥawqal 1938, 152).

The Joseph narrative is clearly of Judeo-Christian origin in which episodes of the Old Testament were associated with physical features of the Egyptian landscape such as pharaonic monuments. The inspiration for the Joseph tradition in late antiquity and in Jewish chronicles can be found in the book of Genesis. Similarly, in Islam, Joseph is an important prophet and it is therefore no surprise that in Islamic histories the pyramids are connected to him, since this would place the pyramids in an Islamic context and would give Egypt a prominent place in the Islamic empire. Despite the symbolic potential of the story of Joseph, it was not widely adopted in Muslim circles perhaps because its Judeo-Christian origin was too alien for Islamic scholars. I have not been able to find any link between Islamic traditions and Jewish and Christian traditions. However, we may assume that later Islamic historians were familiar with the Christian tradition since for example al-Maqrīzī (*d.* 1442) had clearly read Bar Hebraeus, whom he quotes at several occasions.

Hermes Trismegistos

The third narrative is that of the prophet Hermes Trismegistos. According to Islamic historians, Hermes built the pyramids and the temples of Upper Egypt because he had a dream in which the earth would be destroyed (Yāqūt 1984, V, 410; Nuwayrī 1923, I, 388; Abū Jaᶜfar al-Idrīsī 1991, 96, 97; Maqrīzī 2002, I, 319, 322). As he feared that this would mean the loss of all knowledge of the crafts and the sciences he had them recorded on the walls of the pyramids and the temples. Hermes was buried in one of the two great pyramids of Giza. The prophet Agathodaimon, who is in relation to Hermes sometimes seen as the master and sometimes as the pupil, was buried in the other pyramid (Yāqūt 1984, V, 410; Abū Jaᶜfar al-Idrīsī 1991, 22; Maqrīzī 2002, I, 327; Suyūṭī 1967, I, 94). Medieval Islamic historians transmitted this information on authority of the Ṣābians from the Mesopotamian city of Ḥarrān, who will be discussed below. The story of Hermes as part of pharaonic chronology can first be found in the works of al-Masᶜūdī, i.e. the first half of the tenth century. It remained popular since and was transmitted by many scholars working on ancient Egypt.

Hermes is by origin not an Arabic persona but he found his way into Arabic and Islamic thought and literature. The genre of Hermeneutics, named after him, was derived from Hermes Trismegistos (Τρισμέγιστος, the Thrice Greatest) who was the Greek equivalent to the ancient Egyptian deity of wisdom, Thoth. This is well suited because Hermeneutics is the result of a mix of scientific traditions of ancient Egypt on the one hand and Greek, or Hellenistic, traditions on the other, which took place in Alexandria in the first century AD (Fowden 1986, 161). As the arabist Kevin van Bladel puts it, native Egyptian sages in Roman Egypt wrote treatises on science and philosophy in Greek but they remained part of a distinctive Egyptian tradition (2009, 4). Among these sciences were fields like astrology, cosmology, and medicine. In subsequent centuries Hermeneutics found its way into the Coptic language, for example in the Najᶜ Ḥammādī codices of the fourth century AD (Van Bladel 2009, 12).

In late antiquity, Hermeneutics had spread across the eastern Mediterranean and was also known to Christian scholars in Syria. This is shown by the work of the somewhat obscure Ṣābian Ibn Waḥshiyya (*act.* tenth century), who wrote several books but remains otherwise unknown. These works seem to be rewritings of antique scientific and pseudo-scientific works of the Hellenistic world (Fahd 1971, 964). One of his preserved books, called *Kitāb shawq al-mustahām fī maᶜrifat rumūz al-aqlām* (*The Book of the Yearning for the Love of Knowing the*

Symbols of the Scripts), is an Arabic translation of a Chaldean original which has accumulated over ninety ancient scripts and provides a key. One of those scripts is called 'the script of the philosopher Hermes the Greatest, which is the script written on the temples, the pyramids, the sarcophagi, the stones, and ancient shrines' (Ibn Waḥshiyya 1806, 81). In a different sense, this work represents an anti-Arab sentiment, which was expressed by non-Arab, Muslim writers, who were appalled by perceived Arab arrogance. According to non-Arab Muslims, Arabs saw themselves as superior Muslims since they originated from the Arabian Peninsula, the cradle of Islam, but when it came to cultural development the ancient societies of Egypt and Mesopotamia had much more to offer (cf. Goldziher 1966, 147–148).

In Islamic times Hermeneutics was regarded as ancient knowledge from before the revelation of Islam. The influential Baghdadi astrologer Abū Maᶜshar (*d.* 886) was the first to describe Hermes as a prophet who resided in Upper Egypt where he built the temples and filled their walls with depictions of the sciences and crafts known to mankind (Pingree 1968, 14). This was later acknowledged by other astrologers and physicians (Ibn Juljul 1955, 5–10; Ibn al-Qifṭī 1903, 5–6; Ibn Abī Usaybiᶜa 1998, 24–25). Abū Maᶜshar and Ibn Juljul (*d.* 994) can be placed in what is called the translation movement. The translation movement was a tradition in ᶜAbbāsid Baghdad where there was an interest in scientific knowledge in such areas as astronomy, geography, alchemy, and medicine. Arab scholars derived their knowledge primarily from Greek, Persian, and Indian works, which were translated into Arabic on a massive scale. Abū Maᶜshar and Ibn Juljul were part of this tradition and it is here that the Arabic Hermes, upon which the Egyptian Hermes of pharaonic history was based, was born.

I already came to speak of the Ṣābians from the city of Ḥarrān. A discussion of their origins is necessary because they appear to be an authoritative source on the legend of Hermes in pharaonic history. Islamic travellers and geographers mention the Ṣābians performing pilgrimages to the pyramids where they offered roosters and perfume (Gharnāṭī 1925, 227; Abū Jaᶜfar al-Idrīsī 1991, 22). The most striking characteristic of the Ṣābians is that they adhered to their pagan cult despite the Christianisation and subsequent Islamisation of the region. Hermes and Agothodaimon were important prophets in Ḥarrānian belief. They adopted the name 'Ṣābian' only later in accordance with the Quran, which mentions the Ṣābians favourably next to Muslims, Christians, and Jews (Q2:62, 5:69, 22:17). Islamic scholars became better acquainted with Ṣābian religion when the influential Ṣābian family of the philosopher Thābit b. Qurra (*d.* 901) broke with Ḥarrān and relocated to Baghdad. Several Ṣābian scholars have busied themselves with ancient Egyptian history. One of them is Ibn Waḥshiyya, whom I have already mentioned. He collected Egyptian hieroglyphs and provided a translation. Ibn Waṣīf Shāh (*act.* second half or the tenth century) also wrote on pharaonic history but mostly on the Sūrīd narrative, which will be discussed in the next paragraph. It has been suggested that Ibn Waṣīf Shāh was a Ṣābian as well (Sezgin 1993, 10).

In conclusion, the character of Hermes can be traced back to Hellenistic Egypt. The narrative of Hermes, as it was used by Islamic historians, is of Islamic provenance and should be placed within the context of the translation movement. However the spirit in which this narrative was written, is entirely in line with the Hellenistic tradition, which was preserved in the writings of the Ṣābians and presumably other peoples in the eastern Mediterranean. It seems that Islamic historians recognised the importance of ancient knowledge. This knowledge could not have served any practical end since medieval historians were not able to read most ancient scripts and thus ancient scientific corpora remained inaccessible to them. Nevertheless ancient knowledge did serve an ideological purpose. Especially during the translation movement pre-Islamic sciences were valued and several Muslim writers of non-Arab descent, such as Ibn Waḥshiyya, used ancient knowledge as an example in their anti-Arab polemic. For Egypt, Thoth/Hermes was most suitable to fulfil the role of protagonist in this tradition.

The narrative of king Sūrīd and the antediluvian dynasty

The fourth and last narrative is the story of the Egyptian king Sūrīd, who was one of the mythological rulers of the antediluvian dynasty, that is, the dynasty which reigned before the Flood of Noah. This story can first be found in the *Akhbār al-zamān* (*Reports of the Past*) of Ibn Waṣīf Shāh (*act.* second part of the tenth century) (1984). The narratives of the antediluvian dynasty in general and of king Sūrīd in particular became widespread and remained popular in the medieval Near East. This narrative was still being transmitted in the seventeenth century by the Turkish traveller Evliya Çelebi (*d.* 1682) (2010, 403).

Medieval Islamic historians recognise nineteen to twenty antediluvian kings but of most nothing is mentioned but their names (Ibn Waṣīf Shāh 1984, 157–203; Maqrīzī 2002, I, 350–363). Sūrīd is an exception to this and several historians have presented a fairly detailed account of his rule. He was a priest king, who had two dreams in which the earth was destroyed by water and by fire (Ibn Waṣīf Shāh 1984, 182; Maqrīzī 2002, I, 360–361). As he was distressed he sent for the high priests of Egypt. One among them, Philemon, said he had seen a similar dream and he interpreted it literally; the earth would be destroyed. Thus Sūrīd ordered the pyramids and the temples to be built and hid his treasures, the bodies of the kings, and knowledge of the sciences inside the monuments. The actual catastrophe took place 300 years later during the rule of king Firᶜawn (Pharaoh), who was warned by Noah and by a priest, again called Philemon, of an impending disaster (Ibn Waṣīf Shāh 1984, 200–203; Maqrīzī 2002, I, 362–363). The king did not listen and when the Flood came, he tried to reach the pyramids but as he was inebriated he tripped and drowned. In the ears of devout Muslims, the drunken state of the king must have added to the villainous image of the king.

Islamic historians always refer to Coptic sources concerning this history, partially because they saw it as Coptic history. But what is more relevant here is whether Islamic historians consulted Coptic historical data and whether this represented factual historical information. If we take Islamic historians for their word then they were aware of Coptic traditions on pharaonic Egypt. The Egyptian scholar Ibn al-Dawādārī (*d.* after 1335) wrote that he got his information from a Coptic book, which was given to him in the White Monastery of Sohag (Ibn al-Dawādārī 1981, III, 214). Similarly al-Suyūṭī (*d.* 1505) had trouble finding a Copt who was able to read a work on pharaonic history (Suyūṭī 1967, I, 72). Historians also consulted oral sources, thus al-Masᶜūdī (*d.* 956) presents an interview between the Egyptian governor Ibn Ṭūlūn (*d.* 884) and an aged Copt who informs the official of the pyramids (Masᶜūdī 1863, II, 372–374). However, if we want to further identify these Coptic sources we face the problem of their anonymity. Islamic scholars did not name their sources, not even the authors of the Coptic books they consulted. Conversely, Coptic historiographical works only rarely include pharaonic history. When Coptic historians include pharaonic history, it is usually borrowed from Greek material, which presents completely different narratives than Islamic traditions.

Contrary to Coptic and Greek sources, we have evidence that Sūrīd was known in late antique Syria and Mesopotamia and that he was associated with ancient Egypt. Similar to Hermes, Sūrīd was known to Ibn Waḥshiyya, who incorporated the *temple script* (*qalam al-birbāwī*, from the word *birbā*, which was specifically used to designate pharaonic temples), which was attributed to king Sūrīd (1806, 24).

From a linguistic assessment we can conclude that the Arabic accounts of the legend of Sūrīd have Coptic or pharaonic origins as well as Syriac sources. Alexander Fodor has argued that the Greek version of the name of Sūrīd, Σουρίδ, is a corruption of Σουφίς (Souphis), which is the Greek name of Kheops (1973, 357). His conclusion is that medieval historians had at least some knowledge about the builder of the great pyramid. As for the Syriac sources, the arabist Van Reeth has identified several Syriac loanwords words, which were used in medieval Arabic accounts on pharaonic history. One of them is *ḥīd al-maghyār* (the cave of treasure), which is of Syriac origin and is often attested to describe a room underneath the pyramids allegedly filled with treasure (Van Reeth 1994, 227).

There is also a thematic continuity discernable between the ancient and the Islamic Near East. Firstly the interpretation of dreams takes an important role in the narrative of Sūrīd, who had several dreams. In ancient Egypt, indeed in the whole ancient Near East, this practice was very popular. Secondly, there is a similarity between Sūrīd, who hid knowledge of the sciences on the walls inside of the pyramids and temples, and the Demotic story of Setna Khaemwase, who sets out to find the Book of Thoth, filled with ancient wisdom. Lastly I would like to point out the theme of an eschatological Flood, which was a well-known story in Babylonian literature but also in ancient Egypt. Think for example of the primeval ocean, which technically existed before creation, but expresses a contrary situation to Life as did the Flood. This thematic consistency is not only limited to the narrative of Sūrīd but can also be found in those of Shaddād and Hermes as we have seen above.

In short medieval Islamic scholars saw the narrative of king Sūrīd, indeed of his entire dynasty, as genuinely Egyptian. They attributed their sources to Coptic authorities. The name Sūrīd also appears in Arabic translations of late antique texts originally written in Syriac. Although it is difficult to ascertain the degree of continuity in the Sūrīd narrative between pharaonic Egypt and Islamic Egypt, it certainly seems that medieval scholars had at least some knowledge of ancient Egypt via Syriac and Coptic sources.

The king list of al-Bīrūnī

Finally it is interesting to briefly mention the king list of the Persian polymath al- Bīrūnī (*d.* 1048), which presented with some minor inadequacies the actual twentieth to thirtieth Egyptian dynasties (Bīrūnī 1923, 90–91). This work was derived from Eusebius' version of Manetho's well known king list. According to the French arabist Gaston Wiet, al- Bīrūnī copied the list from a Syriac intermediary, which explains most of the inadequacies (Wiet 1953, 28). Although this was a piece of authentic information, it is striking to see that in the Arabic tradition it is only al-Maqrīzī who copied the list (2002, I, 390–391). The wide availability of al-Bīrūnī's work suggests that Islamic historians made deliberate choices on what to transmit and what not to transmit. They did not chose for a historic encyclopaedia presenting all available accounts on pharaonic history, but rather used this history to convey contemporary messages e.g. stressing the importance of collecting and translating knowledge.

Conclusions

I started this paper questioning what the origins of medieval historical accounts of ancient Egypt were and whether there was any sense of continuity with earlier traditions.

The medieval accounts were formed by a mixture of several narratives on pharaonic Egypt. First, the earliest historians such as Ibn Lahīᶜa and Ibn ᶜAbd al-Ḥakam gave prominence to the story of the Arab Shaddād and established a link between Egyptian history and Arab/Yemeni history and between ancient Egypt and Islam. Second, from a Biblical point of view, several pharaonic monuments were associated with episodes of the story of Joseph. This was mostly done by Christian church fathers and by Jews before the dawn of Islam and we rarely see such accounts in medieval Islamic sources. Third, there were the narratives of Hermes and Sūrīd, which were developed in the tenth century AD and which expressed the process of establishing a body of authoritative sources, translating books from older traditions. These traditions, the historians believed, would provide answers to questions, which were raised by the presence of the pharaonic monuments in the Islamic Egyptian landscape.

The narratives were either invented (Shaddād) or restructured (Joseph, Hermes, and Sūrīd) by Islamic historians. However we cannot speak of continuity between Islamic and earlier traditions. The story of Sūrīd may be an exception to this as we find his name in pseudo-scientific works in Syriac. It seems that Hellenistic scientific traditions from Alexandria were adopted in the eastern Mediterranean and kept alive. After the Islamic conquest they were translated into Arabic. Similarly the king list of al-Bīrūnī was translated via a Syriac work. Continuity between Islamic and Coptic traditions is harder to establish. It may have been the case that medieval scholars used Coptic sources, but because of the anonymity of both written and oral sources and the absence of Coptic material – as far as it is known to us – it is almost impossible to present any solid conclusions here.

Although pharaonic history in the Middle Ages was mostly pieced together by Islamic scholars, this history was very much alive. The objective of the historians, however, was not necessarily to present pharaonic history as they deemed it factual. Rather historians tried to bring Egypt's pre-Islamic history under the umbrella of Islam and then used it to define a distinctive Egypt, which was different from the rest of the Islamic Empire. This explains why al-Bīrūnī's king list or the story of Joseph were largely neglected. Islamic historians simply had no use for them.

Finally I would like to stress that medieval interest in ancient Egypt could prove to be useful to Egyptology. Medieval accounts of pharaonic monuments, which are very elaborate at times, describe the monuments in a far better preserved state than in which most monuments are now. These accounts may give an indication where temples and tombs may have been that are now completely erased or have disappeared under more recent constructions. In this regard the material of medieval Islamic historians working on ancient Egypt has still much to offer.

Bibliography

ᶜAbd al-Laṭīf al-Baghdādī (1810) *Kitāb al-ifāda wa-'l-iᶜtibār fī 'l-umūr al-mustāhada wa-'l-ḥawādith al-maᶜāyanna bi-arḍ Miṣr*. Ed. by A.-I. Silvestre de Sacy as *Relation de l'Égypte*. Paris, Treuttel et Würtz.

Abū Jaᶜfar al-Idrīsī (1991) *Kitāb anwār ᶜulūw al-ajrām fī 'l-kashf ᶜan asrār al-ahrām*. Ed. by U. Haarmann as *Das Pyramidenbuch des Abū* Ğaʻfar *al-Idrīsī (st. 644/1251)*. Beiruter Texte und Studien 38. Beirut, Orient-Institut der Deutschen Morgenländische Gesellschaft.

Abū Manṣūr al-Thaᶜālibī (1908) *Thimār al-qulūb fī 'l-muḍāf wa-'l-mansūb*. Cairo, Maktabat al-Isti'nāf.

Benjamin of Tudela (1907) *Sefer ha-massaᶜot*. Tr. by M. N. Adler as *The Itinerary of Benjamin of Tudela*. Oxford, Oxford University Press.

al-Bīrūnī (1923) *al-*Āthār *al-bāqiya ᶜan al-qurūn al-khāliya*. Ed. by E. Sachau as *Chronologie orientalischer Völker*. Leipzig, Otto Harrassowitz.

Cobb P. (2002) 'Iram'. In J. D. MacAuliffe (ed.) *Encyclopedia of the Quran*, II, 559. Leiden, Brill.

Dionysius of Tell Maḥrē (1895) *Chronicle*. Ed. and tr. by J.-B. Chabot as *Chronique de Denys de Tell Maḥré*. Paris, Bouillon.

Evliyā Çelebi (2010) *An Ottoman Traveller*. Tr. by R. Dankoff and S. Kim. London, Eland.

Fahd, T. (1971) 'Ibn Waḥshiyya'. In P. Bearman *et al.* (eds) *Encyclopedia of Islam*, 2nd edition, III, 963-965.

Fodor, A. (1973) 'The Origins of the Arabic Legends of the Pyramids'. *Acta Orientalia Hungaricae* 23, 335-363.

Fowden, G. (1986) *The Egyptian Hermes*. Cambridge, Cambridge University Press.

al-Gharnāṭī (1925) *Tuḥfat al-albāb*. Ed. by G. Ferrand. Paris, Journal Asiatique.

Goldziher, I. (1966) *Muslim Studies*. Vol. I. Tr. by C. R. Barber and S. M. Stern. London, Allen & Unwin.

Ibn ᶜAbd al-Ḥakam (1922) *Futūḥ Miṣr wa akhbāruhā*. Ed. by Ch. C. Torrey as *The History of the Conquest of Egypt, North Africa and Spain Known as the Futūḥ Miṣr*. New Haven, Yale University Press.

Ibn Abī Usaybiᶜa (1998) *ᶜUyūn al-anbā' fī ṭabaqāt al-aṭibbā'*. Ed. by M. B. ᶜUyūn al-Sūd. Beirut, Dār al-Kutub al-ᶜIlmiyya.

Ibn al-Dawādārī (1981) *Kanz al-durar wa-jāmiᶜ al-ghurar*. Ed. by M. al-S. Jamāl al-Dīn. Cairo, Deutsches Archäologisch Institut.

Ibn Ḥawqal (1938) *Kitāb ṣūrat al-arḍ*. Ed. by J. H. Kramers as *Liber Imaginis Terrae*. Leiden, Brill.

Ibn Juljul (1955) *Ṭabaqāt al-aṭībbā' wa-'l-ḥukamā'*. Ed. by A. F. Sayyid. Cairo, Institut Français d'Archéologie Orientale.

Ibn al-Qifṭī (1903) *Ta'rīkh al-ḥukamā'*. Ed. by A. Müller and J. Lippert. Leipzig, Dietrish'sche Verlagsbuchhandlung.

Ibn Waḥshiyya (1806) *Shawq al-mustahām fi maᶜrifat rumūz al-aqlām*. Ed. by J.Hammer as *Ancient Alphabets and Hietoglyphic Characters Explained*. London, W. Bulmer and Co.

Ibn Waṣīf Shāh (1984) L'Abrégé des Merveilles. Paris, Sindbad.

al-Maqrīzī (2002) *al-Mawāᶜiẓ wa-'l-iᶜtibār fī dhikr al-khiṭaṭ wa-'l-athār*. 5 vols. Ed. by A. F. Sayyid. London, al-Furqān Islamic Heritage Foundation.

al-Masᶜūdī (1863) *Murūj al-dhahab wa-maᶜādin al-jawhar*. Vol. 2. Ed. and tr. by C. Barbier de Meynard and P. de Courteille as *Les Prairies d'Or*. Paris, l'Imprimerie Impériale.

al-Masᶜūdī (1864) *Murūj al-dhahab wa-maᶜādin al-jawhar*. Vol. 3. Ed. and tr. by C. Barbier de Meynard and P. de Courteille as *Les Prairies d'Or*. Paris, l'Imprimerie Impériale.

Michael the Syrian (1905) *Chronicle*. Vol. 3. Ed. and tr. by J.-B. Chabot as *Chronique de Michel le Syrien. Patriarche Jacobite d'Antioche*. Paris, Leroux.

al-Muqaddasī (1903) *Kitāb aḥsan al-taqālīm fī muᶜarifa al-aqlīm*. Ed. by M. J. de Goeije as *Descriptio Imperii Moslemici*. Leiden, Brill.

al-Nuwayrī (1923) *Nihāyat al-arab fī funūn al-ādab*. Vol. 3. Ed. by A. al-Zayn *et al.* Cairo, Maṭbaᶜat Dār al-Kutub.

Pingree, D. (1968) *The Thousands of Abū Maᶜshar. Studies of the Warburg Institute* 30. London, the Warburg Institute.

al-Qalqashandī (1914) *Ṣubḥ al-aᶜshā*. Vol. 5. Ed. by M. Q. Baqlī. Cairo, al-Maṭbaᶜa al-Amīriyya.

Sezgin, U. (1993) 'Al-Masᶜūdī, Ibrāhīm b. Waṣīfšāh und das Kitāb al-ᶜağā'ib. Aigyptiaka in arabischen Texten des 10. Jahrhunderts.' *Zeitschrift für Geschichte der arabisch-islamischen Wissenschaften* 8, 1–70.

Silvestre de Sacy, A.-I. (1905) 'Observations sur l'origine du nom donné par les Grecs et les Arabes aux Pyramides d'Ægypte, et sur quelques autres objets relatifs aux antiquités ægyptiennes'. *Bibliothèque des Arabisants* 1, 223–264.

al-Suyūṭī (1967) *Ḥusn al-muḥāḍara fī ta'rīkh Miṣr wa-'l-Qāhira*. Vol. 1. Ed. by M. Abū 'l-Fadl Ibrāhīm. Cairo, ᶜĪsā al-Bābī al-Ḥalabī.

Thevet, A. (1985) *Cosmographie du Levant*. Ed. by F. Lestringant. Geneva, Librairie Droz.

Van Bladel, K. (2009) *The Arabic Hermes*. Oxford, Oxford University Press.

Van Reeth, J. M. F. (1994) 'Caliph al-Ma'mūn and the Treasure of the Pyramids'. *Orientalia Loveniensa Periodica* 25, 221–236.

Wiet, G. (1953) *L'Égypte de Murtadi, Fils du Gaphiphe. Introduction, Traduction et Notes*. Bibliothèque de l'école nationale des langues orientales vivantes 14. Paris, Librairie Paul Geuthner.

Yāqūt (1984) *Muᶜjam al-buldān*. Vol. 5. Beirut, Dār al-Ṣādir.

8

The applicability of modern forensic anthropological sex determination techniques to ancient Egyptian skeletal remains

Emily J. Marlow

Introduction

Much of what is known about ancient Egyptian civilisation is derived from the study of human remains. When considered in the context of other important sources of information, the human skeleton can provide a unique insight into the biological and cultural characteristics of a population, the former encompassing palaeodemographic parameters (sex, age at death, fertility, migration), disease and diet, the latter pertaining to ancient mortuary practices and their presumed relationship with social organisation (Milner *et al.* 2000, 472). Patterns in skeletal characteristics over time may additionally be mapped and correlated with changes in environmental settings and socioeconomic conditions (Milner *et al.* 2000, 471), allowing an understanding of past human behaviour and the evolution of modern civilisation. While technological advances have expanded the scope of skeletal analysis, the study of both palaeodemography and past cultural processes and practices would be severely limited were it not possible to estimate the sex and age at death of a skeleton with a reasonable degree of accuracy and reliability (Milner *et al.* 2000, 472).

Previous studies examining pathological changes in skeletons from ancient Egyptian cemetery sites highlight the importance of these parameters particularly well. In their study evaluating the presence of osteoporosis among 74 individuals from two social classes from Old Kingdom Giza, Zaki and colleagues (2009, 78) found that the disease occurs at an earlier age and more frequently in females than males. They further found that osteoporosis was more common among male workers compared with male high officials, and in female high officials compared with female workers (Zaki *et al.* 2009, 78). Similarly, Buzon and Bombak (2010, 378) found a significantly higher incidence of ante-mortem tooth loss, tooth decay and wear in males than females from Tombos, a cemetery in Nubia used during the Egyptian colonial occupation (Buzon and Bombak 2010, 371). The authors suggested that these sex-associated differences may have been due to a division of labour that precipitated different diets and unequal access to resources (Buzon and Bombak 2010, 382).

The estimation of sex from skeletal remains

Sex is one of the most biologically basic and important pieces of information about an individual and is usually the first parameter to be assessed whenever human skeletal remains are discovered in forensic or archaeological contexts. Sex may be estimated from skeletal remains by morphological and metric methods, both of which have advantages and disadvantages. Often, the methods available for use will be determined by the state of preservation of the human remains. For well preserved skeletons, morphological examination of the bony pelvis (*ossa coxae* or 'hip-bones' and sacrum) is widely considered to be the most accurate sexing technique, since the form of these bones is directly related to biological function with the adult female bony pelvis exhibiting adaptations for childbirth. In instances where recovered skeletal remains are incomplete or damaged, metric estimations of sex are usually preferred, particularly in forensic investigations, because they are easy to apply, result in fewer indeterminate cases and more readily lend themselves to statistical testing and data manipulation. Levels of accuracy and precision are well documented throughout the literature, and continuous testing and re-evaluation of the methods allows estimates of sex to be made with considerable confidence, in some instances exceeding 90% accuracy (Robling and Ubelaker 1997, 1067).

Metric analysis does, however, have limitations. For example, long bone methods often require measurement of the intact length, as well as additional dimensions, which is often impossible if the bone is broken or parts are missing. In addition, the use of metric techniques is restricted by population specificity. It is well known that human body sizes and proportions vary systematically between populations, partly as a result of climatic adaptation and nutritional effects on growth (Ruff 2002, 211). Therefore, the temptation to diagnose sex based on size differences is prone to significant error since males and females overlap in size and males of one population may actually be smaller than females of another population. Metric methods for determining sex are particularly prone to error because they are based on absolute differences in measured skeletal dimensions and the sectioning points used to separate the sexes are only reliably applied to the population used to create the technique (Rogers 2005, 493).

Metric methods of sex estimation: the role of modern reference collections

The creation of numerous metric sex estimation methods was largely made possible by the establishment of skeletal reference collections consisting of individuals of known sex and age at death. The Terry Collection, for example, amassed by Dr R. J. Terry in the 1920s, consists of skeletons collected from cadavers used in the anatomy classes of medical schools. Individuals were generally White or Black Americans who were born and died during the 19th or 20th centuries. Thus, while the Terry Collection represents an excellent resource for physical and forensic anthropologists to develop and test metric methods of sex determination, it is only really a model for this one modern American sample and cannot realistically be expected to serve as a valid analogue for past human populations. Furthermore, the findings of a recent study suggest that individuals who donate or will their bodies to anatomical collections before their death generally have a higher education level and come from a higher socioeconomic background than individuals who were donated by family members or the legal authorities after their death (Komar and Grivas 2008, 225). Certain comparisons may therefore not represent the same socioeconomic group, suggesting that the Terry Collection may not even be a valid reference sample for near contemporaneous population groups.

Previous research by the author and others has demonstrated that methods used to determine sex in different skeletal samples invariably result in lower accuracy rates than were reported in the original investigation (Marlow and Pastor 2011, 165). Therefore, to obtain the most reliable estimates of sex, the population being investigated should be as similar as possible in proportions to the population used to create the method. Better still, sexing techniques should be devised that are specific to a particular population. This is especially important for unique populations such as the ancient Egyptians, who have been shown in previous research to have possessed more gracile body plans than either American Blacks or Whites (Raxter 2007, 11). The primary aim of this research is to determine the accuracy of modern metric sex determination techniques, commonly developed for use in forensic anthropology, when applied to ancient Egyptian skeletal remains. Other aims are to create population-specific sexing formulae using discriminant function analysis and to investigate temporal and geographic differences in patterns of sexual dimorphism.

Materials and methods

Materials

The sample consists of adult skeletons from the Peabody Museum of Archaeology and Ethnology, Harvard University, Boston MA, US. The ancient Egyptian series curated at the Peabody Museum consists of over 500 skeletons and was primarily amassed by George Reisner during his archaeological expeditions to the country in the early part of the 20th century. Table 8.1 shows the number of skeletons related to a particular period and cemetery site that make up

Region	Period	No. of skeletons
Siwa	400–100 BC	103
Giza	Old Kingdom	61
Keneh	Predynastic	174
Mesaeed	Predynastic	135
Mesaeed	-	18
Sheikh Farag	Middle Kingdom	20
Thebes	21st dynasty	4
Lisht	12th dynasty, *c.* 2000–1950 BC	1
Meir	Late 12th dynasty, 1900–1800 BC	2
Thebes	20th dynasty, *c.* 1160 BC	1
Thebes	18–20th dynasty	1
Meroe	AD 75	3
Nuri	*C.* 362 BC	1
Thebes	-	2
Total		526

Table 8.1: The Egyptian series from the Peabody Museum collection (Source: Personal communication, 2011).

the entire Peabody collection. For this study, the most complete skeletons from Keneh, Giza, Sheikh Farag and Thebes were examined.

Morphological sex estimation

Ideally, standards for sex estimation should be developed using samples of documented sex. However, ancient Egyptian skeletal remains of this type are currently unavailable for study; therefore, the sample was restricted to individuals for which sufficient pelvic and/or cranial material was available to permit the morphological determination of sex. Additional inclusion criteria were:

1. Complete fusion of the rounded ends or 'epiphyses' of long bones to the bone shaft (diaphysis) and obliteration of the growth plate, indicating adult individuals.
2. An unambiguous assessment of sex based on pelvic and/or cranial morphology.
3. No evidence of pathological changes that could alter the proportions of the skeleton.

The *ossa coxae*, more commonly known as 'hip-bones', have been shown to be highly reliable for the determination of sex in modern populations (Phenice 1969, 297; Sutherland and Suchey 1991, 501; Ubelaker and Volk 2002, 19). The skull is also known to possess a high concentration of sexually dimorphic indicators. Using these bones, sex was estimated by two methods:

1. Assessment of the Phenice characteristics of the pubic bone (ventral arc, subpubic concavity and medial aspect of the ischiopubic ramus, shown in Fig. 8.1).
2. Morphological assessment of the skull and bony pelvis. Individual sex indicators were scored after their level of masculinity and femininity in accordance with Buikstra and Ubelaker (1994), where:

   0 = Indeterminate (insufficient data)
   1 = Female
   2 = Probable female
   3 = Ambiguous sex
   4 = Probable male
   5 = Male.

This methodology has been widely used in previous studies and has allowed the creation of metric sex estimation standards for numerous archaeological populations, including prehistoric Scottish (MacLaughlin and Bruce 1985), prehistoric Central Californian (Dittrick and Suchey 1986), New Zealand Polynesian (Murphy 2005), medieval Croatian (Šlaus and Tomičić 2005), Pre-dynastic/Old Kingdom Egyptian (Raxter 2007), and ancient (Jomon period) Japanese (Özer and Katayama 2008).

Metric sex estimation

In forensic contexts, methods of sex estimation are generally considered useful if they are able to produce accuracy rates of at least 80% (Rogers 1999), and estimate the sex of males and females with equal accuracy. The skeletal dimensions measured in this study are therefore based on popularly-used techniques that have demonstrated accuracy rates in excess of this cut-off value when tested on modern populations. Only techniques that were created using a skeletal sample of documented sex were chosen.

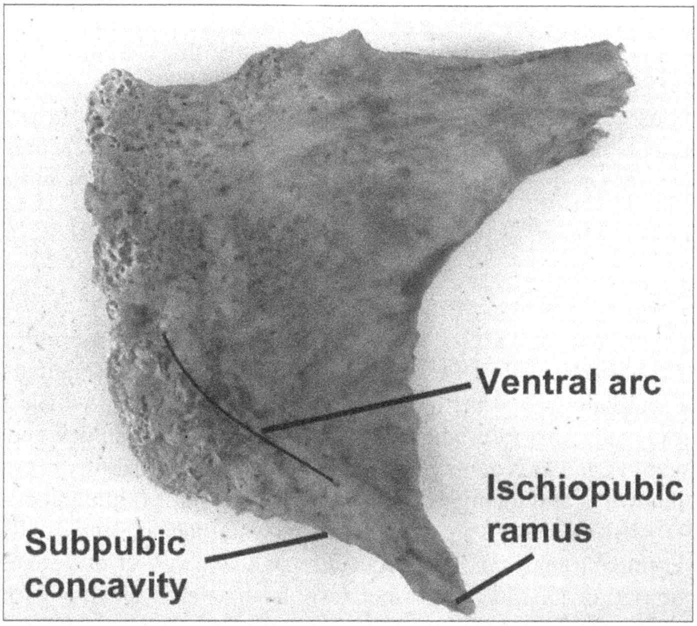

Figure 8.1: The Phenice characters of the pubic bone. The presence of a ventral arc, subpubic concavity and a narrow/sharp ischiopubic ramus indicate a female individual (as shown). The absence of a ventral arc, subpubic convexity and a wide/dull ischiopubic ramus indicate a male individual. Specimen ID: 14-2-50/59001.0. Image © 2013 President and Fellows of Harvard College.

A total of 63 skeletal dimensions (or as many of these that were recordable) were measured for each skeleton. Measurements were taken to the nearest 0.01, 0.1 or 1.0 mm (depending on the equipment used) in accordance with the original studies in which the skeletal dimensions and anatomical landmarks were first described. Measurements were taken using a digital sliding caliper, spreading caliper (for cranial measurements), tape measure, or standard osteometric board (for long bones). For all bilateral elements, the left side was recorded with substitution of the right side in instances where the left side was not recordable.

A total of 12 metric sex estimation methods, formulated using modern population samples, and two methods formulated using ancient Egyptian samples, were selected to be tested. These techniques were developed for use on the: cranium (Giles and Elliot 1963), second cervical vertebra (C2; Wescott 2000), femoral head (Krogman and İşcan 1986), femoral neck (Seidemann *et al.* 1998), femoral shaft (Black 1978), tibia (İşcan and Miller-Shaivitz 1984), humeral head (Spradley and Jantz 2011), humerus, radius and ulna (Holman and Bennet 1991), radial head (Berrizbeitia 1989), metacarpal 1 (Scheuer and Elkington 1993), metatarsal 1 (Robling and Ubelaker 1997), multiple bones including the *ossa coxae* and clavicle (Stewart 1979), scapula (Dabbs 2010), and selected long bones (Raxter 2007).

The original discriminant functions developed for each of these different skeletal elements or combinations of elements were blind-tested using the collected measurements. Where possible, the functions developed for populations of unknown ancestry (i.e. consisting of pooled Black and White individuals) were used. If pooled functions were not available, the equations for Blacks and Whites were tested separately; however, these were not counted as separate techniques. Where multiple functions were available for one technique, the accuracy of each function was calculated separately, as well as a mean accuracy for the technique as a whole. A comparison of the results of sex estimation using morphological *versus* metric methods was only made after all measurements had been collected and all discriminant function scores calculated. The metric sex assessment was deemed to be correct if it was in agreement with the morphological sex assessment.

Statistical analysis

Discriminant function analysis, a procedure that maximises between-group differences, was used to evaluate the effectiveness of various skeletal dimensions at estimating sex. The primary goals of this procedure are to find the dimension or dimensions along which groups differ and to find classification functions to predict group membership (Tabachnick and Fidell 1989). A linear combination of variables is generated that maximises the probability of correctly assigning individuals of unknown group identity to pre-determined groups (Quinn and Keough 2002).

The SPSS 19.0 (IBM, Somers NY) statistical software package for Windows was used to run stepwise discriminant analysis. This procedure selects a subset of variables based on the squared partial correlation and the significance level from an analysis of covariance that has the greatest amount of discriminating ability (Wescott 2000). In other words, the statistical criteria alone determine the order of entry of the variables (Kinnear and Gray 2009). This method is generally used when the researcher requires a reduced set of predictor variables but has no preference among them. Entry of predictors is determined by user-specified statistical criteria, for example Wilks' Lambda, or the values of minimum partial F to Enter and maximum partial F to Remove (Tabachnick and Fidell 1989).

To evaluate the discriminating ability of the variables selected, and reduce bias, a cross-validation procedure was employed. Older studies tended to examine the classification accuracy using the hit rate ratio. However, when the same data that were used to create the discriminant function are also used to generate the hit rate ratio, the outcome will be biased in favour of the function. The cross-validation procedure classifies each individual case based on discriminant analyses run on all other cases, thus the case being classified does not influence the discriminant analysis used to classify it. In this way, a more realistic estimate is gained of the ability of predictors to separate groups and to correctly classify individuals of unknown group identity (Tabachnick and Fidell 1989). The data were analysed both as a combined sample, and according to historical period (Predynastic period *versus* Old Kingdom).

Age at death estimation

For completeness and to determine the demographic profile of the sample, age at death of adult skeletons from the Peabody Museum was estimated using five different methods:

1. Pubic symphysis (Brooks and Suchey 1990)
2. Auricular surface (Buckberry and Chamberlain 2002)
3. Sternal rib end (İşcan *et al.* 1984; İşcan *et al.* 1985)
4. Cranial sutures (Meindl and Lovejoy 1985)
5. Tooth wear (Lovejoy 1985).

An overall age range was derived by considering the results of all five methods. In instances of low levels of agreement between the methods, the greatest weight was given to the pubic symphysis and auricular surface methods since previous studies have found these methods to be the most accurate, albeit using modern population samples.

Results

A total of 105 adult skeletons dating to Predynastic-period Keneh (n=43), Old Kingdom-period Giza (n=47), Middle Kingdom-period Sheikh Farag (n=13) and New Kingdom-period Thebes (n=2) were examined. The sample consisted of 59 male and 46 female specimens, ranging in age from 18 to 55+ years (modal age group, 35–44 years).

Accuracy of discriminant function equations

When tested on ancient Egyptian skeletal remains, only two of the 12 modern metric sex estimation methods (the cranial method developed by Giles and Elliot (1963) and the multiple bones method developed by Stewart (1979)) were able to determine sex with acceptable levels of accuracy, both overall and in males and females separately. None of the remaining 10 methods reached the 80% accuracy cut-off level overall. Some methods produced exceptionally low accuracy rates, overall and for males, as well as high proportions of indeterminate cases – this is due mainly to misclassification of males, as the accuracy rates for females appear consistently high. The accuracy rates of the 12 modern metric sex estimation methods are shown in Table 8.2. As expected, the methods developed by Raxter (2007) and Dabbs (2010) specifically for ancient Egyptian populations produced relatively high levels of accuracy for both males and females when tested on this dissimilar Egyptian sample (Table 8.2).

Statistical analysis of data

Exploration of the data did not reveal any extreme scores or outliers. An independent samples two-tailed t-test demonstrated that the differences between male and female means for all 63 measurements, excluding basion-prosthion length (BP) and maximum width (MW) of the cranium, length of the vertebral foramen (LVF) of C2 and pubic length (PL), were statistically significant ($P \leq 0.05$).

Using the measurements from individual bones and different combinations of bones, a series of discriminant functions were developed that ranged in accuracy from 80.0% using measurements of C2, to 96.7% using measurements from the cranium. The discriminant functions demonstrating the greatest classification accuracy in the present ancient Egyptian sample are shown in Table 8.3.

Discriminant scores are obtained by multiplying each variable with its unstandardised coefficient, summing them and subtracting the constant. The result is then compared to a sectioning point to determine sex. For example, a discriminant equation to determine sex using measurements of the tibia would take the form: $[(MSC \times 0.129) + (PEB \times 0.159)] - 19.976$. A score greater than -0.0835 would indicate a male individual, while a score less than -0.0835 would indicate a female individual.

Bone	Method	Original population	Published accuracy, %	Accuracy in ancient Egyptian sample, %		
				Overall	**Male**	**Female**
Metric sex estimation techniques developed using modern populations						
Cranium	Giles and Elliot 1963	20th C, White and Black, American	84.1*	93.8	85.7	100
Multiple Function 1 Function 2	Stewart 1979	NR	 94.4 94.3	 91.8 88.5	 93.9 93.9	 89.3 82.1
C2	Wescott 2000	20th C, White and Black, American	82.6*	56.1	17.2	96.4
Femoral head diam.	Krogman and İşcan 1986	White and Black, American	90.0	70.2	40.0	100
Femoral neck diameter	Seidemann *et al* 1998	19th and 20th C, White and Black, American	90.0	78.4	67.9	90.9
Femoral shaft circumference	Black 1978	NR	85.0	79.1	90.0[a]	65.9[b]
Tibia (uni.) White Black Tibia (multi.) White Black	İşcan and Miller-Shaivitz 1984	20th C, White and Black, American	 84.4* 89.0*	 67.7 59.1 66.7 60.3	 45.1 27.5 44.2[c] 32.6[d]	 95.2 97.6 94.3 94.3
Humeral head diam. White Black	Spradley and Jantz 2011	20th C, White and Black, American	 83.0 86.0	 55.2 66.7	 13.6 36.4	 97.7 97.7
Humerus, radius and ulna	Holman and Bennett 1991	20th C, White and Black, American	82.6*	56.3	18.4[e]	100
Radial head diam. Max. Min.	Berrizbeitia 1989	20th C, White and Black, American	 83.0 82.0	 50.0 51.1	 15.4[f] 12.0[g]	 95.0[h] 100
MC1	Scheuer and Elkington 1993	White, British	94.0	79.7	80.0	79.3
MT1	Robling and Ubelaker 1997	20th C, White and Black, American	91.5	52.7	16.1	100
Metric sex estimation techniques developed using ancient Egyptian populations						
Scapula	Dabbs 2010	New Kingdom, Egyptian	88.0	89.0	95.1	81.3
Long bones FHD CNF HHD	Raxter 2007	Primarily predynastic-period and Old Kingdom, Egyptian	 89.0 89.0 89.0	 89.4 84.6 86.2	 90.0 93.9 81.8	 88.6 73.8[i] 90.7[j]

C2 = second cervical vertebra; diam. = diameter; uni. = univariate; multi. = multivariate equations; max. = maximum; min. = minimum; MC1 = metacarpal 1; MT1 = metatarsal 1; FHD = femoral head diameter; CNF = circumference at nutrient foramen of tibia; HHD = humeral head diameter; NR = not reported.

*Average of multiple functions.

[a]Using this equation, 4.0% of male skeletons were determined to be of indeterminate sex; [b]7.3% of female skeletons were determined to be of indeterminate sex; [c]2.3% of male skeletons were determined to be of indeterminate sex; [d]14.0% of male skeletons were determined to be of indeterminate sex; [e]2.6% of male skeletons were determined to be of indeterminate sex; [f]80.8% of male skeletons were determined to be of indeterminate sex; [g]76.0% of male skeletons were determined to be of indeterminate sex; [h]5% of female skeletons were determined to be of indeterminate sex; [i]2.4% of female skeletons were determined to be of indeterminate sex; [j]2.3% of female skeletons were determined to be of indeterminate sex.

Table 8.2: Accuracy rates of selected modern metric sex determination methods when tested on ancient Egyptian skeletal remains.

Bone	Variables	Unstandardised coefficients	Sectioning point*	Cross-validated accuracy rate, %		
				Overall	Male	Female
Cranium	BB DB PN Constant	0.268 0.223 0.088 -68.114	0.350	96.7	91.7	100
Scapula	XHS HAX Constant	0.085 0.525 -31.162	0.2285	95.0	87.5	100
Humerus	HHD XHL EWH Constant	0.282 0.059 0.183 -39.527	0.0815	94.0	90.0	97.1
Tibia	MSC PEB Constant	0.129 0.159 -19.976	-0.0835	91.5	90.3	92.9

*A score greater than the sectioning point indicates a male individual, a score lower than the sectioning point indicates a female. BB = basion-bregma height; DB = maximum bi-zygomatic diameter; PN = prosthion-nasion height; XHS = maximum length of scapula; HAX = height of glenoid fossa; HHD = humeral head diameter; XHL = maximum length of humerus; EWH = epicondylar width of humerus; MSC = minimum shaft circumference; PEB = proximal epiphyseal breadth.

Table 8.3: Accuracy rates of selected population-specific equations, created using discriminant function analysis.

Subanalysis of different temporal and geographic samples

A separate analysis of the samples from Keneh (Predynastic period, Upper Egypt; n=43) and Giza (Old Kingdom period, Lower Egypt; n=47) revealed differences in patterns of sexual dimorphism. Statistically significant differences in the Keneh and Giza samples' means were observed for the maximum width of cranium (MW), basion-bregma height of cranium (BB), transverse breadth of tibia (TB), radius semi-bistyloid (wrist) breadth (RSBB) and midshaft diameter of the first metatarsal (MSD; $P \leq 0.039$ for all comparisons). For each of these dimensions, the mean value for the Giza sample was greater than its Keneh counterpart, suggesting that individuals from Old Kingdom-period Giza were larger and more robust than those from Predynastic-period Keneh.

Differences were also observed between the two samples in terms of the skeletal dimensions with the greatest ability to discriminate between the sexes. For the sample from Keneh, the skeletal dimensions best able to separate males from females were derived from the first metacarpal and cranium/C2 combined; for the Giza sample, the skeletal dimensions with the greatest discriminating power were derived from the lower limb (femur and tibia). The formulae exhibiting the greatest classification accuracy in the Keneh and Giza samples are shown in Table 8.4.

Population	Bone	Variables	Unstandardised coefficients	Sectioning point*	Cross-validated accuracy rate, %		
					Overall	Male	Female
Keneh	Cranium + C2	DB PN PB BN XSL Constant	9.628 2.359 -1.243 0.997 0.753 -1303.399	34.3675	100	100	100
	MC1	IAL HML Constant	0.416 0.677 -27.088	0.4945	100	100	100
Giza	Femur	FHD Constant	0.532 -23.221	-0.738	92.3	95.8	86.7
	Tibia	APD Constant	0.410 -13.448	-0.441	91.9	91.3	92.9

C2 = second cervical vertebra; MC1 = metacarpal 1; DB = maximum bi-zygomatic diameter; PN = prosthion-nasion height; PB = external breadth of palate; BN = basion-nasion length; XSL = maximum sagittal length of C2; IAL = interarticular length of MC1; HML = medio-lateral width of head of MC1; FHD = femoral head diameter; APD = antero-posterior diameter of tibia.

Table 8.4: Unstandardised discriminant function coefficients for determining the sex of skeletons from Predynastic-period Keneh and Old Kingdom-period Giza.

Discussion

Previous research has demonstrated that metric sex estimation techniques applied to populations other than that upon which the technique was formulated have less discriminatory power than when tested on the original population. Such techniques are less able to separate the sexes because they are based on skeletal dimensions and measurements that are highly specific to the population used to develop the method. For modern humans, differences in body size and shape are most likely to result from an interaction between long-term genetic factors including climatic adaptation, disease and diet (Ruff 2002, 227). Research has shown that among modern human populations, those from colder climates have relatively shorter limbs and wider bodies than those from warmer environments. This variation is generally viewed as an adaptive strategy to reduce body surface area in colder climates and increase it in warmer ones (Ruff 2002, 220).

The problem of body size variability among different populations and its effect on the accuracy of metric sex determination methods is clearly illustrated by the results arising from this study. Despite reporting accuracy rates in excess of 80% (Berrizbeitia 1989, 1209) or even 90% (Robling and Ubelaker 1997, 1067), the methods involving measurement of the radial head or first metatarsal respectively, were only able to classify sex with around 50% accuracy when tested on ancient Egyptian skeletal remains. The methods were particularly poor at correctly estimating the sex of male skeletons. Using measurements of the maximum and minimum radial head diameter, male skeletons were correctly classified in 15.4% and 12.0% of cases, respectively. A further problem with this method is the non-overlapping sectioning points. For example, while minimum diameter measurements of greater than or equal to 23 mm indicate a male and less than or equal to 20 mm indicate a female (Berrizbeitia 1989, 1210), measurements that fall in the range 20.01 to 22.99 mm cannot be assigned to either group. In the present study, 76% of males were assessed as being of indeterminate sex using the minimum radial head diameter method. This is unfortunate, as the strength of metric sex estimation techniques lies in their ability to produce fewer indeterminate cases compared with morphological techniques. In comparison, the vast majority of metric techniques tested were able to correctly classify females with acceptable or high levels of accuracy; four of the techniques were able to accurately determine the sex of all of the females in the sample.

These findings suggest that the body size and/or proportions of ancient Egyptians were significantly different to those of the modern American population used to create the majority of the metric sex determination techniques tested in this study, and support the notion that ancient Egyptians were smaller and more gracile than American Blacks and Whites. The inability of the techniques tested to correctly classify males, in addition to the high level of accuracy in classifying females, suggests that the sectioning points of the methods are too high for the present population sample. Since to be classified as male a measurement must usually exceed the sectioning point, and to be classified as female it must be below the sectioning point, the pattern of observed results seems hardly surprising.

For these reasons, several other researchers have explored the possibility of producing population specific formulae and metric sex estimation standards are now available for numerous different archaeological populations (MacLaughlin and Bruce 1985; Dittrick and Suchey 1986; Murphy 2005; Šlaus and Tomičić 2005). To date, two independent researchers have developed metric sex estimation equations that are specific to the ancient Egyptians. Dabbs (2010, 413) used a sample of 27 New Kingdom skeletons from the site of Tell El-Amarna to create discriminant functions based on five measurements of the scapula. Although the maximum reported classification accuracy is relatively high (88%), previous experience of the author suggests that the scapula is a fragile bone that often does not survive post-depositional processes intact. Thus, while a useful contribution to the area of research, the utility of this technique in practice may be fairly limited. Furthermore, the size of the sample used in the study was small and therefore cannot account for a wide range of natural human variation.

Raxter (2007) used a wider range of skeletal elements and a larger sample size to produce both univariate and multivariate discriminant functions. The following dimensions were examined for 71 adult ancient Egyptian skeletons dating predominantly to the Predynastic period and Old Kingdom: maximum vertical diameter of the femoral head, maximum femoral length, tibial circumference at the nutrient foramen, maximum tibial length, maximum vertical diameter of the humeral head, and maximum humeral length (Raxter 2007, 10). These dimensions are some of the most commonly used for sex estimation. Therefore, the purpose of Raxter's research was to produce new sectioning points for existing sex estimation techniques (that are specific to the ancient Egyptians) rather than to explore the possibility of sexual dimorphism in other skeletal elements. An accuracy rate of 89% was reported using the sectioning points for single variables (Raxter 2007, 10) and it was noted that sexual dimorphism of long bone widths exceeds that of lengths. The present research extends the findings of these previous studies by presenting a greater range of sex indicators using bones or dimensions that are not commonly used for sex estimation.

A total of four discriminant equations of high accuracy are presented for use by other researchers involved in studies that require analysis of ancient Egyptian skeletal remains. Importantly, the formulae given in Table 8.3 are able to classify the sex of males and females with much more equal accuracy than those created using modern populations and are highly unlikely to result in indeterminate sex assessments. Equations are also presented for use in specific sub-populations from ancient Egypt, namely Predynastic-period Keneh and Old Kingdom-period Giza. The results of this research show that differences in patterns of sexual dimorphism were apparent in these distinct population groups, although it is not possible to determine if the differences are due to time period or geographic location. The increased robustness and greatest degree of sexual dimorphism occurring in the femur and tibia of individuals from Giza could be due to a division of labour that would have arisen as a result of the intensive construction projects (building of the pyramids) that occurred during the Old Kingdom. Further work will focus on an exploration of changes in patterns of sexual dimorphism over time by comparing metric data collected from individuals buried at Giza during the Old Kingdom and Late Period.

Conclusions

With few exceptions, metric sex estimation techniques developed for use in modern populations are highly inaccurate when applied to ancient Egyptian skeletal remains, particularly male individuals, and should not be included as part of the analysis of skeletons from this historical period. The present research highlights the issues regarding population specificity and differences in body proportions that have developed as a result of temporal and geographic separation. Differences in patterns of sexual dimorphism were demonstrated between both modern and archaic populations, and between individuals from the same population group living in different time periods and locations within Egypt. The study further demonstrates the high levels of classification that can be achieved using metric sex determination formulae that have been specifically formulated for a particular population, and a number of equations using different skeletal elements are presented for use by other researchers. A test of these new equations in dissimilar Egyptian populations would be welcomed. Ultimately, it is hoped a complete set of standards may be developed that will facilitate a greater level of accuracy and precision in the analysis of human skeletal remains from ancient Egypt, and allow a greater degree of confidence to be placed in the conclusions arising from studies that require an accurate assessment of biological sex.

Acknowledgements

Thanks are extended to Michele Morgan and Olivia Herschensohn of the Peabody Museum of Archaeology and Ethnology, Harvard University, Boston for granting me access to the collection of ancient Egyptian skeletal remains, and for facilitating my research trip. Thanks are also extended to my supervisors Professor Rosalie David and Dr Ryan Metcalfe for their ongoing support, to Professor Andrew Chamberlain for his comments on the manuscript, and to the KNH Centre for Biomedical and Forensic Egyptology, Manchester University for the generous funding of my research trip to the US.

Bibliography

Berrizbeitia, E. L. (1989) Sex determination with the head of the radius. *Journal of Forensic Sciences* 34, 1206–1213.

Black, T. K. (1978) A new method for assessing the sex of fragmentary skeletal remains: femoral shaft circumference. *American Journal of Physical Anthropology* 48, 227–232.

Brooks, S. and Suchey, J. M. (1990) Skeletal age determination based on the *os pubis*: a comparison of the Ascadi-Nemeskeri and Suchey-Brooks methods. *Human Evolution* 5, 227–238.

Buckberry, J. L. and Chamberlain, A. T. (2002) Age estimation from the auricular surface of the ilium: a revised method. *American Journal of Physical Anthropology* 119, 231–239.

Buikstra, J. E. and Ubelaker, D. H. (1994) *Standards for Data Collection from Human Skeletal Remains.* Fayetteville NC, Arkansas Archaeological Survey Research Series No. 44.

Buzon, M. R. and Bombak, A. (2010) Dental disease in the Nile Valley during the New Kingdom. *International Journal of Osteoarchaeology* 20, 371–387.

Dabbs, G. (2010) Sex determination using the scapula in New Kingdom skeletons from Tell El-Amarna. *HOMO – Journal of Comparative Human Biology* 61, 413–420.

Dittrick, J. and Suchey, J. M. (1986) Sex determination of prehistoric Central Californian skeletal remains using discriminant analysis of the femur and humerus. *American Journal of Physical Anthropology* 70, 3–9.

Giles, E. and Elliot, O. (1963) Sex determination by discriminant function analysis of crania. *American Journal of Physical Anthropology* 21, 53–68.

Holman, D. J. and Bennett, K. A. (1991) Determination of sex from arm bone measurements. *American Journal of Physical Anthropology* 84, 421–426.

İşcan, M.Y. and Miller-Shaivitz, P. (1984) Discriminant function sexing of the tibia. *Journal of Forensic Sciences* 29(4), 1087–1093.

İşcan, M. Y., Loth, S. R. and Wright, R. K. (1984) Age estimation from the rib by phase analysis: white males. *Journal of Forensic Sciences* 29, 1094–1104.

İşcan, M. Y., Loth, S. R. and Wright, R. K. (1985) Age estimation from the rib by phase analysis: white females. *Journal of Forensic Sciences* 30, 853–863.

Kinnear, P. R. and Gray, C. D. (2009) Discriminant analysis and logistic regression. In *SPSS 16 Made Simple,* 525–563. Sussex, Psychology Press Ltd.

Komar, D. A. and Grivas, C. (2008) Manufactured populations: what do contemporary reference skeletal collections represent? A comparative study using the Maxwell Museum documented collection. *American Journal of Physical Anthropology* 137, 224–233.

Krogman, W. M. and İşcan, M. Y. (1986) *The Human Skeleton in Forensic Medicine 2nd ed.* Springfield IL, Charles Thomas.

Lovejoy, C. O. (1985) Dental wear in the Libben population: its functional pattern and role in the determination of adult skeletal age at death. *American Journal of Physical Anthropology* 68, 47–56.

MacLaughlin, S. M. and Bruce, M. F. (1985) A simple univariate technique for determining sex from fragmentary femora: its application to a Scottish short cist population. *American Journal of Physical Anthropology* 67, 413–417.

Marlow, E. and Pastor, R. F. (2011) Sex determination using the second cervical vertebra – a test of the method. *Journal of Forensic Sciences* 56, 165–169.

Meindl, R. S. and Lovejoy, C. O. (1985) Ectocranial suture closure: a revised method for the determination of skeletal age at death based on the lateral-anterior sutures. *American Journal of Physical Anthropology* 68, 57–66.

Milner, G. R., Wood, J. W. and Boldsen, J. L. (2000) Paleodemography. In M. A. Katzenberg and S. R. Saunders (eds) *Biological Anthropology of the Human Skeleton,* 467–497. New York, Wiley-Liss Inc.

Murphy, A. M. (2005) The femoral head: sex assessment of prehistoric New Zealand Polynesian skeletal remains. *Forensic Science International* 154, 210–213.

Özer, I. and Katayama, K. (2008) Sex determination using the femur in an ancient Japanese population. *Collegium Antropologicum* 32, 67–72.

Phenice, T. W. (1969) A newly developed visual method of sexing the os pubis. *American Journal of Physical Anthropology* 30, 297–302.

Quinn, G. P. and Keough, M. J. (2002) Discriminant function analysis. In *Experimental Design and Data Analysis for Biologists*, 435–442. Cambridge, Cambridge University Press.

Raxter, M. H. (2007) Metric sex estimation in an ancient Egyptian skeletal sample. *SAS Bulletin: Newsletter of the Society for Archaeological Sciences* 30(4), 9–12.

Robling, A. G. and Ubelaker, D. H. (1997) Sex estimation from the metatarsals. *Journal of Forensic Sciences* 42, 1062–1069.

Rogers, T. L. (1999) A visual method of determining the sex of skeletal remains using the distal humerus. *Journal of Forensic Sciences* 44(1), 57–60.

Rogers, T. L. (2005) Determining the sex of human remains through cranial morphology. *Journal of Forensic Sciences* 50, 493–500.

Ruff, C. (2002) Variation in human body size and shape. *Annual Review of Anthropology* 31, 211–232.

Scheuer, J. L. and Elkington, N. M. (1993) Sex determination from metacarpals and the first proximal phalanx. *Journal of Forensic Sciences* 38, 769–778.

Seidemann, R. M., Stojanowski C. M. and Doran, G. H. (1998) The use of the supero-inferior femoral neck diameter as a sex assessor. *American Journal of Physical Anthropology* 107, 305–313.

Šlaus, M. and Tomicić, Z. (2005) Discriminant function sexing of fragmentary and complete tibiae from Medieval Croatian sites. *Forensic Science International* 147, 147–152.

Spradley, M. K. and Jantz, R. L. (2011) Sex estimation in forensic anthropology: skull versus postcranial elements. *Journal of Forensic Sciences* 56(2), 289–296.

Stewart, T. D. (1979) *Essentials of Forensic Anthropology.* Springfield, Illinois: Charles C. Thomas.

Sutherland, L. D. and Suchey, J. M. (1991) Use of the ventral arc in pubic sex determination. *Journal of Forensic Sciences* 36, 501–511.

Tabachnick, B. G. and Fidell, L. S. (1989) Discriminant function analysis. In *Using Multivariate Statistics*, 505–596. USA, Harper & Row Publishers.

Ubelaker, D. H. and Volk, C. G. (2002) A test of the Phenice method for the estimation of sex. *Journal of Forensic Sciences* 47, 19–24.

Wescott, D. J. (2000) Sex variation in the second cervical vertebra. *Journal of Forensic Sciences* 45(2), 462–466.

Zaki, M. E., Hussien, F. H. and Abd El-Shafy El Banna, R. (2009) Osteoporosis among ancient Egyptians. *International Journal of Osteoarchaeology* 19, 78–89.

9

Children of Sorrow: Infants and Juveniles in Ancient Egyptian Funeral Processions during the New Kingdom

Emily Millward

Introduction

As part of a wider research project into the gestures and attitudes of mourning in ancient Egypt it has been found that this little studied area has within it a topic that is also worth further study: children, of various ages, as mourners within funeral processions. The aim of this paper is to provide a preliminary insight into the placement, stance, and actions of children in funeral processions during the New Kingdom. Within the scope of this study infants are children who are no older than one year in age whilst juveniles will be split into two groups, younger and older. Both younger and older juveniles are shown walking as part of the funeral entourage, but whilst the younger are depicted unclothed, older juveniles, probably over the age of puberty, are generally depicted in similar garments to their adult counterparts (Rosalind and Janssen 1990, 26–28). Firstly, this paper will present the evidence of children in funeral processions and the issues pertaining to interpreting these sources. The discussion will then focus on the place of infants and juveniles in the funeral processions followed by an analysis of the psychology of being a child mourner in ancient Egypt.

The main body of evidence for this preliminary research will be the wall scenes in a selection of tombs on the West Bank at Thebes. Furthermore, a tomb relief from Abydos and a coffin from Twenty-Second Dynasty Thebes will also support the interpretations discussed here. Issues concerning the reliability of tomb scenes and coffin decoration reflecting the reality of these gestures, as well as concerns over their symbolic and decorative aspects, should be acknowledged. It is implausible that the artists painting these scenes reserved these gestures of grief for purely decorative purposes. Ancient Egyptian artists probably saw funeral processions in reality and therefore would have seen the mourners accompanying the sarcophagus to the tomb. Although these scenes may not represent the exact funeral procession of the owner of a tomb the gestures of mourning displayed within these images are nonetheless reflections of reality. These scenes of funeral processions do contain an amount of artistic license, with the artist surely needing to fill a particular parameter of space on a tomb wall, coffin or relief. Nevertheless, the episodes of the funeral procession were clearly set-out (Hays 2010) and were therefore, familiar to the ancient Egyptian people. Thus it would be a generalization of the evidence to conclude that these images reflected a purely artistic perspective. The symbolic aspects of the scenes should be seen as reflecting the 'ideal' image of an ancient Egyptian funeral procession. Although as representations of the 'ideal' funeral procession, the episodes displayed would have taken place in reality, with the need for the ancient Egyptians to inter their dead in a particular way with certain gestures that are recorded in the scenes.

Mourning or Lamentation?

To set out firmly the context for this study, it should be noted that lamentation is not the same process as mourning within ancient Egypt, a misconception that often results in the two terms being used synonymously. For example, Wickett (2010, 145) described wall scenes in tombs of the Theban elite as depicting 'lamenters engaged in acts of lamenting' whilst she also captions a scene of the funeral from the 18th Dynasty tomb of Ramose (TT55) as displaying 'mourners'. This scene from the tomb of Ramose actually displays a large group of female mourners who can be classed as such because they each adopt one or more of the non-verbal gestures indicating grief. The distinction therefore is that mourning consisted of the non-verbal gestures adopted by ancient Egyptians to express their sorrow, whilst lamentation can be associated with verbal expressions of sorrow. The ancient Egyptian '*im*', which is used to refer to lamentation, is translated as 'whine' or 'wailing moan' (Wörterbuch, 4 Aufl, Bd 1, 77) and the phonetic signs are followed by the determinative of a seated man with one hand to his mouth 𓀁; the use of the determinative in this case indicating a verbal action rather than the actual gesture of putting the hand to the mouth. This word relates to the guttural cries and lengthy dirges carried out by individuals. These wailing cries are evident from the open mouths of some figures in images of the funeral procession from the tombs on the West Bank (Millward 2011, 144). The ancient Egyptian *iꜣkb* is translated as 'mourning', using the determinative of a lock of hair 𓁾 (Faulkner 1962, 9), and *iꜣkyb.t,* translated as 'mourning women', uses the determinative of a female figure with free flowing hair. Mourners in ancient Egypt, particularly females, are known to have unbound and perhaps pulled at their hair in a non-verbal gesture of grief, represented by the dishevelled appearance of two female mourners in the tomb of Neferhotep (TT49) (Davies 1973, pl. IV and pl. V). The contrasting determinatives used for these two words, a seated figure with hand to mouth *versus* a lock of hair, reflect the perspective of the ancient Egyptian people that the words had distinct meanings.

Unlike mourning, lamentation in ancient Egypt also occurred outside the context of the funeral procession and related rituals. A series of lamentation texts have been discovered (Bleeker 1958, 1–170; Faulkner 1936, 121–140; Lichtheim 1980, 116–121; Smith 2009) and one of the best examples is 'The Lamentations of Isis and Nephthys', a text which was recited during the ritual of the Osirian mysteries (Lichtheim 1980, 116). Lamentation, as well as being adopted as an expression of grief during funerals (e.g. the loud wailing cries), had a distinct formulaic nature when used in festival dramatisations. Within the context of the funeral procession it is possible that an individual could be both mourning (i.e. adopting gestures of grief) and lamenting (i.e. letting out wailing cries). However, the clear distinction between these two forms of communicating grief should be recognised by researchers in this area, an aspect that is certainly acknowledged within this study.

The presence of mourners (i.e. those adopting non-verbal gestures of grief) is particularly prevalent in the body of evidence used in this study. Within scenes of funerary processions from elite Theban tombs both male and female mourners are depicted adopting the typical gestures of grief (Millward 2011) such as, raising their arms upwards or female mourners being shown exposing their breasts. An example of this can be seen in the funeral procession from the tomb of Roy (TT255) (Fig. 9.1).

Infants within the Funeral Procession

The analysis of infants with New Kingdom funeral procession is difficult because there is little evidence. Only one scene, from the tomb of Neferhotep (TT49), displays infants as part of the funeral entourage (Davies 1973, pl. XXIII). In the scene four infants are shown being carried in slings. Three of these infants are carried by adult female mourners, who adopt a typical gesture in raising their hands to their faces, and the other is in a sling on the back of an older juvenile girl, who is adopting the same gesture as her adult companions. None of these infants can be classed as mourners as they do not adopt any of the gestures previously referred to. They clearly have an inactive role in the funerary procession and are most likely included within this scene as their mothers and/or sisters are members of the group of female mourners. The young juvenile on the far left of the group has his/her arms raised perhaps representing the typical gesture of

Figure 9.1: Male and female mourners in TT255, the tomb of Roy. Slide 447. Courtesy of das Ramessidenarchiv des Ägyptologischen Instituts der Universität Heidelberg.

mourning. However, the figure's immediate proximity to the adult female in front of her, she is touching her legs, may have a more simple explanation and could be interpreted as request for comfort (Feucht 1995, 347). This theory is certainly possible, especially when remembering that these scenes reflect reality, however, the close proximity could be due to lack of space on the tomb wall and therefore it cannot be concluded one way or the other.

Juveniles in the Funeral Procession

Further to the young female juvenile depicted in the tomb of Neferhotep, other tomb wall scenes represent juveniles within New Kingdom funeral processions. The scene within the tomb of Sharoy (TT13) (Fig. 9.2) depicts the funerary entourage after it has crossed the river Nile and is progressing over the Theban necropolis towards the tomb. The detail of this scene, although somewhat fragmented, shows a group of female mourners adopting the typical gestures of grief that have been referred to above. Alongside this group of female figures at least five younger juveniles are depicted as part of the funeral entourage. Four of these figures appear to be approximately the same height, whilst another is clearly much smaller. This can be interpreted as a representation of the various age ranges of the group, possibly from about two years old to the age of puberty. In terms of the gestures that they display, it is immediately clear that these younger figures are carrying out the same gestures as their female companions. The younger

Figure 9.2: Young juvenile mourners alongside adult female mourners in TT13, the tomb of Sharoy. Slide 2229. Courtesy of das Ramessidenarchiv des Ägyptologischen Instituts der Universität Heidelberg.

juveniles all appear to raise at least one of their hands to their heads, whilst two raise both arms to their heads. The angle of their hands suggests that they are adopting the common gesture of pouring dust or dirt onto their faces and eyes, possibly to induce tears. a gesture which, although not adopted by the female mourners in this image, is commonly seen in other tomb wall scenes, particularly the tomb of Ramose (El-Shahawy 2005, 38). One of the juveniles in the group may also have the dust or dirt actually flowing from their hands, a feature not seen in any of the other images examined as part of this study.

The lack of clothing adorning the children in this image is noteworthy. Imagery dating from the New Kingdom depicts both clothed and unclothed children (Rosalind and Janssen 1990, 27), which will become apparent as this paper continues. Eventhough in the case of funeral processions, artists were influenced by reality, it may be that nudity was used to represent age and also a figure's status as a child. Rosalind and Janssen (1990, 26) state that in a country where "in the winter at least it is distinctly cold in the early mornings and late evenings", nudity is not plausible. Therefore, this nudity should be seen as an indictor of different age ranges of the children within this study and should not be viewed as an indicator of either status, or as a gesture of mourning, as the adoption of white garments by adult mourners is sometimes interpreted (Gardiner 1910, 162–163). Instead it should be viewed as a display of a child's stage of life: distinguishing younger juveniles from older juveniles.

Images from other elite Theban tombs depict juveniles as members of the funeral procession and, as is the case with the figures in the tomb of Sharoy (TT13), adopt the same gestures as the adult mourners surrounding them. Possibly the most well-known image of mourning originates from the tomb of Ramose (TT55). It displays children as part of a group of adult female mourners carrying out the archetypical gestures of mourning (El-Shahawy 2005, 34–35). This group includes several older juveniles and, in a way, these girls are 'miniature' versions of the adult mourners surrounding them, even down to their white garments and hair styles, which are very similar. An addition to this group is a naked younger female juvenile, possibly at the same stage in life as the children shown in the tomb of Sharoy (TT13). Although clearly much younger in age than those figures surrounding her, she can still be defined as a mourner from the gestures that she adopts. She is shown with both of her arms raised upwards and has her face tilted slightly upward, as do several figures at the back of the group. Similarly, to the other mourners in the group, this younger juvenile also has thin black lines, representing tears, painted onto her cheeks.

Therefore, as demonstrated by the tombs of Sharoy (TT13) and Ramose (TT55), it is clear that juveniles took an active part as mourners in the funeral procession in the New Kingdom. However, one particular source, dating to the later Twenty Second Dynasty, also provides an, albeit much later, insight into the presence of children within a funeral procession. The source is a coffin (Fig. 9.3), also from Thebes, which shows a group of mourners preceding the sarcophagus in the funeral procession (British Museum EA22941; Taylor 2000, 189). Amongst the adult female mourners, two older juvenile females are depicted and, despite their significantly smaller scale in comparison to the figures surrounding them, their actions are clear. The child on the left adopts a more unconventional gesture by pulling at her hair which, although infrequently shown in earlier New Kingdom scenes, is alluded to by the disheveled appearance of two female mourners in the tomb of Neferhotep (TT50) (Davies 1973, pl. XXIII). The second child shown on the coffin adopts a more typical gesture in raising both of her hands to her face. The age of these mourners, the gestures that they adopt, and the context within which they appear (from the images in the New Kingdom tombs and on this Twenty-Second Dynasty coffin) suggests

Figure 9.3: Detail of mourners on the Twenty-Second Dynasty coffin of Amenemipet. British Museum EA 22941. Courtesy of British Museum Trustees.

that the raising of the arms and the throwing of dust onto the face, were by no means reserved for the New Kingdom period only.

The sources discussed so far depict female juveniles alongside female adults in funeral processions; however, we must not assume that this combination was the only one that occurred. The wider research into ancient Egyptian mourning has confirmed that scenes of funeral processions show more female mourners than male, but male mourners are still depicted, as are juvenile boys (Werbrouck 1938). For example the tomb of Nakhatamun (TT341) (Fig. 9.4), displays an unclothed young juvenile boy alongside an adult male mourner. These figures' actions are almost a mirror of each other: both figures raise their hands upwards to the crown of their heads, although the young juvenile does appear to have his right hand slightly closer to his head than the adult male, but this is a small detail. This stance is similar to another image shown in the tomb of Samut (TT409), in which two older male clothed juveniles, although not in close proximity to any adult mourners, adopt the typical gestures of grief in raising their arms to their heads (Negm 1997, pl. XXIII). A late Eighteenth-Dynasty tomb relief (British Museum EA326) which shows the part of the funeral procession can also be examined here. Although the relief originates from Abydos rather than Thebes it is still a relevant source as it depicts a procession very much like the one shown in the tomb of Samut. The relief displays a group of at least five female mourners following the entourage of three male mourners and two bearers carrying a chest, possibly the canopic chest holding the embalmed organs of the deceased. Amongst this part of the procession, accompanying the bearers are two older juvenile boys adopting exactly the same gestures that we have seen in the two previous examples. The juvenile underneath the

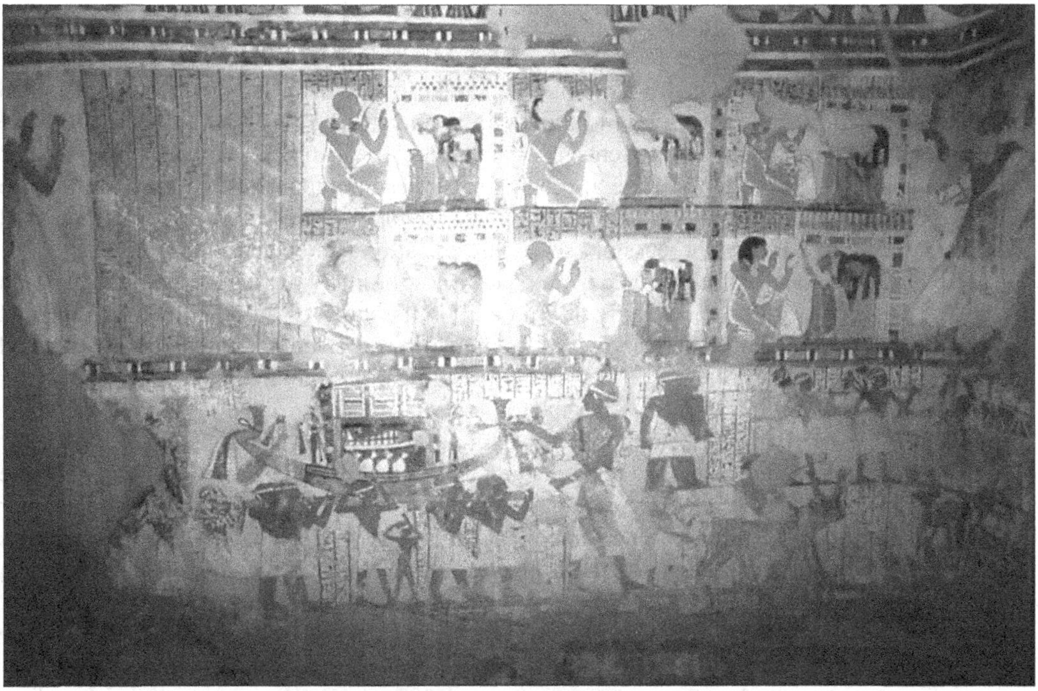

Figure 9.4: Funeral procession of Nakhatamun, TT341. Slide 3597. Courtesy of das Ramessidenarchiv des Ägyptologischen Instituts der Universität Heidelberg.

chest is slightly smaller in scale to the other child, possibly to indicate that he is at the lower end of the age range for the 'older juvenile' than his counterpart.

The aforementioned images illustrate that the gestures of mourning were not exclusive to female juvenile mourners, just as they were not only adopted by female adult mourners but by male adult mourners also. However, there does appear to be a difference between specific types of gestures adopted by the different genders: only female mourners, whether adults or children, appear to bend to the ground to pick up dust or dirt, and evidently the exposure of breasts only applies to females. However, as the primary focus of this paper is the gestures made by child mourners, the comparison between mourners of different genders does not infringe to a large extent upon the analysis, which will now be considered further from the examination of infants within funeral procession.

Analysis of Data

The evidence examined above firmly establishes the presence of children within funeral processions of the Theban elite during the New Kingdom. The Twenty-Second Dynasty coffin from Thebes (British Museum EA22941; Taylor 2001, 189) also suggests children continued to be part of ancient Egyptian funeral processions in subsequent eras. Both older and younger juveniles appear to have played an active role as mourners during these events because the images shown previously depict examples of a variety of juveniles, both male and female, younger and older, adopting the common gestures of grief. Establishing the presence of children within funeral processions and the actions that they undertake is one step, the next is to understand what these depictions tell us about child-mourners in ancient Egypt. To what extent did these younger individuals understand the events going on around them and, moreover, what emotional attachments did they have to the funeral procession? These points are much more difficult to examine, especially when studying images, but by understanding these scenes as a reflection of the episodes of a real funeral procession, some interpretation can be attempted.

As explained above, within this paper juveniles are split into two categories – younger and older. The age category in which the figure of a child falls indicates those children who would have a better psychological understanding of the funeral procession and the emotions attached to such an event. For example, it is implausible to suggest that an infant of younger than a year would have understood the events of the funeral procession and to have responded using the gestures of mourning that we see children 10 years older than them adopting.

All together the scenes discussed above depict twenty-six children (Fig. 9.5). Five of these are the infants shown in the tomb of Neferhotep (TT49) (Davies 1973, pl. XXIII). The remainder can be broken down into thirteen older juveniles and eight younger juveniles. The data shows that all of the younger juveniles from these images are represented directly accompanying an adult mourner during the procession along the west bank, meaning that they are within immediate proximity to them (Fig. 9.6). Although analysis also shows that eleven of the older juveniles are accompanying adult mourners on-route to the tomb, it is important to note that the two older juvenile boys from the tomb of Samut (TT409) (Negm 1997, pl. XXIII), are not within immediate

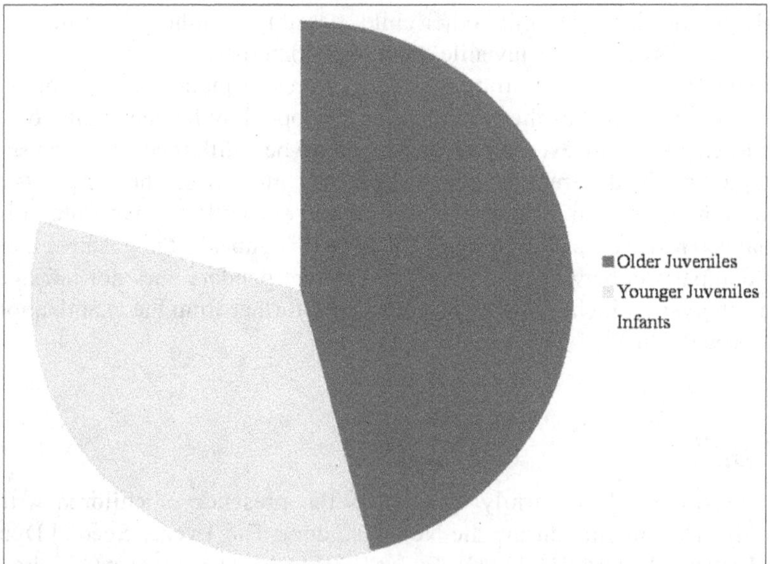

Figure 9.5: Pie chart showing the proportion of infants, younger juveniles and older juveniles in the examples discussed in the paper.

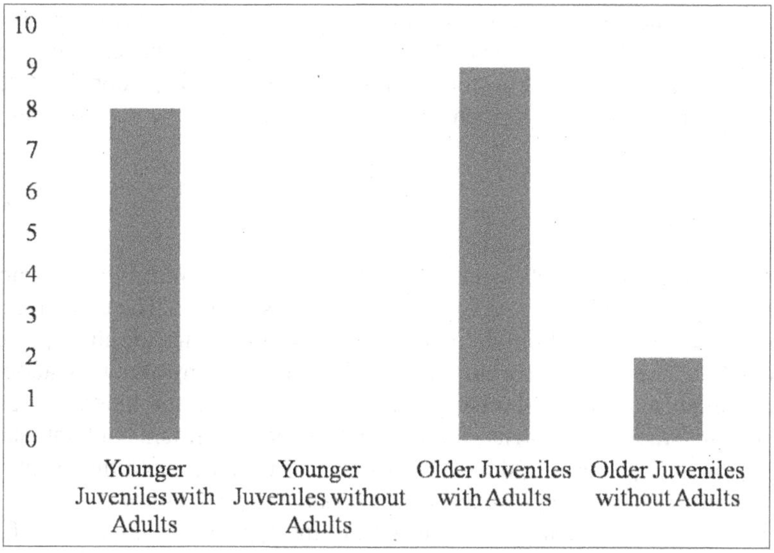

Figure 9.6: Graph displaying the number of younger and older juveniles accompnaied with and without adult mourner in the examples discussed in the paper.

proximity of any adult mourners and that their actions show that they themselves are mourners. The older juvenile shown beneath the canopic chest on the Eighteenth Dynasty relief from Abydos is positioned a little distance away from the male mourners behind him, but he is not as separated as the older juveniles in the tomb of Samut. We cannot discount the possibility that the older juvenile's positioning on the relief could be due to artistic or ideological reasons such as the aesthetic need to space the figures out or the ancient Egyptian worry of *horror vacui* and the subsequent need to fill an empty space. Factors such as these need to be considered during analysis and, of course, conclusions can be altered with the collation of more data. These initial findings however may suggest that due to their age, older juveniles could walk the processional route at a distance away from any adult mourners and adopt the gestures of grief of their own accord, rather than mimicking their adult counterparts, as some of the images examined above strongly suggest, particularly the detail from the tomb of Nakhatamun (Fig. 9.4). In doing so, these older juveniles may highlight a true understanding of the gestures of mourning in the minds ancient Egyptian older juveniles. Of course, they would be aware of the other adult mourners around them and would to some extent imitate their gestures, but it is clear that they have a higher level of understanding of the funeral procession than their younger counterparts.

Other details from these scenes studied above also support this theory of the active and possibly more emotionally motivated actions of older juveniles. In the previously studied scene from the tomb of Ramose (El-Shahawy 2005, 34–35), one older female juvenile can clearly be seen in a more spontaneous and, perhaps more emotional, action of grasping the waist of the much older female mourner in front of her (Feucht 1995, 345). The image of the older juvenile on the Twenty Second Dynasty coffin (British Museum EA22941; Taylor 2000, 189) pulling at her hair, has already being highlighted as a rarely depicted gesture. However, these are also details which may indicate the level of understanding of these older juveniles about the events going on around them and they may provide an insight into how a connection was made between the emotional motivation behind a gesture of mourning and the deep-rooted ideologies that led these juveniles to understand that in such circumstances, this was the way to express your grief.

Conclusion

The wall scenes, coffin, and reliefs examined within this study confirm the presence of children within ancient Egyptian funeral processions in the New Kingdom. The evidence also provides an understanding of the role of children within this event, illustrating their placement within the wider context of the funeral procession and the gestures, if any, that they adopted. It can be concluded that infants are rarely shown within images depicting the funeral procession during the New Kingdom, when the majority of the evidence dates to. Infants did not take active parts in the procession, simply because they were too young to understand the events in the world around them, and did have the physical means to adopt such gestures of grief. On the other hand, both younger and older juveniles carried out the typical gestures of grief, raising their arms to their heads, throwing dust onto their faces and, in the case of older juvenile females, exposing their breasts. Further analysis needs to be carried out in this area, with a range of sources from a wider chronological period, being examined, as well as an examination of why children were present during funeral processions. Were they simply accompanying family members to the burial of a beloved deceased? Or were they taken by their mothers, who may have been professional mourners, to the event? In studying these areas an idea of how younger mourners fitted into the funeral procession, and the extent to which they understood and acted upon the emotions of such an event, can be grasped, and the preliminary ideas presented within this paper can be concluded.

Bibliography

Assmann, J. (2005) *Death and Salvation in Ancient Egypt.* New York NY, Cornell University Press.

Bleeker, C. J. (1958) Isis and Nephthys as Wailing Women, *Numen* 5, 1–17.

Davies, N. de G. (1973) *The Tomb of Neferhotep at Thebes.* New York NY, Metropolitan Museum of Art.

El-Saady, H. (1996) *The Tomb of Amenemhab.* Warminster, Aris & Phillips Ltd.

El-Shahawy, A. (2005) *The Funerary Art of Ancient Egypt: a Bridge to the Realm of the Hereafter.* Cairo, Dar al-Mushaf.

Erman, A. and Grapow, H. (1982) *Wörterbuch der ägyptischen Sprache*, 4 Aufl, Band 1. Berlin, Akademie-Verlag.

Faulkner, R. O. (1962) *A Concise Dictionary of Middle Egyptian.* Oxford, Griffith Institute.

Feucht, E. (1995) *Das Kind im Alten Ägypten.* Frankfurt, Campus.

Gardiner, A. H. (1910) The Colour of Mourning, *Zeitschrift für ägyptische Sprache und Altertumskunde* 47, 162–163.

Hays, H. M. (2010) Funerary Rituals (Pharaonic Period). In J. Dieleman and W. Wendrich (eds) *UCLA Encyclopedia of Egyptology*. Los Angeles CA, UCLA.

Lichtheim, M. (1980) *Ancient Egyptian Literature: Volume III The Later Period.* Berkeley CA, University of California Press.

McDermott, B. (2006) *Death in Ancient Egypt.* London, Sutton Publishing Ltd.

Millward, E. (2011) Visual and written evidence for mourning in New Kingdom Egypt. In N. Andrews, M. Correas-Amador, H. Abd El Gawad and V. Tamorri (eds) *Current Research in Egyptology 2011: Proceedings of the Twelfth Annual Symposium Durham University 2011, 141–146.* Oxford, Oxbow Books.

Negm, M. (1997) *The Tomb of Simut called Kyky: Theban Tomb 409 at Qurnah.* Warminster, Aris & Phillips Ltd.

Rosalind, M. and Janssen, J. J. (1990) *Growing Up in Ancient Egypt.* London, Rubicon Press.

Smith, M. (2009) *Traversing Eternity: Texts for the Afterlife from Ptolemaic and Roman Egypt.* Oxford, Oxford University Press.

Taylor, J. H. (2001) *Death and the Afterlife in Ancient Egypt.* London, British Museum Press.

Taylor, J. H. (2010) The Day of Burial. In J. H. Taylor (ed.) *Journey through the afterlife: Ancient Egyptian Book of the Dead, 82–103.* London, British Museum Press.

Werbrouck, M. (1938) *Les Pleureuses dans l'Egypte ancienne.* Bruxelles, FERE.

Wickett, E. (2010) *For the Living and the Dead : the Funerary Laments of Upper Egypt, Ancient and Modern.* London, I. B. Tauris.

British Museum Collection Catalogue. EA22941. www.britishmuseum.org/collection,

British Museum, last modified 24/01/2010. Online. Last accessed 18/05/2011.

British Museum Collection Catalogue. EA326. www.britishmuseum.org/collection, British Museum, last modified 25/09/2011. Online. Last accessed 30/09/2011.

Das Ramessidenarchiv des Ägyptologischen Instituts der Universität Heidelberg. Last accessed 10th, 11th, 12th October 2011.

10

Skeletal Health in Early Egypt

Sarah Musselwhite

Introduction

This paper uses skeletal data to investigate how health varied among Predynastic and Early Dynastic Egyptian populations as the Egyptian state formed and new social classes emerged. These early periods were characterised by profound economic, political and social changes: agriculture was introduced into the Nile Valley from the Fertile Crescent and allowed the production of surplus food to support craft specialisation, foreign trade flourished and allowed exotic raw materials to be imported into Egypt for the manufacture of elite prestige items, urban centres developed and acted as important arenas of elite activity, and social stratification became increasingly pronounced. These changes culminated in the rise of several different 'proto-states', the most significant of which were centred on the Upper Egyptian sites of Nagada, Hierakonpolis and This (Kemp 2006, 76) and ultimately provided the ideological foundations for later Egyptian kingship. Cultural unification of Egypt was complete by the Nagada II period, followed by political unification in the Nagada III period (Wilkinson 2000, 377) and the establishment of a new political capital at Memphis. However, little is known about how all of these processes affected the physical wellbeing of people and how their relationship with their physical environment changed over time.

Before the emergence of the state in Egypt the introduction of agriculture into the Nile Valley had already brought the potential for substantial health changes in society. It led to a change in diet and its nutritional value and allowed greater quantities of food to be produced (Bard 2008, 83), all of which would have influenced the levels and types of nutritional disorders that people could experience and their ability to deal with disease. A new type of economy emerged based on agricultural surplus and foreign trade (Hassan 1988, 157; Wengrow 2006, 75). The latter would have allowed the exchange of ideas that may have benefited medical practices but would also have increased the likelihood of new diseases and disease strains being introduced into Egypt to which no immunity existed. Agriculture also increased the potential for disease to spread through greater animal to human contact and exposure to Nile floods, with the latter increasing exposure to diseases such as schistosomiasis which thrives in stagnant water (Keita 2003, 211). Further changes in population health would be expected as agriculture intensified and new crops and animals were introduced.

The cultural changes brought about by the emergence and subsequent unification of the Egyptian state would also have provided great potential for health change over time, bringing both new health risks and new ways of dealing with the stresses of the environment. As communities became increasingly sedentary and focused on key political centres, the spread of medical knowledge would have been favoured. However, the associated increases in population density, along with the unsanitary living conditions that are often associated with urbanisation (Kjellstrom *et al.* 2008, 11–12), would have further increased the potential for disease spread; some regions may have been more affected than others. One would expect to see some kind of temporal change in the general level and type of health problems people were experiencing, both after the initial introduction of agriculture and the subsequent development of the state.

The emergence of the state was characterised by increasing social stratification and the growing power of a social elite (Wilkinson 2000; Wengrow 2006; Bard 2008). The rise of social inequality may have resulted in some groups of people being deprived of the essential resources needed to maintain good health, such as food with good nutritional content, adequate healthcare and a clean and safe living environment (Crooks 1995, 61). Conversely, other groups of higher social status may have had better access to essential resources and consequently been able to produce a better biological response to environmental stress, i.e. have a higher immunity against disease (Cucina and Işcan 1997, 213).

Some studies have revealed a link between high status and a lack of visible skeletal and dental pathology in the archaeological record (e.g. Cook 1981). However, there are also studies which have shown no such health distinctions between higher and lower status groups from the same society. Robb *et al.* (2001, 218) found no significant association between various skeletal health indicators and social status as defined by grave goods from the Italian Iron Age site of Pontecagnano. Cucina and Iscan (1997, 215) found that disruption in childhood growth was common among high-status individuals from the Fort Center site in Florida, US, dated to AD 200–800. This variation indicates that the relationship between social status and health depends very much on the particular social context from which the studied groups originate and the specific mechanisms in place to control resource distribution. The present paper ensures that the social context of each skeletal collection sampled is investigated in detail so that the relationship between social status and health can be examined.

This paper addresses two key questions. Firstly, did health change over time from the beginning of the Predynastic Period to the Early Dynastic Period and if so, why? Secondly, were social status and health correlated in these early periods? By considering the health and therefore, the relationship of populations to their biological and social environments, this paper aims to shed light on the human experience of state formation in Egypt.

There are several sources of information we can use to investigate health and nutrition in Egypt: artistic depictions and medical papyri can inform us about the diseases present, medical care and diet. However, these sources are not present for early Egypt. Mummified and skeletal remains are the only real source we have for investigating disease prevalence and growth disruption in these early periods and more importantly, they allow us to quantify health differences between populations. In general, much of our existing evidence of Predynastic and Early Dynastic Egypt has come from studies of material culture associated with burials or changing cemetery patterns, although these are limited in what they can tell us about societal change and are biased towards representation of the deceased in the afterlife. Skeletal health can provide information about people's lives which may have some bearing on the key political, economic and social changes occurring within Egypt during these periods. It can also provide insight into whether the changes brought to society by state formation had the same effects on everyone, regardless of the social group to which they belonged.

Health can be assessed from the skeleton by measuring the presence, distribution and severity of the lesions which diseases and nutritional disorders leave behind, commonly referred to as skeletal stress markers. They are often visible by eye. Some stress markers can be caused by specific diseases or conditions whereas others are more general responses to infection or malnutrition. By measuring the frequency of different stress markers within a skeletal sample it is possible to gain a general idea of the level and types of environmental stress that that population was experiencing while they were living. For this study, three stress markers were measured: cribra orbitalia, porotic hyperostosis and linear enamel hypoplasia (LEH), all of which give an idea of environmental stress experienced during childhood. These will be discussed in more detail below.

Previous studies of health in Egypt have tended to investigate very broad periods of Egyptian history (Duhig 2000; Zakrzewski 2003). Although such broad comparisons are useful for pinpointing time periods that warrant more detailed study, failure to fully take into account the variation in the physical and social environments of the archaeological contexts sampled reduces the accuracy with which any observed health changes can be interpreted. In relation to early Egypt, there have been a few detailed studies involving skeletal material from individual archaeological contexts, including those from Hierakonpolis and Nagada (Greene 2006; Kumar 2009), and some temporal studies which have suggested an improvement in health sometime after the Badarian period (Keita 2003; Keita and Boyce 2001; Starling and Stock 2007). These studies have focused mainly on the effects of dietary change with agriculture on health, but there has been less emphasis on the effects of societal context. The present paper aims to reconstruct the social context of each population sampled and to consider this as a significant variable in the interpretation of the biological data collected.

Material

Skeletal remains from six archaeological contexts were sampled, each from sites of major socio-political importance in the emergence of the Egyptian state, and dating to different cultural phases within the overall Predynastic and Early Dynastic period. The sites are: El-Badari (Badarian), Hierakonpolis (probably mainly Nagada II), Nagada, from which two contexts were sampled (Nagada II and III), Abydos (First Dynasty) and Tarkhan (mainly Nagada III). All of these sites, apart from Tarkhan, are located in Upper Egypt, whereas Tarkhan is in Lower Egypt. Details of the contexts sampled are summarised in Table 10.1, along with a map of their locations in Fig. 10.1. Only cranial material, i.e. skulls, was used due to the rarity of postcranial material in the collections. All of the skeletal material is held in the Duckworth Collection of the Department of Archaeology and Anthropology at the University of Cambridge. Where possible, individuals were traced to the original excavation reports using information such as grave numbers written on the skeletal material or boxes. The Duckworth Collection's records were also consulted. Tables linking the skeletal material with burial information, if recorded, were made.

It is possible to identify two higher or special status groups: those from cemetery T at Nagada and Abydos. Cemetery T at Nagada, excavated by Petrie and Quibell (1896), was mainly in use during the Nagada II and III periods (Bard 1994, 81). It was the smallest cemetery at Nagada, with

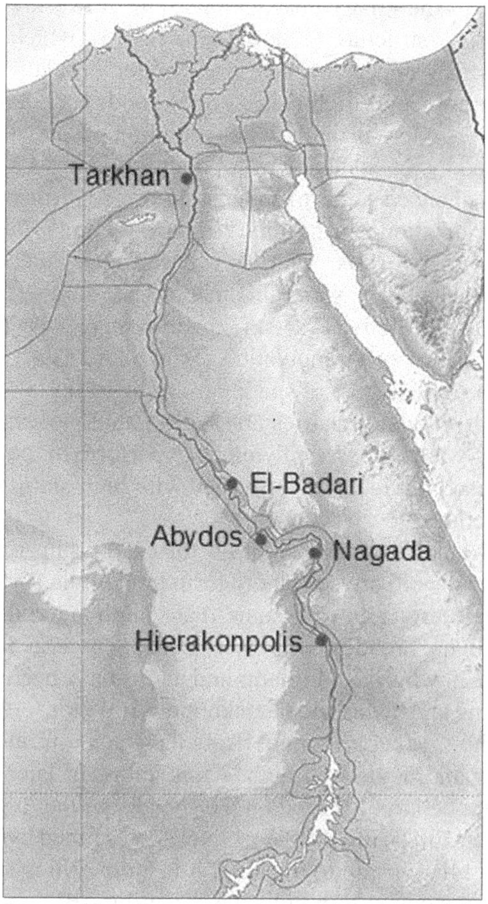

Figure 10.1: A map showing the locations of the archaeological contexts sampled (adapted by author).

just 69 graves (*ibid.* 79–81). It seems to be well accepted in the literature that cemetery T was a high-status, elite burial ground, perhaps even where the early leaders of Nagada were buried (Case and Crowfoot Payne 1962, 11; Kemp 1973, 42). As well as its separate location, this cemetery had the lowest density of graves out of all of the Nagada cemeteries, the largest average grave size and, in the Nagada II period, the highest average number of pots per grave (Bard 1994). Many of the tombs contained large quantities of pottery and luxury goods, including slate palettes, beads made of precious stones and shell, and hard stone vessels (Baumgartel 1970; Petrie and Quibell 1896), all representing a significant investment of resources. There were also several larger, brick-lined tombs containing multiple burials, including those of children; indeed, it was noted from the Duckworth material that adults and infants were often buried in the same tomb. The similar treatment of subadults to adults in burial suggests a degree of inherited rather than acquired status (Wilkinson 2000, 380).

The skeletal material from Abydos, excavated by Petrie (1924), is from the subsidiary burials situated around the funerary enclosures of three First Dynasty kings of Egypt: Djer, Djet and Merneith (the majority from the former two). Similar subsidiary

Origin of skeletal material	**Approximate date of skeletal material**	**Excavator(s) of skeletal material and publication date of excavation report**
El-Badari – Badarian graves	Badarian period	Brunton and Caton-Thompson (1928)
Hierakonpolis – Prehistoric and possibly the 'Fort' cemeteries	Mainly Nagada II period, with possibly some Nagada I and III	Quibell and Green (1902)
Nagada – cemetery B	Mainly Nagada II period	Petrie and Quibell (1896)
Nagada – cemetery T	Nagada II and III period	Petrie and Quibell (1896)
Tarkhan	Mainly Nagada III period, with some First Dynasty	Petrie (1914)
Abydos – 'Tombs of the Courtiers'	First Dynasty	Petrie (1924)

Table 10.1: The skeletal material used.

burials were also found around several royal tombs of the First Dynasty kings. The graves are brick-lined, possibly once surmounted by a brick superstructure (Kemp 1966, 14–15), which suggests a high resource investment. Some individuals appear to have been minor officials, on the basis of titles such as 'seal-bearer' and the presence of high-status burial goods such as ivory combs and cosmetic implements (Petrie 1924, 3). More recently it has been proposed that many of the individuals were court artisans, suggested by the inclusion of copper tools in burials (Bestock 2007, 116–17; O'Connor 2009, 173). The enhanced status of some is suggested further by names of individuals appearing on tools and the association with specific kings (Valbelle 1997, 36). Kemp (1967, 22) suggests that the purpose of the subsidiary burials was for individuals to serve the kings in the afterlife and, although it is debated, it is possible that at least some of these individuals were killed for this purpose (O'Connor 2009, 172–3) (Lovell has suggested that the teeth of some of the individuals show evidence of strangulation (Bard, 2002, 72)). Bestock (2007, 117) has also suggested that there is some degree of spatial grouping of burials containing specific types of objects, e.g. arrowheads, model granaries and ivory game pieces, possibly relating to different functions that the kings wanted these individuals to perform in the afterlife. All of this evidence would suggest that these individuals were buried with high-status and presumably were accorded this during their lifetime.

However, as will be discussed in detail later, the health profile built up for each group is based on childhood health data; the stress markers measured are thought to form predominantly in childhood. For Nagada cemetery T, it would be reasonable to assume that childhood and adulthood social status were linked, as social status in the broadest sense was probably inherited rather than acquired in early Egypt (for example, wealthy burials of infants and adults have been found in several Predynastic elite cemeteries, including at Abydos and Hierakonpolis) (Wilkinson 2000, 380, 388). At Abydos, officials working for the royal court would likely have come from families who had a similar relationship to the king and associated high social status. In later periods, the social standing of a typical family would be largely based on the social standing of the male head of the household, e.g. Heqanakht (Allen 2002); this was most likely determined by his position within the administrative hierarchy and relationship to the king. It is more difficult to say whether Egyptian artisans in general would have come from high-status families. But, as specialised craftsmen working for the king (Valbelle 1997, 36), the artisans buried at Abydos may have been specifically chosen from families who had a history of providing services for the king and the special status that went with this. Thus, such individuals may have had this special status during childhood.

Two of the groups studied were of lower status than the Nagada cemetery T and Abydos groups, namely those from Tarkhan and cemetery B at Nagada. The material from Tarkhan was excavated by Petrie (1914) from a large cemetery of over 2000 graves dating to the Nagada III period and the First Dynasty. The Duckworth material sampled from Tarkhan is mainly from the Nagada III period, with a small number of individuals from the First Dynasty (five of the sampled individuals did not have individual entries in the excavation report but it was assumed that they were from either the Nagada III period or the First Dynasty) (a table linking the individuals sampled to their respective graves in the excavation report could not be included here but is available on request). Most of the sampled graves were square or oval pits and commonly contained pottery and beads (Petrie 1914). Other items included were slate palettes, stone vessels, and sometimes copper and ivory objects (*ibid.*). Grajetzki (2004, 5) states that the cemetery at Tarkhan is notable for the range of different social classes that its graves represent; the poorest graves were just 1.5–1.8m deep and contained pottery and sometimes jewellery, and the richest ones had coffins and/or large mud-brick superstructures (*ibid.* 13). The most important people had their tombs carved into rocks overlooking the valley whereas the densely distributed graves occupying the middle valley were for poorer people (*ibid.* 6). Given that the graves of the individuals sampled in this study are from a variety of different locations within the cemetery (as determined by examining maps in the excavation report detailing the locations of all the published graves) and contain different types and numbers of grave goods, the sample is likely to contain individuals from a range of different social classes, and overall probably represents a more varied and lower-status group than those from either Abydos or cemetery T at Nagada.

Cemetery B at Nagada dates predominantly to the Nagada II period (Bard 1994, 81) and contains 144 graves (*ibid.* 80) excavated by Petrie (Petrie and Quibell 1896) alongside the other Nagada material discussed earlier. Most cemetery B graves were rectangular pits, with some oval or round ones (Bard 1994, 84). Grave goods included pottery, particularly of the red and black type, beads, shell, stone vases and slate palettes (Baumgartel 1970; Petrie and Quibell 1896). A detailed comparison of mortuary practices in the three different cemeteries at Nagada by Bard (1994) strongly suggests that cemetery B was for lower-status individuals than cemeteries T and N West; cemetery B had a smaller average grave size, a greater density of graves and a lower number of 'rich' graves than the other cemeteries. Bard (1994, 96, 103) suggests that the cemetery was a burial ground for middle-class individuals living in a nearby farming village.

It was not possible to define the social status of each of the two remaining groups from El-Badari and Hierakonpolis, but some information on social context could be discerned. The material from El-Badari is from several Badarian period cemeteries excavated by Brunton and Caton-Thompson (1928), specifically cemeteries 5100, 5300, 5400, 5600, 5700 and 5800. Badarian period graves generally consisted of one or more individuals buried in an oval or rectangular pit (Trigger 1983, 27). The body was wrapped in matting, cloth or animal skin and was placed in a contracted position (Midant-Reynes 2000, 153). Some graves contained the remains of reeds which probably formed some kind of roofing over the body (*ibid.*), or matting cover. Graves were generally rich in burial goods: a variety of pottery types including 'red-polished, black-topped' vessels, bone tools, various ivory items such as bracelets and rings, bone and ivory combs, siltstone palettes, ostrich egg shell vessels, shell and stone beads, and copper items such as pins (Brunton and Caton-Thompson 1928; Midant-Reynes 2000, 153–5). There has been debate as to the level of social stratification that Badarian period graves represent: Trigger (1983, 27) has argued that although graves were differentiated in size, there were no strong wealth distinctions in terms of burial goods whereas Anderson (1992, 66) argues against this and the traditional view of Badarian society being largely egalitarian in structure. What is clear is that social status differences in Egyptian tombs became much more evident in the latter half of the Predynastic Period, as the ideological foundations of Egyptian kingship were developing among a powerful elite class.

There was very little information available on the material from Hierakonpolis. It is likely that it mostly originates from Quibell and Green's excavations at the end of the 19th century (Quibell 1900; Quibell and Green 1902). They investigated two main Predynastic burial areas, one within the Fort region, in use during the Nagada I and II periods, and one at the south of the desert site which dates to the Nagada II period (Wilkinson 2000, 384). The latter contained the 'Painted Tomb' (100) (*ibid.*), which possibly belonged to an early king (Case and Crowfoot Payne 1962, 18). It was the main Predynastic cemetery area and so the most likely place from which the material originates. In this case, most individuals sampled were probably of lower social standing than the individuals buried in tomb 100 and the few other large tombs found. However, it is possible that at least some of the sampled material may have come from the Fort cemetery, and so the Hierakonpolis group has been labelled broadly as mid Predynastic-Protodynastic in date.

Methods

A total of 179 individuals were sampled across the six archaeological contexts (Table 10. 2), with individuals only being included if they met the minimum criteria for preservation. Individuals were assigned a sex and rough age category (either adult or subadult) using standard osteological methods (outlined in Buikstra and Ubelaker 1994, 19–21, 49, 51), and adapted by Dr J. T. Stock (*pers. comm.*) and Starling (2005, 45–6). Where possible, only adults were sampled, though for some populations a small number of subadults had to be included; although all three stress markers used are generally thought to form in childhood, porotic hyperostosis and cribra orbitalia can remodel and heal later in life (Stuart-Macadam 1985, 392). The age distribution of a sample could therefore influence the perceived frequencies of stress markers in a population. Minimising age variation in the way described reduces this influence. Individuals were then assessed for the presence and severity of three different skeletal stress markers that appear on the skull and that are among the most common indicators of skeletal health used by osteoarchaeologists: porotic hyperostosis, cribra orbitalia and linear enamel hypoplasia (LEH).

LEH is a defect in the tooth enamel caused by stunted growth during childhood (Fig. 10.2). The defect appears as a roughly horizontal groove or linear sequence of pits on the enamel surface (Goodman and Rose 1990, 65–6) and is normally visible with the naked eye. It is likely to appear on most or all teeth developing in a period of metabolic stress (*ibid.* 64). LEH is not correlated with a specific disease or medical condition but rather gives an indication of *general* episodes of severe physiological disturbance during childhood, which can be the

Archaeological context	**Total number of individuals sampled**	**Number of individuals observable for porotic hyperostosis**	**Number of individuals observable for cribra orbitalia**	**Number of individuals observable for LEH (at least 1 scorable tooth)**
El-Badari	30	30	30	30
Hierakonpolis	39	39	39	29
Nagada B	24	24	20	24
Nagada T	24	24	23	15
Tarkhan	30	30	29	28
Abydos	32	32	30	31
TOTAL	**179**	**179**	**171**	**157**

Table 10.2: The skeletal sample taken.

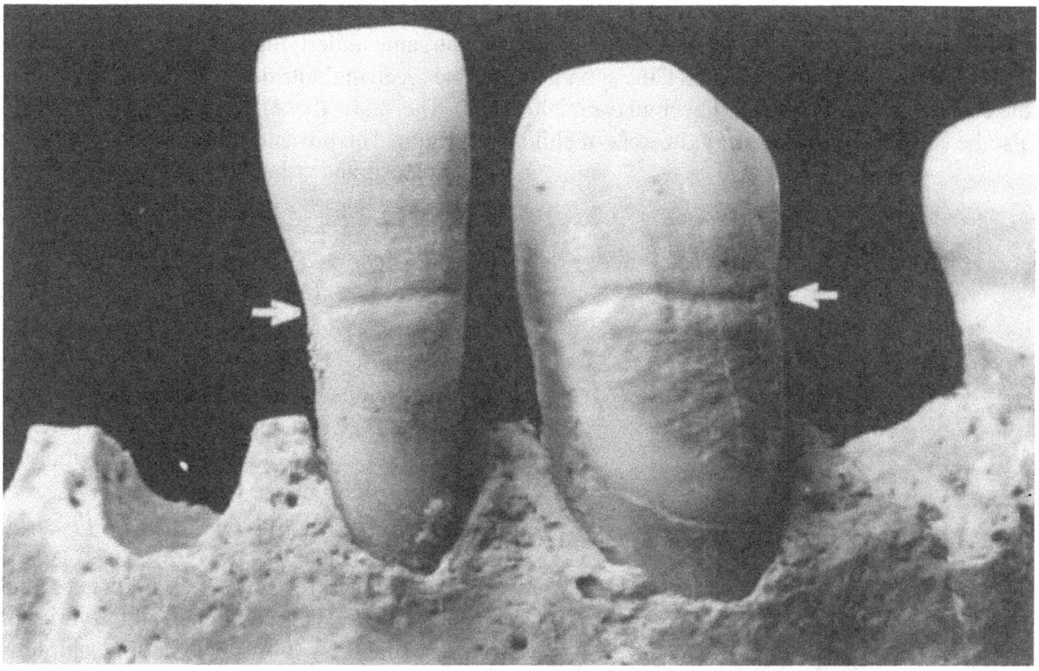

Figure 10.2: Linear enamel hypoplasia bands (Mays 2002, 156) (Copyright © 1998, Taylor & Francis Group).

result of disease, malnutrition, or more likely a combination of both (Keita and Boyce 2001, 735; Lovell and Whyte 1999, 70). Studies of modern populations have frequently linked high enamel hypoplasia prevalences to poor living conditions and low socio-economic status because they promote poor diet and/or high disease prevalence (Larsen 1997, 50). For each individual sampled, all scorable teeth were scored for the presence of LEH bands using the methods described by Starling (2005, 47–9). Only posterior teeth (molars and premolars) were included in the analysis as these were preserved in more equal numbers across populations than anterior teeth (incisors and canines) and therefore allowed more accurate comparisons of LEH prevalence to be made.

Porotic hyperostosis and cribra orbitalia are both characterised by the appearance of porous lesions on the surface of the skull. In the former case they appear on the cranial vault (most commonly the parietal bones) and in the latter they appear on the roofs of the orbits (eye sockets) (Stuart-Macadam 1989, 187–8; White and Folkens 2005, 320) (Figs 10.3 and 10.4). It is thought that they most commonly form during childhood (Stuart-Macadam 1985, 392), although a survey of the literature does not provide unanimous support for this. The most commonly cited and long-established view is that both stress markers are caused by iron-deficiency anaemia, a condition which can be caused by dietary deficiency in iron and/or disease which results in the loss of iron (Keita and Boyce 2006, 65; Larsen 1997, 29–30). In the case of ancient Egypt, the parasitic disease schistosomiasis, which has been identified in mummified remains from the Predynastic Period (Deelder *et al.* 1990), could have been a significant risk factor for this. However, some recent studies have suggested that a wider range of metabolic disorders can be responsible for the stress markers (Walker *et al.* 2009) and that porotic hyperostosis and cribra orbitalia may not always have the same underlying cause (Stuart-Macadam 1989, 187). Furthermore, like LEH, the synergetic link between malnutrition and disease in causing the conditions is emphasised (Facchini *et al.* 2004, 127). Therefore, these two stress markers should also be considered as *general* indicators of childhood health. The presence and severity of porotic hyperostosis and cribra orbitalia were measured using the same scoring system, 0–4, based on severity, developed by Ubelaker and Buikstra (1994, 120–121, 151–3). In the analysis, a severity score of 2 or above was used as the threshold for porotic hyperostosis and cribra orbitalia presence.

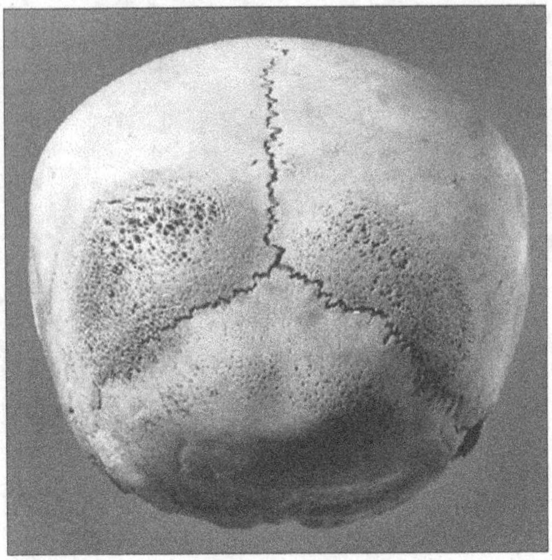

Figure 10.3: Porotic hyperostosis (White and Folkens 2005, 322) (Copyright © 2005, Elsevier).

The frequency of each stress marker was compared between populations and any trends in the data were identified and tested for statistical significance using *Microsoft Excel* (Microsoft Inc., Redmond WA) and *SPSS 19.0* (SPSS Inc., Chicago IL). Average severity was also calculated for porotic hyperostosis and cribra orbitalia. The frequency and severity of a stress marker within a population sample is an indicator of how much environmental stress that population was experiencing, particularly during childhood.

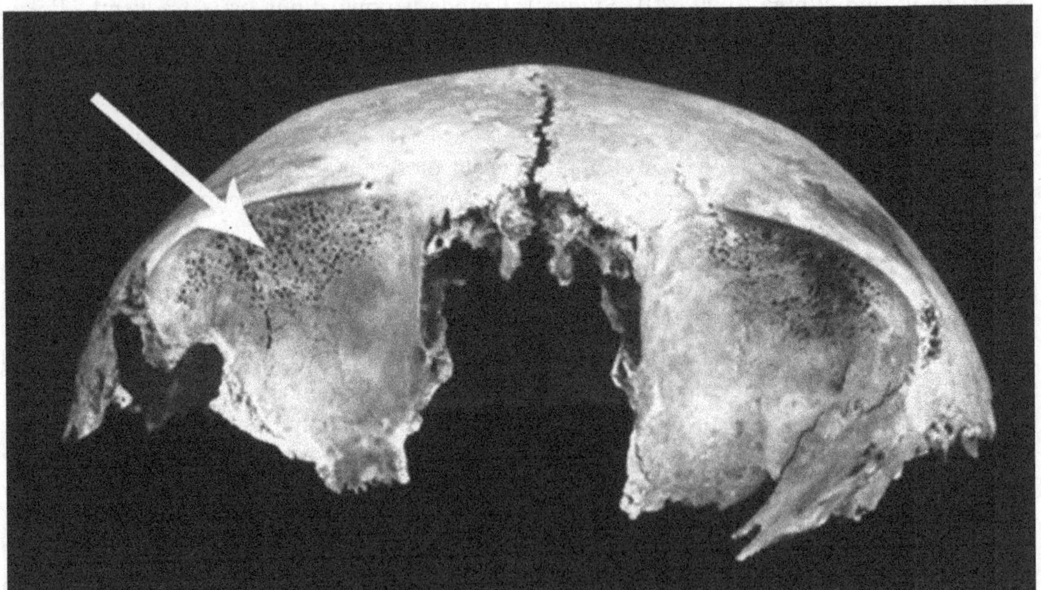

Figure 10.4: Cribra orbitalia (Aberdeen Art Gallery and Museums' Collections).

Results and Discussion

Temporal Trends

The results were analysed temporally to see whether early Egyptian populations experienced any changes in health over time. The six populations were grouped into three time periods: early Predynastic (El-Badari), mid Predynastic–Protodynastic (Hierakonpolis, Nagada B and Nagada T), and Protodynastic–Early Dynastic (Tarkhan and Abydos). Figs 10.5–7 clearly show that all three stress markers exhibited their highest prevalence in the earliest, Badarian period, and then decreased to the mid Predynastic-Protodynastic. The same trend apparent in all three stress markers suggests that overall health was initially poor within the Badarian group, but then there was a general improvement in health after the Badarian period. The same pattern is also apparent for the average severity of porotic hyperostosis and cribra orbitalia. It is also interesting that the decrease occurs in all three populations that make up the mid Predynastic-Protodynastic group, which, given they represent a variety of different social groups, suggests that the overall improvement in health occurred regardless of social status.

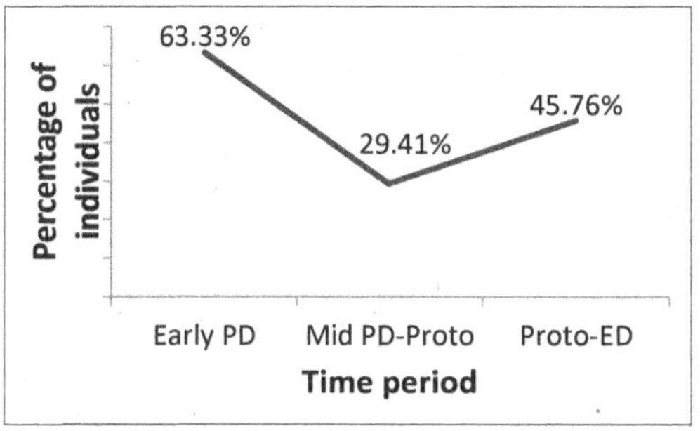

Figure 10.5: The percentage of individuals with linear enamel hypoplasia (posterior teeth only), by time period (the difference between the Early Predynastic and Mid Predynastic-Protodynastic was statistically significant, Mann-Whitney test: $U=674.000$, $Z=-3.146$, $p<0.0025$; and the difference between the Mid Predynastic-Protodynastic and Proto-Early Dynastic was nearly significant, Mann-Whitney test: $U=1678.000$, $Z=-1.896$, $p=0.059$).

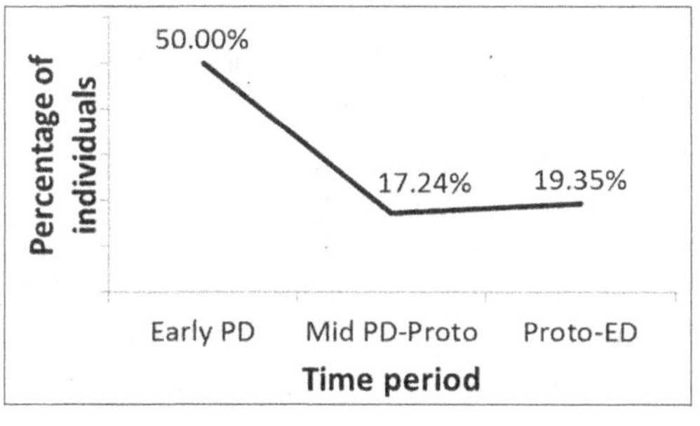

Figure 10.6: The percentage of individuals with porotic hyperostosis (severity score 2 or above), by time period (the Early Predynastic was statistically different to both later groups, Mann-Whitney tests: $U=877.500$, $Z=-3.528$, $p<0.001$; $U=210.000$, $Z=-3.245$, $p<0.001$).

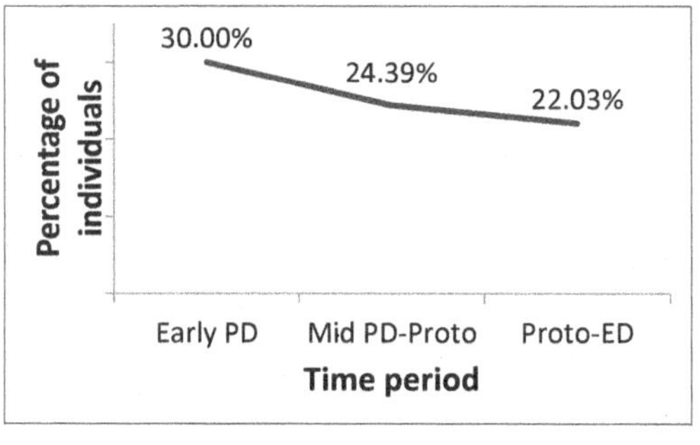

Figure 10.7: The percentage of individuals with cribra orbitalia (severity score 2 or above), by time period (the differences were not statistically significant, for all comparisons, overall Kruskal-Wallis test: $X^2=0.680$, $df=2$, $p=ns$).

The Badarian population was the first predominantly agricultural group to inhabit Upper Egypt, and these results further support current thinking that the transition to agriculture resulted in an initial decline in health in many regions of the world. A similar high level of skeletal stress within the Badarian population was found by Starling and Stock (2007, 525). Documented health problems that arose with agriculture include increased prevalence of dental caries (cavities) due to the increase of starch-based foods in the diet, increased prevalence of infectious disease as a result of increased population density and sedentism, and an increase in nutritional disorders because of reduced diversity and nutritional content of some agricultural products (Larsen 1995, 187–8, 198–9).

The suggested general improvement in health after the Badarian period is most likely nutritional in origin as there is evidence for dietary diversification throughout the Predynastic Period. Greene's (2006, 39) review of recent evidence suggests that a variety of new fruits and vegetables appeared during the Predynastic Period including those rich in iron such as pea, lentil and watermelon. A greater bioavailability of iron may explain why the prevalence of porotic hyperostosis and cribra orbitalia decreased after the Badarian period. There is no firm evidence of increased meat consumption but it is plausible that as agriculture became better established within the Nile Valley animal protein became a more regular part of the diet. Beer, made from fermenting barley, was also another important addition to the mid Predynastic diet, as it was nutritionally-rich, contained vitamins, protein and starch, and had disinfecting properties (Greene 2006, 54; Samuel 1993, 161–2). The earliest evidence comes from beer residues found in a brewery at Hierakonpolis, dating to the transition between the Nagada I and Nagada II periods (Geller 1992, 23). Along with bread, beer became a dietary staple for the ancient Egyptians. Perhaps we should also consider that as agriculture intensified and became better established in the Nile valley, people were increasingly able to produce food surplus which would have brought greater nutritional security against unpredictable Nile flooding and thus alleviated severe nutritional stress. The large reduction in LEH prevalence observed after the Badarian period signifies that fewer children were suffering from severe growth disruptions which could have been caused by nutritional stress.

It is more difficult to explain the second temporal change in stress marker prevalence seen in Fig. 10.5–7. After the mid Predynastic-Protodynastic, the prevalence of porotic hyperostosis and LEH increased, but there was a decrease in cribra orbitalia prevalence. However, only the LEH increase is of some magnitude and very close to statistical significance. This result must be viewed with caution because the average number of scorable teeth per individual also increased after the mid Predynastic-Protodynastic (Table 10.3), meaning that LEH had an increased chance of being observed; but if LEH prevalence did increase to some extent, it might suggest a decline in overall health between the Nagada I/II and Early Dynastic periods.

Urbanisation offers the most plausible explanation for this decline in health. There is a well-established link between health and urbanisation among both ancient and modern societies. Population aggregation favours the spread of infectious diseases. Urbanism can be accompanied by decreased sanitation (Kjellstrom 2008, 11–12) and increased potential for resource competition between individuals. There is some evidence for a change in the pace and pattern of urbanisation in the Protodynastic Period (Nagada III) in Egypt, the period in which the decline in health is observed, with a noticible increase in the density and tightness of settlement evident at Hierakonpolis (Hoffman *et al.* 1986, 184–5). The increase in population density that this suggests would have increased the potential for disease spread and thus the risk of disruptions in child growth that LEH represents. The sites used for the Protodynastic-

Time period	Average number of scorable posterior teeth per individual
Early Predynastic (El-Badari)	12.93
Mid Predynastic-Protodynastic (Hierakonpolis, Nagada B and Nagada T)	3.55
Protodynastic-Early Dynastic (Tarkhan and Abydos)	9.32

Table 10.3: The average number of scorable posterior teeth per individual, by time period.

Early Dynastic time period in this study were important urban centres around the time of state formation, i.e. Tarkhan (Grajetzki 2004, 5) and Memphis (presumably where the individuals buried at Abydos lived for a large proportion of the year because it was the state capital). The site of This (just north of Abydos), the capital of one of Kemp's 'proto-states' around the time of state formation, must also have been a significant urban centre and an important residence for people associated with the royal family (*pers. comm.* Dr K. E. Spence).

One caveat is that it is solely the Abydos sample which is contributing to the increase in LEH prevalence. Perhaps this indicates that the effects of urbanisation on health depended on the location; it would be expected that Memphis, as the capital, would have been more densely populated than Tarkhan, and Tarkhan was probably not as densely populated during the Protodynastic/Nagada III period as regions further south in Upper Egypt, such as This. Clearly this is an issue that needs more detailed study using more collections of skeletal material from this time period.

Social Status

A primary aim of this paper is to test for a correlation between social status and health. Of particular interest are the two higher-status groups from cemetery T at Nagada and Abydos. Table 10.4 shows the prevalences and average severities for each of the three stress markers in all populations. A comparison between cemetery T and the 'middle-class' group from cemetery B reveals that high social status did not necessarily confer good health; such a comparison minimises environmental differences between the groups so that the effects of social status on health can be assessed more accurately. There is little or no differentiation in either porotic hyperostosis or cribra orbitalia prevalence or average severity between cemeteries T and B. Cemetery T has a slightly higher LEH prevalence, which is in contrast to what you might expect. Differential tooth preservation between the groups is unlikely to have had a large effect on the observed differences as it was cemetery B that had a higher number of scorable posterior teeth per individual and therefore the higher chance of LEH being observed. When all results are considered together, it is apparent that individuals from the higher-status cemetery T did not benefit from a better level of health than those from the lower-status cemetery B and, in fact, it could be tentatively suggested that their health was poorer.

The most likely reason for high-status elites having similar stress marker frequencies as lower-status individuals is their common environment. Nagada was an important urban centre during the development of the Egyptian state, and in fact was one of the proto-states put forward by Kemp (2006, 76). It is plausible that both groups living in the Nagada region would have been subjected to the same health risks that living in an urban environment entailed, discussed earlier. But, if

Archaeological context	PH prevalence (%)	PH average severity (scores 0–4)	CO prevalence (%)	CO average severity (scores 0–4)	LEH prevalence (%)
El-Badari	50	1.5	30	1.1	63
Hierakonpolis	28	1.2	28	1.1	31
Nagada B	8	0.8	20	1.0	25
Nagada T	8	0.8	22	0.8	33
Tarkhan	20	1.1	28	1.1	18
Abydos	19	0.8	17	0.6	71

Table 10.4: The percentage of individuals with porotic hyperostosis, cribra orbitalia (severity score 2 or above) and linear enamel hypoplasia (posterior teeth only), and the average severity score of porotic hyperostosis and cribra orbitalia in each population.

porotic hyperostosis and cribra orbitalia are indeed caused by iron-defiency anaemia, it is surprising that they did not occur at significantly lower prevalences among the cemetery T individuals. One would expect that as children they would have had access to a more nutritionally-rich diet with more iron-rich foods. Even if the anaemia was caused predominantly by parasitic disease rather than dietary deficency in iron, it would still be expected that the cemetery T group would be able to buffer themselves more effectively against this threat from their physical environment.

The Abydos group have either the lowest or among the lowest porotic hyperostosis and cribra orbitalia prevalences and severities. In particular, they are lower than Tarkhan, the closest group temporally and which most likely represents a range of different social classes (low values of cribra orbitalia and porotic hyperostosis were also found by Keita and Boyce (2006, 68) using the same material from Abydos). However, in contrast LEH prevalence is very high. As mentioned earlier, there was differential tooth preservation between populations, but a figure of 71% of individuals with at least one tooth with LEH is still high for any population. Overall, this suggests that the people buried at Abydos did not have as good a level of health as might be expected given their apparent special status.

Moreover, the disparity between the different stress markers could reflect differences in their underlying causes. Perhaps these individuals received better food resources because of their enhanced family status, explaining the low porotic hyperostosis and cribra orbitalia rates, but were still predisposed to high disease levels because they lived in a high-density settlement. Under this scenario, the LEH could have been caused predominantly by high infectious disease rates associated with living in an increasingly urban environment. Evidence from later Dynastic tomb scenes certainly indicates that high status individuals would have eaten well and that their diet would have provided adequate nutrients (including enough iron) to ensure good health (Duhig 2000, 4). That high status individuals 'ate well' is also indicated by some relief and sculptural depictions of tomb owners in which they are portrayed as being overweight (Darby *et al.* 1977, 59–60).

Conclusions

This study has measured skeletal stress markers caused by disease and malnutrition to quantify health differences between populations occupying Egypt during the emergence and formation of the state. The results have suggested a temporal change in health throughout the Predynastic and Early Dynastic periods. After initially high levels of childhood skeletal stress apparent among the first agriculturalists, levels decreased in the mid Predynastic, and it has been suggested that this could have been due to dietary diversifiation. Skeletal stress then increased in the Protodynastic, possibly due to the negative effects of urbanisation on health. The period of political unification in Egypt appears to have been a difficult time for its inhabitants. The results have also suggested that high social status did not necessarily confer better health on individuals in early Egypt and it has been tentatively suggested that urbanisation negatively affected the health of groups regardless of their perceived social status.

The relationship between health and the environment is complex and there are obviously limitations in what skeletal stress markers can reveal about the physical stresses that individuals suffered during their lifetimes. Multiple interpretations are also possible from the measurement of stress marker frequencies as their exact causes are still debated, but by linking this data closely with other archaeological evidence, the most important and likely causes of any observed differences can be suggested with much greater confidence.

The results and conclusions of this study have raised several issues that need to be addressed in more detail in future research. More skeletal data could be incorporated into the study using material from other collections, including that held at the Natural History Museum in London and that which has been recently excavated from sites such as Hierakonpolis and Abydos. In particular, work should focus on increasing sample sizes of LEH measurements using recently excavated material which has better levels of tooth preservation than material excavated during Petrie's time; this would allow more accurate conclusions to be made regarding LEH prevalence over time and between different social groups. Moreover, it is hoped that this study will encourage further research into the effects of urbanisation on health and whether it was experienced in the same way by everyone during state formation, as well as a closer examination of the relationship between social status and health, particularly in the later periods of Egyptian history where we have more archaeological evidence available for reconstructing social status.

Acknowledgements

I would like to thank my supervisors Dr Kate Spence and Dr Jay Stock for their advice and support throughout, and for reading drafts of this paper. Thanks also goes to Dr Marta Mirazon Lahr, Director of the Duckworth Laboratory in Cambridge, and Maggie Bellatti for allowing me access to the skeletal material. I would also like to acknowledge Daniel Strange and Lucy Musselwhite for proofreading and technical assistance. Finally, thank you to the whole CRE XIII committee for creating such a welcoming environment in which to present and discuss research.

References

Allen, J. (2002) *The Heqanakht Papyri*. New York, Metropolitan Museum of Art.

Anderson, W. (1992) Badarian burials: evidence of social inequality in Middle Egypt during the early Predynastic era. *Journal of the American Research Center in Egypt* 29, 51–66.

Bard, K. A. (1994) *From Farmers to Pharaohs: Mortuary Evidence for the Rise of Complex Society in Egypt*. Sheffield, Sheffield Academic Press.

Bard, K. A. (2002) The emergence of the Egyptian state (*c.* 3200–2686 BC). In I. Shaw (ed.) *The Oxford History of Ancient Egypt*, 61–88. Oxford, Oxford University Press.

Bard, K. A. (2008) *An Introduction to the Archaeology of Ancient Egypt*. Oxford, Blackwell Publishing.

Baumgartel, E. (1970) *Petrie's Naqada Excavation A Supplement*. London, Quaritch.

Bestock, L. (2007) *The Development of Royal Funerary Cult at Abydos: Two New Funerary Enclosures from the Reigh of Aha*. Unpublished thesis, New York University.

Brunton, G. and Caton-Thompson, G. (1928) *The Badarian Civilisation and Predynastic Remains Near Badari*. Publications of the Egyptian Research Account and British School of Archaeology in Egypt 46. London, Quaritch.

Buikstra, J. E. and Ubelaker, D. H. (eds) (1994) *Standards for Data Collection from Human Skeletal Remains*. Fayetteville, Arkansas Archaeological Survey.

Case, H. and Crowfoot Payne, J. (1962) Tomb 100: The decorated tomb at Hierakonpolis. *Journal of Egyptian Archaeology* 48, 5–18.

Cook, D. C. (1981) Mortality, age-structure and status in the interpretation of stress indicators in Prehistoric skeletons: a dental example from the Lower Illinois Valley. In R. Chapman and K. Randsborg (eds) *The Archaeology of Death*, 133–44. Cambridge, Cambridge University Press.

Crooks, D. L. (1995) American children at risk: Poverty and its consequences for children's health, growth, and school achievement. *American Journal of Physical Anthropology* 38 (S2), 57–86.

Cucina, A. and Işcan, Y. M. (1997) Assessment of enamel hypoplasia in a high status burial site. *American Journal of Human Biology* 9 (2), 213–222.

Darby, W. J., Ghalioungui, P. and Grivetti, L. (1977) *Food: The Gift of Osiris*, Vol. 1. London, Academic Press.

Deelder, A. M., Miller, R. L., De Jonge, N. and Krijger, F. W. (1990) Detection of schistosome antigen in mummies. *Lancet* 335, 724–5.

Duhig, C. (2000) *They Are Eating People Here! Skeletal Indicators of Stress in the Egyptian First Intermediate Period*. Unpublished thesis, University of Cambridge.

Facchini, F., Rastelli, E. and Brasili, P. (2004) Cribra orbitalia and cribra cranii in Roman skeletal remains from the Ravenna area and Rimini (I–IV century AD). *International Journal of Osteoarchaeology* 14 (2), 126–136.

Geller, J. (1992) From prehistory to history: beer in Egypt. In R. Friedman and B. Adams (eds.) *The Followers of Horus: Studies Dedicated to Michael Allen Hoffman 1944–1990*, 19–26. Oxford, Oxbow Books.

Goodman, A. H. and Rose, J. C. (1990) Assessment of systemic physiological perturbations from dental enamel hypoplasias and associated histological structures. *Yearbook of Physical Anthropology* 33 (S11), 59–110.

Grajetzki, W. (2004) *Tarkhan: A Cemetery at the Time of Egyptian State Formation*. London, Golden House Publications.

Greene, T. R. (2006) *Diet and Dental Health in Predynastic Egypt: A Comparison of Hierkonpolis and Naqada*. Unpublished thesis, University of Alaska Fairbanks.

Hassan, F.A. (1988) The Predynastic of Egypt. *Journal of World Prehistory* 2(2), 135–85.

Hoffman, M. A., Hamroush, H. A. and Allen, R. O. (1986) A model of urban development for the Hierakonpolis region from Predynastic through Old Kingdom times. *Journal of the American Research Center in Egypt* 23, 175–87.

Keita, S. O. Y. (2003) A study of vault porosities in early Upper Egypt from the Badarian through Dynasty I. *World Archaeology* 35 (2), 210–222.

Keita, S.O.Y. and Boyce, A. J. (2001) Diachronic patterns of dental hypoplasias and vault pororosities during the Predynastic in the Naqada region, Upper Egypt. *American Journal of Human Biology* 13, 733–743.

Keita, S. O. Y. and Boyce, A. J. (2006) Variation in porotic hyperostosis in the royal cemetery complex at Abydos, Upper Egypt: a social interpretation. *Antiquity* 80, 64–73.

Kemp, B. J. (1966) Abydos and the royal tombs of the First Dynasty. *Journal of Egyptian Archaeology* 52, 13–22.

Kemp, B. J. (1967) The Egyptian 1st Dynasty royal cemetery. *Antiquity* 41, 22–32.

Kemp, B. J. (1973) Photographs of the decorated tomb at Hierakonpolis. *Journal of Egyptian Archaeology* 59, 36–43.

Kemp, B. J. (2006) *Ancient Egypt: Anatomy of a Civilisation*. London, Routledge.

Kjellstrom, T. (2008) *Our Cities, Our Health, Our Future: Acting on Social Determinants for Health Equity in Urban Settings*. Kobe, WHO Centre for Health Development.

Kumar, A. (2009) *Health at Hierakonpolis, a Predynastic settlement in Upper Egypt*. Unpublished thesis, University of Arkansas.

Larsen, C. S. (1995) Biological changes in human populations with agriculture. *Annual Review of Anthropology* 24, 185–213.

Larsen, C. S. (1997) *Bioarchaeology : Interpreting Behavior from the Human Skeleton*. Cambridge, Cambridge University Press.

Lovell, N. C. and Whyte, I. (1999) Patterns of dental enamel defects at ancient Mendes, Egypt. *American Journal of Physical Anthropology* 110 (1), 69–80.

Midant-Reynes, B. (2000) *The Prehistory of Egypt*. Oxford, Blackwell Publishing.

O'Connor, D. (2009) *Abydos: Egypt's First Pharaohs and the Cult of Osiris*. London, Thames & Hudson.

Petrie, W. M. F. (1914) *Tarkhan II*. Publications of the Egyptian Research Account and British School of Archaeology in Egypt 26. London, Quaritch.

Petrie, W. M. F. (1924) *Tombs of the Courtiers and Oxyrhynkhos*. Publications of the Egyptian Research Account and British School of Archaeology in Egypt 37. London, Quaritch.

Petrie, W. M. F. and Quibell, B. A. (1896) *Naqada and Ballas*. Publications of the Egyptian Research Account and British School of Archaeology in Egypt I. London, Quaritch.

Quibell, B. A. (1900) *Hierakonpolis I*. Publications of the Egyptian Research Account and British School of Archaeology in Egypt 4. London, Quaritch.

Quibell, B. A. and Green, F. W. (1902) *Hierakonpolis II*. Publications of the Egyptian Research Account and British School of Archaeology in Egypt 5. London, Quaritch.

Robb, J., Bigazzi, R., Lazzarini, L., Scarsini, C. and Sonego, F. (2001) Social 'status' and biological 'status': a comparison of grave goods and skeletal indicators from Pontecagnano. *American Journal of Physical Anthropology* 115, 213–22.

Samuel, D. (1993) Cereal foods and nutrition in ancient Egypt. In W. V. Davies and R. Walker (eds) *Biological Anthropology and the Study of Ancient Egypt*, 156–64. London, British Museum Press.

Starling, A. P. (2005) *Dental Indicators of Health and Stress in Ancient Egypt and Nubia*. Unpublished thesis, University of Cambridge.

Starling, A. P. and Stock, J. T. (2007) Dental indicators of health and stress in early Egyptian and Nubian agriculturalists: a difficult transition and gradual recovery. *American Journal of Physical Anthropology* 134 (4), 520–258.

Stuart-Macadam, P. (1985) Porotic hyperostosis: representative of a childhood condition. *American Journal of Physical Anthropology* 66, 391–98.

Stuart-Macadam, P. (1989) Porotic hyperostosis: relationship between orbital and vault lesions. *American Journal of Physical Anthropology* 80 (2), 187–193.

Trigger, B. G. (1983) The rise of Egyptian civilisation. In B. G. Trigger, B. J. Kemp, D. O'Connor and A. B. Lloyd (eds) *Ancient Egypt: A Social History*, 1–70. Cambridge, Cambridge University Press.

Valbelle, D. (1997) Craftsmen. In S. Donadoni (ed.) *The Egyptians,* 31–59. Chicago, University of Chicago Press.

Walker, P. L., Bathurst, R. R., Richman, R., Gjerdrum, T. and Andrushko, V. A. (2009) The causes of porotic hyperostosis and cribra orbitalia: a reappraisal of the iron-deficiency-anemia hypothesis. *American Journal of Physical Anthropology* 139 (2), 109–125.

Wengrow, D. (2006) *The Archaeology of Early Egypt: Social Transformations in North-East Africa, 10,000 to 2650 BC.* Cambridge, Cambridge University Press.

White, T. D, and Folkens, P. A. (2005) *The Human Bone Manual.* Amsterdam, Elsevier Academic Press.

Wilkinson, T. A. H. (2000) Political unification: towards a reconstruction. *Mitteilungen des Deutschen Archäologischen Instituts Abteilung Kairo* 56, 377–95.

Zakrzewski, S. R. (2003) Variation in ancient Egyptian stature and body proportions. *American Journal of Physical Anthropology* 121 (3), 219–229.

11

The Medjay leaders of the New Kingdom

Rune Olsen

Introduction

Not much is known about the term Medjay before the New Kingdom. Early examples from the Old and Middle Kingdoms, such as the 6th dynasty autobiography of Weni (Lictheim 1973, 19) and the 12th dynasty Semnah Dispatches (Smither 1945) apply the term for an area in Nubia and its inhabitants. During the Second Intermediate Period the Medjay appear as Nubian mercenaries assisting the Egyptian forces under Kamose and Ahmose in their war against the Hyksos rulers (Goedicke 1995, 49). When the latter were finally expelled from Egypt the Medjay settled in the country and by the mid-18th dynasty they are attested in connection with the royal tombs in the Valley of the Kings (Černý 1973, 261). Two centuries later they seem to have very little in common with the Medjay of the Old and Middle Kingdoms.

During the New Kingdom, the word Medjay becomes a title, distinct from the ethnic appellation of the Nubian mercenary group, and the term could thus designate Nubians and Egyptians alike. This is also the case for the title Medjay leader (*ḥry Mḏ3yw*), though the majority of the title bearers seem to have been Egyptian (Černý 1973, 261–262). The Medjay and their leaders have usually been referred to as a police force, but what exactly did their function entail?

The aim of the present article is to shed light on the title of Medjay leader and the functions and areas of responsibility with which it is associated. For this purpose, all published material with reference to the title (mainly written documents on ostraca and papyri, but also tomb decorations and stelae) has been examined. This analysis produced a list of 32 individuals bearing the title, some of which are only known from a single source while others can be found in a variety of sources covering their entire career. The article exclusively focuses on the Medjay leaders due to the fact that they are prominently represented in the sources, as opposed to their subordinates, the Medjay.

Material

The archaeological material which involves the Medjay leaders exclusively derives from the New Kingdom, the majority being written documents, which date to the Ramesside Period.

This is mainly due to the discovery and excavation of the workmen's village of Deir el-Medina that yielded a multitude of documents, without which relevant information would have been almost non-existent.

The material is also geographically limited, as only two sources mention Medjay leaders outside the Theban area: part of the tomb decoration of Menkheperreseneb (TT86) depicts a Medjay leader of Coptos, and the tomb of Mahu (AT9), who was the Medjay leader of Amarna. The lack of material from the rest of Egypt makes a focus on Thebes a necessity, or rather western Thebes as most of the sources are directly from or have a contextual relation to this area. The existence of the two aforementioned tombs confirms that the title was not only local to the Theban area, however, nothing is known of any Medjay leaders in other places than Thebes, Coptos and Amarna.

The written documents are comprised of no less than 66 ostraca and 23 papyri. As mentioned above, all the documents are from the Theban area and all except one date to the period after the 18th dynasty. Sources concerning the 18th dynasty Medjay leaders are on the other hand limited to tombs, stelae or funerary cones, the information of which requires a high degree of interpretation. Only 5 of the 32 named Medjay leaders belong exclusively to the 18th dynasty. The remaining 27 are from the 19th or 20th dynasties (Fig. 11.1). Thus, in accordance with the available material, any thorough analysis of the office of Medjay leader has to be limited to the Ramesside Period. The bulk of the material is from Deir el-Medina, which means that the Medjay leaders for the most part were connected in some way to the village.

The classification and division of the written documents into categories, defined by the present author, provide an outline of the responsibilities and functions of the Medjay leaders. As mentioned earlier, the Medjay and their leaders are often regarded as a police force, however, there seems to be surprisingly little actual 'police work' to be found in the sources. If they were a police force, one would have expected a report of the arrest of thieves, an investigation of a murder, or at least an account of some attempt to break into the Valley of the Kings. If any such report existed, one would assume that the Medjay leaders would have been mentioned, but that is not the case. Instead, the 3 most extensive document categories by far are 'Communication', 'Distribution Lists' and 'Legal Procedures'.

'Communication' contains documents describing messages, announcements and letters to or from the inhabitants of Deir el-Medina, 'Distribution Lists' include descriptions of rations, salaries and taxes, while 'Legal Procedures' consist of lawsuits and disputes between people from the workmen's village. Indeed, one would think that such 'court cases' could sometimes fall under the jurisdiction of the police, but the Medjay leaders only play a peripheral role in these documents.

Another substantial category is the 'Middlemen', which contain documents describing private trade agreements, arranged by the Medjay leaders on behalf of the villagers and the surrounding world. The remaining categories, which will not be touched upon in this article, are: 'Oracles', 'Name lists', 'Payments and trade', 'Lists of debt', 'Fragments' and 'Family relations'.

The Medjay leaders in the 18th dynasty

The earliest source to mention a Medjay leader is the Leiden F 1996/1.1 papyrus (Demarée 1999, 77–78), which is a letter from the Medjay leader Didu to the Medjay Nebseny, in which Didu reproaches his subordinate for not doing as he had been told. The letter does not convey

Medjay leader chronology

Thutmose III + Amenhotep II		?: Didu		
Thutmose IV + Amenhotep III		?: Nebamun	?: Teri	?: Turo
Ahkenaten		?: Mahu		
Tutankhamun				
Horemheb		7(?): Miniwy		
Rameses I				
Sety I	?: Mentuemheb			
Rameses II	15 (c.): Pashed 66: Nakhtmin	?: Miniwy ?: Sobekhotep ?: Khaemnun	36: Nakhtsobek ?: Sobekmose	?: Mentuturech
Merenptah		8: Hori		
Sety II	6: Nakhtmin	6: ***Mentumose***		
Siptah				
Sethnakht		*c. 50 years*		
Rameses III	?: Pentaweret 29: Nebsemen		?: Wia 31:Nebsemen s. Pacher	20: Khonsuemheb
Rameses IV				
Rameses V		1: ***Mentumose***		
Rameses VI	*c. 30 years*			*c. 44 years*
Rameses VII				
Rameses VIII				
Rameses IX	2: Nebsemen 4-16: Bakinwerenel 16: Pawero + Mentukhepeshef + Nesyamon ?: Sermonthu		17: Sahenefer	7: Khonsuemheb 17: Nakhtemhatef ?:Pairy
Rameses X	*c. 21 years*		*c. 25 years*	
Rameses XI	15: Pawero + Sermonthu 12-15: Amenwahsu		19: Nesyamon ?: Anubisnakhte	?: Amenemipet

Numbers are regnal years of the king
Numbers are approximate length of Medjay leader career

Figure 11.1: Chronological table of all the named Medjay leaders, inspired by a similar table done by Černý (1973, 269).

any detailed information on the office of 'Medjay leader' and neither do the two other sources in which Didu is mentioned. At any rate, he can in all probability be identified as the owner of TT200, from which a funerary cone bearing Didu's name and titles, such as 'Overseer of Western Thebes', most likely originates. However, his tomb inscription does not mention the title 'Medjay leader' and the tomb scenes only depict Didu's earlier career and titles as a soldier. The same titles, along with 'Medjay leader', are indeed found on the funerary cone, but nothing else is written on it. The only thing linking the funerary cone and the letter with the tomb, besides the name Didu, is a tomb scene depicting a standard with a gazelle bearing the feather of Maat, or 'truth', on its back. This standard might be the symbol of the Medjay in Thebes, as it is also depicted in TT90, where it is presented to the tomb owner, Nebamun, along with the office of 'Medjay leader' (Garis Davies 1923, IX–XXXVIII). Both standard and office are given by royal decree through a royal scribe by the name of Iwny.

Another Medjay leader, Teri, is represented in the tomb scene behind Nebamun, standing with a line of men, probably the subordinate Medjay, the first of which, the '*Idnw* Medjay', Mana, is holding the aforementioned gazelle standard. This indicates that this standard is the official heraldry of the Medjay of Western Thebes and/or the Necropolis, including the Valley of the Kings. It is worth noting that Nebamun received the title after a long career in the army and navy. His many titles include 'Royal adjutant', 'The head of many soldiers', 'Standard bearer for the royal ship, Mery-Amun', 'Captain for the archers' and 'Veteran-soldier', which is equal to having received the 'Golden fly of valour'. Interestingly, Nebamun was not 'Overseer of Western Thebes' (presumably a title of high administrative responsibility) like Didu, but neither is any other Medjay leader. This suggests that the earliest 18th dynasty Medjay leaders were given the responsibility of leading the Medjay only at the end of their career, perhaps as preparation for retirement.

In TT86, belonging to a man called Menkheperreseneb (Garis Davies 1933, IX) who was High Priest of Amun during the reign of Thutmose III, several officials with various titles are illustrated as they approach him to pay tribute. One of these is a Medjay leader of Coptos:

( *ḥry Mḏ3yw n Gbtw*). He is not mentioned by name, but it seems clear that he must have been responsible for the area in or around Coptos. He was probably also part of the mining expeditions, which set off from Coptos via Wadi Hammamat to the Eastern Desert where Egyptian copper and gold could be mined (Bradbury 1988, 132). In the tomb scene the Medjay leader has prostrated himself on the ground along with an 'Overseer of the gold lands of Coptos';

(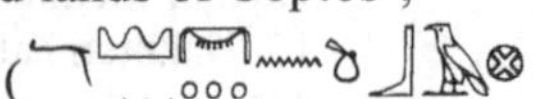 *Ỉmi-r3 ḫ3swt nbw n Gbtw*) in front of the High Priest of Amun. Since both individuals are from Coptos and as they both are prostrate before the High Priest, it may be interpreted that they are present in the same capacity. It is evident that the title 'Overseer of the gold lands' must have been responsible for the mining expeditions, and the Medjay leader could have been in charge of the security and protection on these expeditions.

In AT9 (Garis Davies 1906, XIV–XXIX), the only source in the material that is not linked to the Theban area, the tomb owner, Mahu, is depicted in various scenes evidently performing his duties as Medjay leader. However, the accompanying texts in the tomb decorations are not very informative as they are mostly titles and names, and at no point do they mention any official functions or responsibilities. In one scene Mahu delivers two men of 'the group from the foreign countries' to the vizier, but it is unclear why this is done. They could be criminals or trespassers on Egyptian territory, or even foreign officials. Whatever the case, it was clearly a moment Mahu wanted memorialized alongside scenes of worshipping Akhenaten and driving a chariot, which was a great privilege, for his eternal sleep. Fortunately, Mahu also had the standard of the Medjay of Akhetaten (Amarna) portrayed. It consists of a square featuring a man, most likely the king, in the typical Egyptian smiting-of-the-enemy position, holding a foe by the hair. The square is topped by a feather of Maat, which, along with the above-mentioned gazelle standard, suggests that the Medjay are identified by, and somehow connected to, that goddess or concept.

Geographical distribution

Apart from Mahu in Amarna and the unnamed person from Coptos, Thebes is the only location where the title 'Medjay leader' is attested. However, 5 variations of the title were in use in the area during the Ramesside Period, although no source mentions them all together.

The three most common of these are:

'Medjay leader of Thebes' ( *ḥry Mḏj3yw ḥr W3st*)

'Medjay leader of Western Thebes' ( *ḥry Mḏ3yw ḥr imnt niwt*)

'Medjay leader of the Necropolis ( *ḥry Mḏ3yw n p3-ḫr*)

These designations are more or less self-explanatory regarding the area the Medjay leaders were assigned and responsible for, the first being the city of Thebes itself, and the second the fertile part of the Theban West bank. The third must as a minimum refer to the areas of the Valley of the Kings and Deir el-Medina, but perhaps it includes all of the Theban Necropolis with private tombs and mortuary temples alike.

In ostracon Ashmolean Museum 0130 (Kitchen 1989, 304), which is a list of various officials from the reign of Rameses III, the first two entries are the 2 Medjay leaders of the Necropolis and the 2 Medjay leaders of the South:

( *ḥry Mḏ3yw 2 rsy*)

What exactly the title 'Medjay leader of the South' designated and where the titleholders' area of responsibility precisely was, is not known. It could be all of Egypt south of Thebes, or perhaps a certain and much more limited area south of the city. The usual number of Medjay leaders, including both Thebes and Western Thebes, in the Ramesside period was 2 (Davies 1994, 37). This is also true of the fifth title found during and after the reign of Rameses IX, the 'Medjay leader of the temple':

( *ḥry Mḏ3yw n t3 ḥwt*)

It is mentioned in a list on Papyrus Mayer A (Kitchen 1983b, 803–828). The temple referred to is probably the mortuary temple of Rameses III, Medinet Habu, as a large part of the administration for the West Bank at the end of the 20th dynasty actually moved inside the temple (Taylor 2000, 350). This was most likely done due to the increased threat of hostile Libyans in the western desert, but also due to internal political struggles. In any case, the result was that the number of both Medjay leaders and Medjay was doubled (Černý 1973, 270) and security was heightened.

Houses

The recto of Papyrus BM 10068 (Peet 1930, IX–XVI) concerns the tomb robberies during the reign of Rameses IX, but the verso is dated to the 12th year of Rameses XI (Helck 2002, 26), and it contains a registry of houses situated between the mortuary temples of Sety I and the settlement of Maiures. Two Medjay leaders and seven regular Medjay are mentioned in the list, which contains 182 houses and their owners. The interesting aspect about the list is that it provides some idea about the geographical location of these houses. The list is, according to Peet (1930, 82–87), organized from north to south, starting with the mortuary temple of Sety I. Between this temple and the Ramesseum allegedly stood 10 houses, two of which belonged to the Medjay named Wserankh and Hori. Between the Ramesseum and Medinet Habu were another 14 houses, mainly owned by priests. Between Medinet Habu and Maiures were the remaining 158 houses, two of which belonged to the Medjay leaders Nesyamon and Amenwahsu. Peet (1930, 84) describes how Herbert Winlock tried to find these houses in a continuing line from the Ramesseum to Medinet Habu and further south, without finding any remains. Winlock suggests that the list in P.BM 10068 would have taken a westward turn from Medinet Habu, and that the houses should rather be found in the area between the mortuary temple and Deir el-Medina, where, apparently, a French excavation found several houses from the same period (Peet 1930, 84).

"Police Work"

There are only two recorded instances of what can be labelled 'Police Work' for the Medjay leaders. The first is on ostracon Florence 2621 (Allam 1973, 36–39; Kitchen 1983a, 478–480), which dates to the 21st year of Rameses III. The text is unfortunately not complete, but from what is left it becomes clear that it is an investigation of a plundered tomb belonging to a man called Amonemipet. It recounts, in short, that the Medjay leader Mentumose descended and inspected the tomb and informed officials waiting above that, apart from a coffin, there was nothing to be found in it. It is worth noting that Mentumose was not the leading investigator, but only part of the inspection group.

The second example dates to the late 20th dynasty in a group of papyri that describe the famous tomb robberies including, for example, papyrus BM 10068 and the Abbott Papyrus (Peet 1930, I–IV). In Papyrus Mayer A (Kitchen 1983b, 803–828) the Medjay leader Nesyamun claims to have arrested no less than 6 robbers by himself. This act, bordering the heroic, unfortunately becomes a bit diminished as Nesyamun is revealed to have been an accomplice to the robberies himself, and only escapes severe punishment by naming the other conspirators.

The remainder of the "police work" performed by the Medjay leaders in the Tomb Robbery Documents classified as, like in the case of Mentumose, passive members of affiliation with a committee or group, which was always led by a higher ranking official.

The documents above only amount to two out of a total of 89, which means that investigating and arresting criminals cannot have been the primary function of the Medjay leaders. However, if they were not policemen in that sense, their primary task must have been something else.

Communication

The Medjay leaders were among the few who had access to the village of Deir el-Medina and as such their job was to convey communication between the workers and the outside world. They did this by delivering letters and oral messages, which were later recorded in detail by the workers. A few of these will be presented here. Ostracon Cairo CG. 25237 (Kitchen 1980, 529–530) from the reign of Merenptah reads:

> *'Year 8, 2nd month of* ***Akhet****, day 13. On this day the scribe Inpuemhep, the scribe Paser, the Medjay leader Nakhtmin and the Medjay leader Hori arrived and said: "The Overseer of craftsmen, Rema, arrived to the 'Sealed' of the Necropolis". The Captains were brought before him and he said to them: "Pharaoh, L.P.H., has sent the vizier, Pensekhemet, the Overseer of the Treasury, Meryptah, and scribe of the House of Gold, Hui". And they arrived at the entrance of the valley with Pharaoh's letter.'* (Author's translation)

The first impression of the scribes and Medjay leaders is that they are rather redundant. They proclaim the arrival of Rema and bring the captains of the workers before him, at which point Rema announces the immediate arrival of the vizier and his high ranking officials. It would have been easier to let Rema find the captains himself, or just pass on his message, but in this context it is important to remember the secluded and special status of the village. Indeed, very few people from the outside had access to it, and all had to register with the scribes and the Medjay leaders at the 'Sealed of the Necropolis' (*ẖtm n p3-ẖr*) (Ventura 1986, 83–106). The 'Sealed' was located somewhere along the path leading from Deir el-Medina down to the Ramesseum (McDowell 1990, 93–94), as this was the main access road to the village. Its exact location and function is still unknown, but it was certainly a major checkpoint for anyone wishing admittance. The privilege of being part of this control point provided the Medjay leaders quite a bit of bureaucratic power and they made good use of it by acting as middlemen in trade relations between the workers and the outside world (discussed in detail below).

In the 29th regnal year of Rameses III the workers of Deir el-Medina went on strike, because they apparently no longer received their rations. This event is described in detail on the famous Strike Papyrus (Gardiner 1948, 45–58). An interesting passage of the text falls into the document category 'Communication'. Here the vizier sends a message to the workers using the Medjay leader Nebsemen son of Panehsy:

> *'Year 29, 4th month of* ***Peret****, day 28. The vizier Ta travelled north after he had taken the gods of the South to the Sed Festival. The Medjay leader Nebsemen, son of Panehsy, arrived to tell the three captains and the workers, while they were standing by 'The Sealed' of the Necropolis. "Thus says the vizier: "Was it for no reasons that I did not come to you? It was not because there was nothing to bring you that I did not come. Concerning your saying "Do not take our rations", am I the vizier who was appointed to take away (from you)?"""'* (Author's translation)

It is peculiar that the vizier himself did not deliver the message. He had obviously been to Thebes, but had not set aside the time for a visit to or inspection of the village, which he would have been expected to do, seeing that he had the overall responsibility of the Necropolis. As Frandsen (1990, 93–105) explains it, the text gives the impression that the vizier was afraid of confronting the workers. Rather, he preferred to send Nebsemen with the cryptic (but grammatically interesting) message. The fact that he sent a Medjay leader indicates that they were in direct contact, and at hand to execute his commands.

Two documents commemorate the announcement of the death of the pharaoh. The first is ostracon Cairo CG 25515 (Černý 1930, 11*–12*; VIII–IX), a journal of workdays and days of rest, but it also includes the following line:

> *'1st month of* ***Peret****, day 19. The day where the Medjay leader Nakhtmin arrived to tell that the Falcon, Sety II, has flown up to the sky. Another has risen in his stead.'* (Author's translation)

The second, P. Turin Cat. 1946 and P. Turin Cat. 1949 (Černý 1936, 110–111), documents the announcement of the death of Rameses III, which happened in his 32nd regnal year. The task of announcing his death was given to Mentumose, who at the time would have been the senior of the two Medjay leaders. When the events in ostracon Cairo CG 25515 took place he would have been the junior while Nakhtmin was the senior. The relevant part of the Turin Papyrus reads:

> *'3rd month of* ***Shemu****, day 16 at this place. The day where the Medjay leader Mentumose arrived to tell the people of the Necropolis that the Falcon of (His) Majesty, king Usermaatra Meriamun, son of Ra, Rameses Hekaiunu, L.P.H., has flown to heaven, and that king Usermaatra Setepenamun, son of Ra, Rameses Meriamun, L.P.H., the ruler, has seated himself on the throne of Ra (in) his place. And the workers of the Necropolis spend the day in joy until (sun-) set.'* (Author's translation)

Unlike the message delivered in ostracon Cairo CG. 25237 the death of a pharaoh was important enough to let the Medjay leaders convey the news directly to the inhabitants of Deir el-Medina, instead of having them find the captains of the workers and bring them to the 'Sealed of the Necropolis'.

Legal Procedures and distribution lists

The documents of '*Legal Procedures*' are in themselves very interesting in terms of content, but the role of the Medjay leaders is always limited to the function of witnesses, jury members or being part of the local '*qnbt*', the local court (Vleeming 1982, 183). Except, of course, when a Medjay leader himself was taken to court by a worker of Deir el-Medina, a point that will be discussed further below.

The Medjay leaders often feature in documents dealing with the distribution of rations to the workers, but it is unclear whether they did the actual distributing themselves or were only present as a security measure. They are, however, often mentioned together with scribes and could have been with them to ensure their safety from potentially angry and dissatisfied workers. It is further possible that the Medjay leaders were present to ensure that the distribution was done correctly and without any 'tampering' with the rations.

The distribution lists also concern the salary of the Medjay leaders, which was paid in grain, provided by the same administration that paid the workers of Deir el-Medina. This means that the Medjay leaders were under the authority of the Necropolis administration, which in turn was led by the vizier. The salary is described on one document, P. BM 9997 (Kitchen 1989, 389–394), which shows that the Medjay leaders at the end of the 20th dynasty were paid a total of 72 *khar* (1 *khar* is about 75 litres grain (Warburton 1997, 20)). Calculations show that one person consumes about 1 *khar* each month (Haring 1997, 177). However, the Medjay leaders did not receive an equal amount of grain and the document does not reveal whether it was a monthly or yearly salary. Still, the Medjay leaders were not solely dependent on their salary from the administration. As ostracon IFAO 0855 (Černý 1972, 52; XVI) reveals, the Medjay leaders also had their own fields, but a more common, and probably more lucrative, income source was from providing the inhabitants of Deir el-Medina with goods as middlemen.

Middlemen

As has already been mentioned, the Medjay leaders were some of the few who had access to the workmen's village and as such were able to profit from this privilege. As middlemen, the Medjay leaders were the source to which the inhabitants of Deir el-Medina turned when they wished to procure products that the administration did not provide them with, as seen, for example, in ostracon Turin N. 57456 (López 1984, TAV. 155–155a).

Several documents, for example ostracon DeM 0261 (Kitchen 1983a, 580) and ostracon UC 39649 (Kitchen 1983b, 869–870), also show that the Medjay leaders were storing possessions for the workers, presumably at the 'Sealed'. This can be seen as an expression of loyalty on the part of the Medjay leaders and as an expression of trust on the part of the workers.

Two documents reveal that the Medjay leaders were not exempt from being judged in front of the '*qnbt*'. In the first document, ostracon Torino 9611/57381 (Allam 1973, 68–71; Kitchen 1983a, 469–470), which is dated to year 18 of Rameses III, the worker Menna claims that the Medjay leader Mentumose, mentioned above, had taken his goods 11 years earlier to procure other commodities for him in return, but that this never happened and that Mentumose had still not returned them to Menna. Mentumose tried to turn the situation around by taking an oath of Amun, claiming that the fault was with Menna and that he (Mentumose) did indeed repay him. The Medjay leader then presented a list of a variety of products and their '*deben* value', but if this tactic succeeded in the short run, it was by no means the end of the legal issue.

About 18 years later, Menna again accused Mentumose with the same crime. The new lawsuit is depicted on ostracon OIM 12073 (Černý and Gardiner 1957, LXXVII) which is from the 4th year of Rameses IV reign. It describes how Mentumose was supposed to have arranged a purchase between Menna and an unnamed third party, and that Menna had complained about the missing result to the '*qnbt*' 3 times already. The Medjay leader maintained that he could not be held accountable for the inadequacy of a third person. However, in the end Mentumose conceded to pay the debt, which amounted to 65 *deben*, probably because Menna couldn't legally prosecute the unidentified third person (Manning *et al.* 1989, 122).

The reason why Mentumose did not tell Menna the name of this person is unknown, but Menna and other workmen appear to have used the Medjay leader as a middleman on several other occasions. This points to a special connection between the villagers and Mentumose, as they must have trusted him to correct his mistakes, even if this took several decades. The nature of this relationship is never explained in full, but it was rather unique and for that reason, if for none other, Mentumose appears in no less than a third of all documents mentioning Medjay leaders, and is thus the best known of the titleholders.

The Strike papyrus

The special relationship between Mentumose and the workers of Deir el-Medina is best revealed in Papyrus Turin Cat. 1880 (Gardiner 1948, 45–58), more commonly known as the Strike Papyrus. In the first of several relevant parts of the text, which is dated to day 12, 2nd month of *Peret*, year

29 of Rameses III, Mentumose is only sympathetic towards the workers and their situation. He offers to bring the mayor of Thebes, but what exactly he plans to do with him is unfortunately lost. Perhaps the Medjay leader only wants to bring the mayor in front of the workers so they can complain directly to the highest authority of the region, as the vizier evidently was not in the area, and when he did arrive two months later, he was unwilling to meet with them. This already seems an unusual initiative by a Medjay leader, but the local administration clearly hasn't thought it beyond the authority given to Mentumose. It is interesting to consider why Mentumose acts in this manner. He could easily have stood by and let the villagers handle the problem on their own, seeing that he wasn't a part of the actual village itself. He must have had an excuse or at least a motive for his way of handling the case, even more so when considering the next part of the text:

> *'Year 29, 2nd month of* ***Peret****, day 13 by the 'Sealed' of the Necropolis. The Medjay leader Mentumose says: "Look! I will tell you my opinion. Go up and gather your things, lock your doors and bring your wives and children, and I shall go in front of you to the temple of Menmaatra (Sety I), and I will let you sit (there) until morning."'* (Author's translation)

This suggestion has to be an expression of more than just common sympathy towards the workers. Mentumose chose sides in the conflict and probably went beyond what the administration would accept.

Reading between the lines in this part of the papyrus, the strike is not so much about vital provisions like grain, bread and water, but what the workers are actually asking for is clothing, ointments, fish and vegetables. They are hardly threatened by famine but only a lack of more luxurious commodities. In addition, the strike only started three days before the above-mentioned part of the text, i.e. on the tenth day (Gardiner 1948, 52). Every tenth day was a day off from work in the Valley of the Kings (Vleeming 1982, 183) and thus the strike cannot be labelled a true strike that particular day, since the workers were not supposed to be working. It becomes a real strike when the workers continue their 'sit down' the following days. The famine motive for the strike becomes further weakened by taking the regnal year into account. It is the 29th year of Rameses III's reign and the tomb of the king should in all likelihood already have been built. However, the words of the vizier given to the workers through the Medjay leader, Nebsemen son of Panehsy, should be noted, which show that the granaries two months later were in fact empty, or so the vizier claims. Whether this is true for every granary in Egypt, in the Theban area or only those which supplied Deir el-Medina remains a matter of debate. The question is whether the strike was instigated because the workers were bored and because they were used to a higher standard of luxury supply. If this is the case, then the actions of Mentumose become even harder to understand, unless he himself was a victim of the decreased supply.

Ostracon Cairo CG 25588 (Černý 1930, 54*; XLVI) and ostracon Cairo CG 25597 (Kitchen 1983b, 129) mention a worker by the name of Hori, which could potentially explain the problem, as he is described as the son of Mentumose. This could mean that the Medjay leader was married to the daughter of a workman, which is plausible seeing as the Medjay leaders were highly regarded and respected in the community, and was thus tied to the village to a greater degree. The trouble is that the two documents do not label Mentumose a Medjay leader, which could mean that it is an entirely different person with the same name. That being said, I have not come across any other document mentioning the name Mentumose without the Medjay leader title.

The initiative and actions of Mentumose does not seem to have destroyed his career (Frandsen 1990, 199) as he continues as a Medjay leader for several years afterwards, but he does seem to have been silenced by the administration, as he does not appear in the Strike Papyrus again.

The Medjay leaders

Based on the document analysis, labelling the Medjay leaders as 'Chiefs of Police' is not correct. The closest a Medjay leader comes to performing any form of 'police work' is as a subordinate member of an investigating committee. Only one document concerns the arrest of tomb robbers by a Medjay leader, but here the Medjay leader in question seems to have been implicated in the robbery himself. The 'police' aspect only appears in 2 documents, which in addition describe unusual circumstances (O. Florence 2621 and P. Mayer A), i.e. 2 of 89, which equals 2.25%. Though equally extraordinary, documents like the Strike Papyrus show that the Medjay leaders probably were under the direct command of the vizier and this affiliation to the highest official in the country might, in part, explain why the functions, roles and responsibilities of the Medjay leaders were of a more administrative character, rather than carrying out 'police work'.

In their role as mediators between the workmen's village and the outside world, the Medjay leaders had two primary functions. First, they acted as couriers relaying urgent messages and news to the villagers, as for example the death of a pharaoh. Second, the Medjay leaders would establish contact on behalf of various officials who were in need of speaking with one or more of the workers. The officials presented themselves at the 'Sealed of the Necropolis', where they would put forth their request to the Medjay leaders who would then find the individual(s) from the village. Because of the nature of the closed society of Deir el-Medina, the officials were not permitted to enter the village and the Medjay leaders would act as envoys bringing the two parties together, presumably at the 'Sealed of the Necropolis'. This was also the place where the Medjay leaders would act as middlemen in the trade arrangements between the villagers and the outside world, although this was most likely not an official function. It was rather an opportunity for making extra earnings, a principle which is not unknown from modern day Egypt.

The Medjay leaders were guardians and administrators alongside the scribes of the 'Sealed of the Necropolis', safeguarding the daily life of the workers of Deir el-Medina, while also leading and administrating the Medjay for the protection of the pharaohs' mummified bodies in the Valley of the Kings. How exactly the latter function was organized remains unclear, but a study of the Medjay and their functions may reveal other, but also very different aspects of the Medjay leaders, and give a more complete picture of the overall Medjay organization during the New Kingdom.

Bibliography

Allam, S. (1973) *Hieratische Ostraka und Papyri. I, Transkriptionen aus dem Nachlass von J. Černy.* Tübingen, Selbstverl.

Bradbury, L. (1988) Reflections on Traveling to "God's Land" and Punt in the Middle Kingdom. *Journal of the American Research Center in Egypt* 25. 127–156.

Černý, J. (1930) *Ostraca Hiératiques (Nos 25501–25832). Catalogue Général des Antiquités Égyptiennes du Musée du Caire*. Cairo, L'Institut Français D'Archéologie Orientale.

Černý, J. (1936) Datum des Todes Ramses III und der Thronbesteigung Ramses IV. *Zeitschrift für Ägyptische Sprache* 72, 109–188.

Černý, J. (1972) Troisième série de questions adressées aux oracles. *Bulletin de L'Institut Français D'Archéologie Orientale* 72, 49–70.

Černý, J. (1973) *A Community of Workmen at Thebes in the Ramesside Period*. Cairo, Institut Français D'Archéologie Orientale du Caire.

Černý, J. and Gardiner, A. (1957) *Hieratic Ostraca vol. I*. Oxford, Charles Batey.

Davies, B. (1994) Two or Three 'Chiefs of Medjay': A Conundrum of Nebsmens. *Göttinger Miszellen* 143, 37–39.

Demarée, R. J. (1999) A Letter of Reproach. In E. Teeter and J. A. Larson (ed.) *Gold of Praise. Studies on Ancient Egypt in Honor of Edward F. Wente*, 75–82. Chicago, The University of Chicago.

Frandsen, P. J. (1990) *Editing Reality: The Turin Strike Papyrus. Studies in Egyptology. Presented to Miriam Lichtheim vol. I*, 166–199. Jerusalem, The Hebrew University.

Gardiner, A. (1948) *Ramesside Administrative Documents*. London, Oxford University Press.

Garies Davies, N. (1906) *The Rock Tombs of El Amarna. Part IV – The Tombs of Penthu, Mahu, and Others. Archaeological Survey of Egypt Sixteenth Memoir*. London, The Egypt Exploration Fund.

Garis Davies, N. (1923) *The Tombs of Two Officials of Thutmosis the Fourth (nos 75 and 90). The Theban Tomb Series Third Memoir*. London, The Egypt Exploration Society.

Garis Davies, N. (1933) *The Tombs of Menkheperrasonb, Amenmose and another. The Theban Tombs Series Fifth Memoir*. London, The Egypt Exploration Society.

Goedicke, H. (1995) *Studies about Kamose and Ahmose*. Baltimore, HALGO, INC.

Haring, B. J. J. (1997) *Divine Households*. Leiden. Nederlands Instituut voor het Nabije Osten.

Helck, W. (2002) *Die datierten und datierbaren Ostraka, Papyri und Graffiti von Deir el-Medina*. Wiesbaden, Harrasowitz Verlag.

Kitchen, K. A. (1980) *Ramesside Inscriptions III*. Oxford, B. H. Blackwell.

Kitchen, K. A. (1983a) *Ramesside Inscriptions V*. Oxford, B. H. Blackwell.

Kitchen, K. A. (1983b) *Ramesside Inscriptions VI*. Oxford. B. H. Blackwell.

Kitchen, K. A. (1989) *Ramesside Inscriptions VII*. Oxford. B. H. Blackwell.

Lichtheim, M. (1973) Ancient Egyptian Literature, Volume I: The Old and Middle Kingdoms. Los Angeles, University of California Press.

López, J. (1984) *Ostraca Ieratici N. 57450–57568*. Milan, Instituto Editoriale Cisalpino – La Goliardica.

Manning, J. G., Greig, G. and Uchida, S. (1989) Chicago Oriental Institute Ostracon 12073 once again. *Journal of Near Eastern Studies* 48, 117–124.

McDowell, A. G. (1990) *Jurisdiction in the Workmen's Community of Deir el-Medina*. Leiden, Nederlands Instituut voor het Nabije Oosten.

Peet, T. E. (1930) *The Great Tomb Robberies of the Twentieth Egyptian Dynasty I–II*. Oxford, Clarendon Press.

Smither, P. (1945) The Semnah Dispatches. *Journal of Egyptian Archaeology* 31, 3–10.

Taylor, J. (2000) The Third Intermediate Period. In I. Shaw (ed.) *The Oxford History of Ancient Egypt*, 330–368. Oxford, Oxford University Press.

Ventura, R. (1986) *Living in a City of the Dead*. Freiburg, Universitätsverlag.

Vleeming, S. P. (1982) The Days on which the qnbt used to gather. In R. J. Demarée and Jac J. Janssen (ed.) *Gleanings from Deir el-Medina*, 183–192. Leiden, Nederlands Instituut voor het Nabije Oosten.

Warburton, D. A. (1997) *State and Economy in Ancient Egypt. Fiscal Vocabulary of the New Kingdom*. Freiburg, University Press.

12

The functional context of 18th Dynasty marks ostraca from the Theban Necropolis

Daniel Soliman

Introduction

The Theban necropolis workmen living in the village now known as Deir el-Medina employed a system of identity marks which were used on various media. The identity of each workman was represented by a different mark, and these identity marks form the focus of a research project at Leiden University. Part of the project deals with the function of the marks and their historical context. This article will mainly discuss ostraca containing workmen's marks of the 18th Dynasty and will present some preliminary ideas regarding their function. As pointed out by Haring (2009, 152), marks ostraca of the 18th Dynasty are recognizable by the repertory of signs and by their style. It remains very difficult to interpret 18th Dynasty marks ostraca because of the lack of written administrative texts from that time. In general, knowledge of the workmen's community prior to the Amarna period is relatively limited.

At the time of writing, the corpus of marks ostraca from the 18th Dynasty consists of fifty-four pieces. This number is extremely small considering the period under examination. The earliest known marks ostracon is JE 72490 which is tentatively dated to the reign of Thutmosis III, while the latest pre-Amarna period ostraca are connected to the reign of Amenhotep III (see below). We are therefore dealing with a period that probably spans at least 125 years. Although the current corpus of workmen's marks of the 18th Dynasty is rather small, not only do marks ostraca continue to be found by excavations in the Valley of the Kings, but unpublished ostraca may also still be awaiting rediscovery in museum collections.

A number of ostraca discussed here are unpublished or are referred to by names that require some clarification. In some cases photographs of the ostraca were kindly provided by the excavation directors or the persons responsible for the publication of these finds. What is here called "the Bruyère ostracon" is a piece found by the excavations of the IFAO and published by Bruyère (1953, pl. XVIII, top right). ARTP stands for Amarna Royal Tomb Project under the direction of Nicholas Reeves. The Brock ostracon is a piece discovered by Edwin C. Brock's excavations (1999–2001) in the Valley of the Kings, and Cilli 278 is an ostracon discovered by the Basel University mission which belongs to a corpus of objects to be published by Debora Cilli.

Four ostraca discovered by the Waseda University excavations (three are published (Yoshimura and Kondo 1995)) are here named WV 22.1-4. Ostraca BTdK 832 and 833 were discovered by the Basel University mission and have recently been published (Dorn and Paulin-Grothe 2011), while ostraca with the prefix 'KV' refer to those discovered by the SCA excavations in the Valley of the Kings (Hawass 2011).

Provenance, material and seriation

The exact provenances of eleven ostraca are unknown. The only published 18th Dynasty marks ostracon with a secure provenance in the workmen's village itself is the aforementioned Bruyère ostracon, discovered among the debris from the Great Pit. Turin N 57310 might have come from the village or from the Valley of the Queens, but thirty-eight ostraca and perhaps three more come from the Valley of the Kings. The provenances of twenty-four ostraca from this latter group can be determined more specifically:

KV 10002, -04, -10, -11, -12:	branch leading to KV 30
JE 72490 and 72494:	between KV 30 and KV 26
CG 25321:	near KV 37
JE 72498:	end of branch leading to KV 34
CG 24105-8:	probably entrance of KV 35
JE 96650:	south side of KV 35
JE 72492:	east of KV 47
Cilli 278:	near KV 47
Brock ostracon:	in front of KV 17
BTdK 832-3:	not *in situ*; among pottery fragments dated to the time of Thutmosis III
WV 22.1-4:	area between WV 22 and WV A.
ARTP 02-236:	site 2 (between KV 47 and KV 37) or site 4 (between KV 11 and KV 57)

The first nine ostraca from this list come from a branch in the Valley of Kings where a number of 18th Dynasty tombs are located and which ultimately leads to KV 34. The two ostraca found near KV 47 can also be connected to this branch. The ARTP ostracon comes from that branch as well, or might be connected to KV 58 dating to the late 18th Dynasty. BTdK 832 and 833 were found out of their archaeological context near KV 18 among pottery datable to the reign of Thutmosis III and so perhaps they originate from the vicinity of KV 21, an anonymous 18th Dynasty tomb. The same may be true for the Brock ostracon. Four ostraca are clearly connected to KV 35, the tomb of Amenhotep II and to this group JE 96650 should be added as it was discovered near KV 35 and contains many marks that are typical for the KV 35 ostraca. Finally, four ostraca were discovered near WV 22, the tomb of Amenhotep III. Marks ostraca of the 18th Dynasty thus seem to have come mostly from the worksite of the crew: the Valley of the Kings. This suggests that they deal with matters related to the construction of royal tombs.

Besides the general provenance, the corpus is even more homogeneous in terms of material used for the ostraca. There is only one instance of a ceramic ostracon (JE 72492). The others are of stone: flint in two cases, limestone in all other cases (the material of four ostraca is unknown). Comparing this corpus to the 20th Dynasty figured, hieratic and marks ostraca found in the workmen's hut settlement in the Valley of the Kings, we observe the same preference for limestone over ceramics (Dorn 2011, 74).

A tentative, relative dating sequence of the ostraca can be established by means of ostraca (groups) which are datable through their provenance. These serve as anchor points to which the remaining ostraca can be compared. The seriation is to a large extent based on the idea that the greater the number of shared marks between two ostraca, the closer they should be dated together. Another important criterion is the sequences of marks: when the same sequence of marks is found in two different ostraca, they are believed to belong to the same period. Yet, however tempting both criteria might be, they are not necessarily true. A major obstacle is the fact that the same mark may be made in different ways by different 'scribes' (see Figures 12.1 and 12.2). Hence one cannot always be sure whether a mark on one ostracon is the same as a mark on another ostracon when it is executed slightly differently. Moreover, the poor state of preservation of some ostraca makes comparison difficult. The relative seriation is therefore, still preliminary.

On the following pages the ostraca will be analysed by looking at nine features. As the reader will notice, different aspects are often interconnected and cannot be discussed in isolation.

Lay-out

A horizontal arrangement of marks is typical for the 18th Dynasty (forty-two instances, 78%). In most cases the marks are equally spaced on a horizontal line, but there are five ostraca with relatively large marks in which the horizontal 'lines' are far from straight. In these cases it seems it is rather the shape of the ostracon that dictates the lay-out of the document. Ostraca JE 96603 and MMA 09.184.786 display what seem to be vertically arranged marks next to horizontally placed marks. In about a quarter of the corpus we see marks which are arranged rather differently from regular hieroglyphic or hieratic documents; in eight ostraca and on the reverse of an ostracon with a horizontal lay-out on the obverse (*c.* 17%), we find the marks scattered over the ostracon without any evidently logical distribution pattern, as on the unpublished ostracon Cairo JE 96587. In four ostraca (*c.* 7%) marks are inscribed along the edge of the ostracon, leaving the centre blank, see for example CG 24105 (Fig. 12.3).

Within horizontally arranged marks ostraca, two marks are sometimes placed over each other to form a neat block. A striking example can be found in the third row of the Bruyère ostracon (Fig. 12.4). Here, two horizontal marks 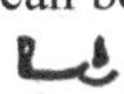 and  are grouped together in a manner that is very reminiscent of hieroglyphic texts. Since there is plenty of writing space left on the ostracon this was seemingly done only for aesthetic reasons.

In seven ostraca with horizontally arranged marks horizontal lines are used to separate one row from the other, as in Stockholm MM 14130 (Peterson 1973, pl. 79). Six cases display a single sequence of marks. This does not seem to be the case in Ashmolean HO 1114: three marks found in the upper row return in the same relative position in the lower row, so the dividing lines may have been used to separate two different records. Something similar could also be happening in seven other ostraca, where a small horizontal line (one instance), a vertical line (three instances), a box (two instances) and a curved line (one instance) are used to separate a group of marks from others on the same ostracon.

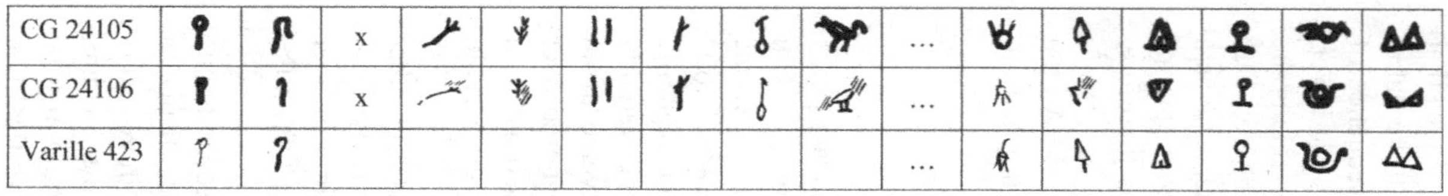

Figure 12.1: Table illustrating the sequence of marks found in ostraca CG 24105-6 and Varille 423. (Marks by Kyra van der Moezel)

Figure 12.2: Table illustrating the sequence of marks found in ostraca Bruyère, Stockholm MM 14130, UC 31988, WV 22.3, MMA 09.184.700 and UC 45709. (Marks by Kyra van der Moezel)

Figure 12.3: O. Cairo CG 24105. (after Daressy 1902, pl. XVIII).

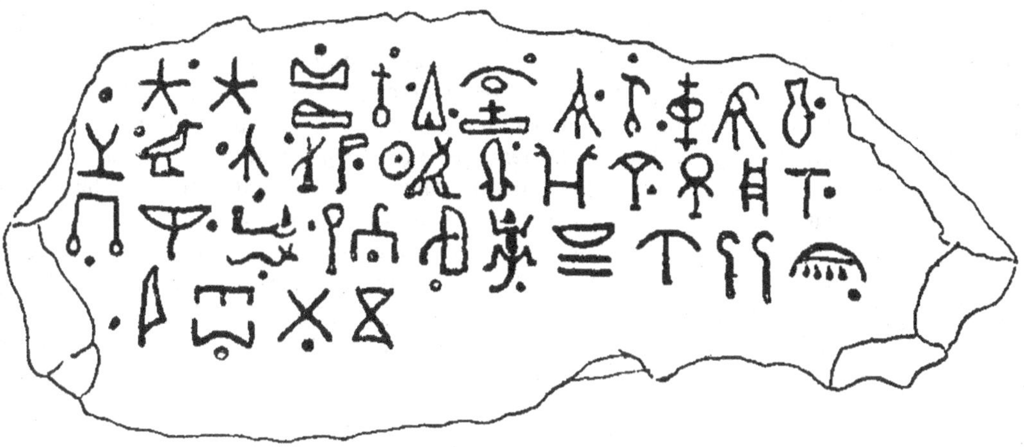

Figure 12.4: The Bruyère ostracon from the Great Pit. (after Bruyère 1953, pl. XVIII).

Recurring sequences of marks

An important aspect is the recurrence of (almost) the same sequence of marks on different ostraca. As mentioned, such sequences may be used to date ostraca. Moreover, ostraca which share a sequence of marks make it possible to compare the hand of the 'scribe', the exact form of the marks, the direction in which the ostracon is to be read, and other features which will be discussed below. One sequence of marks is found in ostraca CG 24105, CG 24107 (both found near KV 35) and Varille 423 (Fig. 12.1). The second and longest sequence is found in six ostraca which are thought to be of a relatively late date (Fig. 12.2).

Orientation of marks

As we can recognize the same sequence of marks in several ostraca, it is possible to observe how the same mark is drawn differently in these instances. Particularly remarkable is the fact that marks are orientated in various ways. Figures 12.1 and 12.2 illustrate how marks can be rotated 90 degrees and or mirrored and . It seems that orientation of marks was of no importance on ostraca. Even within a single ostracon, marks with a clear front and back could be differently orientated. For example, in CG 24105 the bird is orientated to the right, while the *w3s* sceptre left of it is orientated to the left.

Reading direction

Despite the flexibility in the orientation of marks, the majority of marks with a clear front and back (body parts, animals, staffs etc.) are orientated to the right. This would suggest, on the analogy with hieroglyphs and hieratic, that ostraca with a horizontal arrangement of marks are to be read from right to left. The ends of lines in ostraca with more than one line are also illustrative in this respect; the majority of the ostraca in which this part is preserved (Ashmolean HO 892, the Brock ostracon, JE 72490, perhaps JE 72492, JE 96603 upper line, UC 45683 and WV 22.4) indicate that a new line started on the right and therefore the ostracon was probably read from right to left. The reading direction of two ostraca (JE 96631 and WV 22.1) in which this part is not preserved can still be demonstrated to be right to left because marks close to the left edge of the ostracon are drawn with less space between it and the neighbouring mark and/or are partly written on the edge of the ostracon. These ostraca are thus likely to have been inscribed from right to left and should probably be read in the same way.

The right–left orientation of the majority of the 18th Dynasty marks ostraca corresponds to the way hieratic was written, yet there are also ostraca which seem to have been written from left to right. This is indicated by a new line starting on the left side of an ostracon, as in the Bruyère ostracon, KV 10004, and the right lower section on JE 96603. The upper line in Varille 423 shows part of the same sequence of marks as in CG 24105, which must be read from right to left. However, the sequence on Varille 423 (Kunicki *et al.* 2007, 85 nr. 423) is reversed and might therefore have been read from left to right as well.

Even further removed from hieratic in terms of reading direction are four, perhaps five ostraca which seem to have been written in boustrophedon. Marks on these ostraca are sometimes written along the edge of the ostracon (see above) but not necessarily so. The clearest example of a boustrophedon is CG 24105 (Fig. 12.3). The sequence of marks starts at the top right, continues to the left, then turns a corner, and at the bottom of the ostracon the sequence goes on from left to right. Although CG 24107 (Fig. 12.5) is written in two rather neat horizontal rows, the sequence of marks overlaps for a great part with that of CG 24105 indicating that here the upper row is read from right to left as well, but the lower row from left to right. The lay-out of CG 25321 and JE 72450 suggest that these ostraca too should be read in boustrophedon. Their respective sequence of marks is however not (yet) known from other ostraca and so it is unclear from what point one should start reading them.

Figure 12.5: O. Cairo CG 24107. (after Daressy 1902, pl. XVIII).

Occurrence of double marks

As mentioned in the introduction, each mark represents a different workman. There are, however, instances in which a particular mark appears twice on the same ostracon. In three ostraca this can be explained by arguing that the ostracon is divided into two or more different sections which represent different records within the same document. In ostracon Varille 423 (Kunicki *et al.* 2007, 85 nr. 423) the repeated marks are found in a line written at an angle of 180 degrees from the first line, in Ashmolean HO 1114 the marks repeated in the second row are divided from the first row by a horizontal line, and in JE 96603 the repeated marks are in sections separated from each other by empty space and a vertical line. Yet in eight other ostraca the repeated marks clearly belong to one and the same sequence. These double marks can be interpreted in two ways: either a single person is mentioned twice within one ostracon, or there are two people who employed the same mark.

Although there is no evidence for either option, the latter is preferred. In six ostraca (Ashmolean HO 892, the Bruyère ostracon, UC 45709, Stockholm MM 14130, Ashmolean HO 1114 and perhaps also WV 22.2) the repeated mark immediately follows the first mark. Because the double marks are attested on their own in other ostraca, and because they have their own dots or strokes (see below), when they appear next to each other it is certain that they constitute two different marks. One way to explain such double marks would be to attribute them to a senior workman and his assistant, perhaps his son. There are indications that in the 20th Dynasty a son could inherit his father's mark (Haring 2009, 149) and so perhaps we see something similar in the 18th Dynasty ostraca, although a counterargument would be that double marks appear relatively infrequently. Yet, the fact that there are no instances of more than two of the same marks supports this interpretation. In three other ostraca (JE 72490, JE 96590 and KV 10002 (Hawass 2011, 66)) the double mark is not written immediately next to its counterpart, but is removed from it by several other marks. Remarkably, in all three instances it is the very last mark of the sequence. If the interpretation of the repeated mark as being that of an assistant is correct, these three ostraca may reflect the standing of these individuals in respect to the other crew members. As foremen and scribes of the crew usually head hieratic workmen's lists, the young assistants are here found at the end of the sequence of workmen's marks.

Dots and strokes

It has already been mentioned briefly that in the 18th Dynasty, marks on ostraca are sometimes found in combination with one or more strokes or dots, or with a combination of both. They display no further symbols as in some Ramesside marks ostraca (Haring 2009, 146, group 13; 148). Marks ostraca of the 18th Dynasty with added dots and/or strokes form just over a third of the current corpus. There are three instances with strokes added to marks, fourteen with dots, and two with both strokes and dots. Together, this group of nineteen ostraca are either of a horizontal lay-out (eleven instances), have marks following the edge of the ostracon (three instances), or have marks scattered over the ostracon (five instances). Marks with more than one added dot or stroke appear to count something related to the workman represented by that mark. As almost all marks ostraca come from the worksite of the crew it is plausible that they relate to their activities there. It has been suggested that the dots and strokes count the workmen's days of presence or absence at work, or denote numbers of commodities or tools distributed to the workmen (Dorn and Paulin-Grothe 2011, 18). In the absence of information about the administration of the 18th Dynasty necropolis workmen this can unfortunately not be proven. However, ostraca with dots and/or strokes display a relatively large number of marks per ostracon: the average is *c.* eighteen marks, compared to an overall average of fifteen (see below). In reality however the average number of marks on ostraca with dots and/or strokes must be considerably higher as the corpus includes incompletely preserved ostraca. Because these ostraca show a high number of marks, they could well have presented an overview of the entire crew of workmen, as one would expect in ostraca recording presence of workmen.

Still, the use of dots and strokes on marks ostraca remains a difficult topic. The number of ostraca in which dots and strokes feature is relatively small, and these do not display enough consistency to explain their underlying system. Ostraca with only dots added to marks can be divided into two groups. The first consists of three instances (CG 24107, BTdK 832, UC 31988 obverse) in which great numbers of dots are added around a mark. For example, the mark representing a snake in the first row of CG 24107 is provided with about twenty dots. The cluttered arrangement of the dots does not convey a very administrative appearance and it could be that such ostraca were used during a longer period in which a dot was added in between intervals of time. The second group consists of ostraca with marks combined with one or two dots. In KV 10011, MMA 09.184.700, JE 72450, Turin CG 57310, BTdK 833, the Bruyère ostracon, and WV 22.2 a single dot is added to one or more marks. In a group of ostraca from the last quarter of the relative seriation, belonging together on the basis of shared sequences of marks, we find marks with one or two dots. These are Stockholm MM 14130, UC 45709, and WV 22.3. The reverse of UC 31988 should perhaps be added to this group, and interesting in this context is also the Bruyère ostracon. In this group of ostraca, up to two red or black dots are added to a mark and the combination of one red and one black dot occurs as well. This might perhaps mean that a four quarter system is being used, where two red dots represent the highest value and one black dot the lowest.

In Ashmolean HO 892 some marks are combined with up to two strokes, while in O. Varille 423 some marks show a single stroke. In these two ostraca strokes may have been used in the same way as in the second group of ostraca with dots. In CG 24108 we see marks combined with up to five strokes, a number which agrees better with the first group of ostraca with dots.

If ostraca with strokes can indeed be divided into two similar groups (cf. ostraca with dots), then perhaps there is no essential difference between the use of strokes on one hand and dots

Figure 12.6: O. Cairo CG 24106. (after Daressy 1902, pl. XVIII).

on the other. When we turn to the two ostraca in which strokes and dots are combined, one may come to the same conclusion. In CG 24105 (Fig. 12.3) strokes are used only for the very first mark. It would almost seem as if the scribe absentmindedly continued with dots after this mark. In CG 24106 (Fig. 12.6) dots seem to be used either for very large numbers or when they are added inside a mark. In both cases it is easier to use dots than strokes. Yet, the mark representing a snake shows both dots and strokes and cannot be explained in the same way.

Number of marks per ostracon

The total number of marks on an ostracon – or in some cases, the total number of marks in a specific section on an ostracon – provides some insight into the manner in which the marks based administration functioned. Ostraca which are complete (fourteen pieces) and those which presumably are complete (nine pieces) display an average of about fifteen marks per ostracon. In reality this number could well have been higher, because there are six incompletely preserved ostraca which display more than fifteen marks. The total number of marks on completely preserved ostraca fluctuates greatly (Fig. 12.7). Among complete ostraca, the minimum of marks is five or six marks (five instances). Complete ostraca with the highest total of marks contain twenty-six marks (two instances), thirty marks (one instance) and forty-four marks (one instance).

As has been demonstrated previously (Haring 2009, 153), complete ostraca such as the Bruyère piece and groups of ostraca, which must date to the same period on account of their provenance, allow an estimation of the size of the crew of workmen. The ostraca from around the tomb of Amenhotep II (CG 24105-8 and JE 96650) display thirty-nine or forty different marks; the four ostraca from around the tomb of Amenhotep III (WV 22.1-4) display thirty-four or thirty-five different marks; and the Bruyère ostracon contains forty-four marks. These figures suggest a crew of thirty-five to almost forty-five men, or an average of *c.* forty men. If these estimated totals are correct, then apparently the majority of all 18th Dynasty marks ostraca deal with only a part of the entire crew per ostracon.

It thus seems that inscribing ostraca with the marks of all crewmembers is the exception rather than the rule, since we have only one clear example: the Bruyère ostracon. Ostraca with ten or less marks are then more likely to record only men who are absent from work. If they record the presence of workmen, we would have several cases where less than a quarter of the

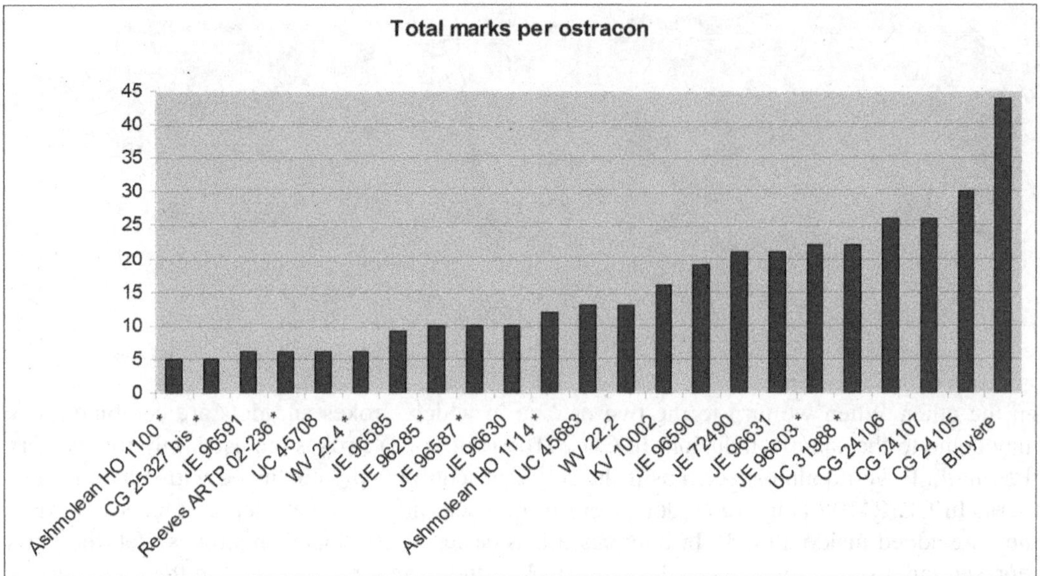

*Figure 12.7: Graph showing the total amount of marks per complete ostracon. The asterisk * indicates ostraca which are presumed to be complete.*

crew showed up. Interestingly, five out of twenty-three (presumably) complete ostraca display a total number of marks that approaches half the estimated size of the crew:

KV 10002:	16 marks (half of 32)
JE 96590:	19 marks (half of 38)
JE 72490:	21 marks (half of 42)
JE 96631:	21 marks (half of 42)
JE 96603:	22 marks (half of 44)
UC 31988:	22 marks (half of 44)

It is well known that from the 19th Dynasty onwards, the crew was divided into two equal halves, or 'sides'. Since we lack any written documentation about the organization of the 18th Dynasty crew it is unknown whether this division was made in that period as well. According to Cathleen Keller, such a division would have been practical in the construction of some royal tombs of the 18th Dynasty (Kozloff and Bryan 1992, 238 n. 18). Marks ostraca do not prove that it existed but such a division could explain these particular totals. Ostraca with totals of nine to sixteen marks may discredit such an interpretation and are themselves not easily explained. They could relate to a part of the crew that had a common job and worked together.

Different hands and different stages

A close inspection of the ostraca reveals a few interesting features of the usage of the objects as documents. First of all, by merely comparing the hand of the marks in Figures 12.1 and 12.2, it becomes clear that these ostraca were composed by different persons. This is best noticeable by comparing the more intricate marks such as birds or lizards. In at least four ostraca, traces demonstrate that marks have been erased. In MMA 09.187.700 and Ashmolean HO 892, perhaps also WV 22.3, a single mark has been erased. Ostraca CG 24106 and CG 24107 seem to be palimpsests: a previous record was entirely erased and the ostracon was reused. The original ostracon was inscribed with marks as well. Palimpsests are regularly found among hieratic administrative ostraca (the Deir el-Medina Database currently contains 212 examples found on ostraca and weights) and in this respect marks ostraca are no different from hieratic documents. Unfortunately we do not know how much time passed between the composition of the original ostracon and the marks that are legible today. In any case, it demonstrates that some marks ostraca were of a temporary nature. The document only served its purpose for a certain period (perhaps only a day) during which it was apparently kept in a place where it could be retrieved again to be reused.

In two instances, the ostracon was inscribed by at least two different scribes. A very clear example is WV 22.3 (Yoshimura and Kondo 1995, 18).The red marks in the upper line are smaller, more neatly arranged, and display more of a hieroglyphic ductus than the other marks on the ostracon. As the black mark at the left end of the first row – written in the second hand – was added in line with the red marks, it is probable that the first and second scribe worked on one and the same record. It remains unclear exactly why two persons worked on the same document, but the fact in itself is striking. Apparently the marks based administration was not kept by a single person at a time. Unfortunately WV 22.3 is not completely preserved. The rightmost marks are partly damaged and it is unknown whether further marks preceded those which are still visible. Nevertheless, it is interesting to see that the two scribes of WV 22.3 – as it has survived – each wrote down eleven marks. This could be yet another indication of a crew divided into two halves. If this were so, it would seem that two different individuals were responsible for one part of the crew each. This would be analogous to indications of the existence of two senior scribes attached to the crew in the19th Dynasty (McDowell 1990, 86–89).

Colour use

Marks on ostraca appear in red or black. The colour of the marks could not be determined in three instances. Among the remaining fifty-one ostraca we find slightly more ostraca with black marks exclusively (twenty-four instances, *c.* 47%; perhaps three more) than ostraca with exclusively red marks (twenty instances, *c.* 39%). There are four ostraca with both red and black marks. In these four cases differently coloured marks may alternate within the same row, although in MMA 09.184.700 and WV 22.3 (Yoshimura and Kondo 1995, 18) – both from the later quarter of the seriation – marks of the same colour are clustered together. In CG 24106 (fig. 9) and in MMA 09.184.700 the ratio of red and black marks is almost equal (fifteen black – fourteen red; eight black – seven red respectively). Once again, a division of the crew into two 'sides' springs to mind, but in JE 96590 and WV 22.3 the ratio is very different (three black – sixteen red; six black – sixteen red respectively).

Two ostraca with both red and black marks come from relatively well dated ostraca groups (CG 24106 and WV 22.3) and allow an investigation into the use of colour. Among the WV 22 group there is unfortunately very little overlap in terms of shared marks, and even less in terms of shared marks with the same colour. Among the six ostraca associated with KV 35 there is little consistency as well. Ostraca CG 24105 and CG 24107 display only red marks and both contain about twenty-six marks. They are unlikely to record the workmen of one particular 'side', as that would mean the entire crew consisted of fifty-two men. Therefore in these ostraca, colour does probably not distinguish workmen from different 'sides'. Theoretically this could be the case in CG 24106, with its fifteen black and fourteen red marks. Comparison of this piece to the other ostraca from the same group does not elucidate things. Ostracon CG 24108 contains only black marks. It (probably) shares ten marks with CG 24106, of which eight are black on both ostraca. JE 96650 is also inscribed with all black marks. It (probably) shares seven marks with CG 24106, of which only four are black on both ostraca. All marks in Varille 423 are red. It shares fourteen marks with CG 24106, yet only four marks are red on both ostraca.

The attribution of a specific colour to a mark is therefore unlikely to reflect a supposed division of the crew into two halves. A specific mark can be red on one ostracon and black on the next. Moreover, if the red marks on for example CG 24106 or WV 22.3 were to belong to a specific half of the crew, one would expect to find these marks on other ostraca without marks belonging the supposed other half. Yet this is never the case. Whatever the meaning of the use of red and black marks may be, it is not evident at this point of our research.

Marks on other objects and in graffiti

Thus far this article has discussed workmen's marks that are employed on ostraca. The same 18th Dynasty marks also occur on other objects used by the workmen where they serve as property markers. The marks are mostly attested on pottery fragments recovered by the excavations of the IFAO at Deir el-Medina and published by Bruyère, B. (1924–1930; 1933–1934; 1937; 1939; 1948; 1952–1953). Their archaeological context confirms that the ostraca discussed here belong to the 18th Dynasty. Objects with marks often come from a funerary context, but only in one case has it been possible to associate a workmen's mark with an individual who is known by name (Haring 2009, 154): the "Overseer of construction in the Great Place" Kha probably used the mark .

Objects found in the same tomb shaft at Deir el-Medina often bear different marks; apparently these items did not all belong to the deceased but were given to him at the time of his funeral, or the burial could have belonged to various individuals with their own items. In some cases one could argue that the mark represented by the highest number of samples belongs to the owner of the tomb. An interesting case in point is tomb shaft 1099. The published pottery from this site includes six items with a workman's mark, of which four are the same (Nagel 1938, 53 n. 1; 54 n. 6; 55 n. 12, n. 17). They represent the mirror-shaped mark  which is known from at least nine ostraca. Shaft 1099 was attributed to a Nekhunefer by Bruyère (1928, 11–12) on account of a vase inscribed for this person. It could thus be this Nekhunefer who is represented by mark  in some, if not all of these ostraca.

Apart from ostraca, pottery and other objects, workmen's marks are abundantly present as graffiti in the Theban mountains (Fronczak and Rzepka 2009). Remarkably, none of them can be securely dated to the 18th Dynasty. Some marks etched into the rock do occur as identity marks on ostraca of the 18th Dynasty, such as the frequently attested mark  (see for example graffito no. 101, 158, and 1222). However, such marks were used throughout the 19th and 20th Dynasty as well and so these graffiti may also date to later periods. Marks which are found exclusively on 18th Dynasty ostraca are not attested in graffiti. The absence of marks in graffiti in the 18th Dynasty is paralleled by the lack of textual graffiti from the same time. This leads to the assumption that the workmen's practice of using their spare time to create graffiti which represented their own identity – through script or through marks – began somewhere after the Amarna period. Yet identity marks were already well in use for administrative purposes. The absence of textual graffiti has previously puzzled scholars. Tentative explanations attribute it to a more limited access to the valleys in the 18th Dynasty, and the increase of literacy in the 19th Dynasty (Peden 2001, 136–138 and 147–148). Only the former argument may be used to explain the absence of workmen's marks.

Conclusions

The small number of 18th Dynasty marks ostraca we possess remains very enigmatic at the moment. Nevertheless, these documents are an important source on the activities and particularly the administration of the necropolis workmen of the time. A better understanding of the 18th Dynasty marks will also contribute to the study of the development of the use of marks in Deir el-Medina in general and may provide insights as to the origins of the use of marks and their relation to writing.

The provenances of the ostraca suggest that they were composed during work on the royal tomb and record matters related to workmen's activity there. The ostraca usually do not record all workmen of the crew. Ostraca with a low number of marks are less likely to record presence, while ostraca with a high number of marks are less likely to record absence. Very little is clear about the use of colour and the addition of dots and strokes, but it is possible that dots have the same meaning as strokes.

Marks ostraca were probably produced by more than one person at a given time, and some were perhaps made as part of a private administration. Other ostraca appear to be of a more official nature, based on the appearance of the same sequence of marks on different ostraca. Palimpsests and ostraca with marks surrounded by a great amount of dots may have been stored and reused at different times. Double marks on the same ostracon may belong to a senior and his assistant. If this is correct, some sequences of marks may also reflect the social status of the workmen and list the assistants in the last position. This would also imply that, as in later times, workmen could inherit an identity mark from their predecessors.

Analysis of the 18th Dynasty ostraca reveals the heterogeneity of the system. Marks could be arranged in a variety of ways and were read in different directions. Marks within a sequence on an ostracon could be orientated to the right or to left and the same mark could be drawn differently by different scribes. It would thus seem that, although some of the ostraca might be recording official administration, the marking system itself was not very much bound to rules. The system is in all these aspects quite different from writing. This could be explained by the supposed illiteracy of the 18th Dynasty workmen, as has been done to understand the absence of hieratic graffiti. Nevertheless, there are similarities to hieratic ostraca, such as the use of limestone for ostraca from the Valley of the Kings and the predominantly right to left reading direction. The use of horizontal lines between rows of marks may have been inspired by the lines which separate registers of texts in royal tombs.

As mysterious as the marks ostraca still are, they have been shown to be informative about the size of the crew of workmen. Moreover, ostraca with totals that match with the number of half the crew, as well as ostraca written by two scribes can be used as arguments for a division of the crew into two sides. It is hoped that when more marks ostraca become available our understanding of the 18th Dynasty community of workmen will grow.

Acknowledgements

I wish to thank Dr Ben Haring, Joost Kramer and Jurgen van Oostenrijk for reading an earlier draft of this paper and for their valuable remarks.

Bibliography

Bruyère, B. (1924–1930, 1933–1934, 1937, 1939, 1948, 1952–1953) *Rapport sur les fouilles de Deir el Médineh (1922–1923), (1923–1924), (1924–1925), (1926), (1927), (1928), (1929), (1930), (1931–1932), (1933–1934), (1934–1935), (1935–1940), (1945–1946 et 1946–1947)* and *(1948 à 1951)*. Fouilles de l'Institut Français d'Archéologie Orientale du Caire 1–8, 10, 14–16, 20–21 and 26. Cairo, l'Institut Français d'Archéologie Orientale.

Daressy, G. (1902) *Fouilles de la Vallée des Rois (1898–1899). Catalogue general des antiquités égyptiennes du Musée du Caire. Nos 24001–24990.* Cairo, l'Institut Français d'Archéologie Orientale.

Dorn, A. (2011) *Arbeiterhütten im Tal der Könige. Ein Beitrag zur altägyptischen Sozialgeschichte auf grund von neuem Quellenmaterial aus der Mitte der 20. Dynastie (ca. 1150 v. Chr.).* Aegyptiaca Helvetica 23. Basel, Schwabe & Co. AG.

Dorn, A. and Paulin-Grothe, E. (2011) Zwei Ostraka der 18. Dynastie aus dem Tal der Könige mit Namenszeichen (O. BTdK 832 und O. BTdK 833). *Göttinger Miszellen* 231, 17–23.

Fronczak, M. and Rzepka, S. (2009) "Funny signs" in Theban rock graffiti. In P. Andrássy, J. Budka and F. Kammerzell (eds) *Non-textual marking systems, writing and pseudo script from prehistory to modern times.* Lingua Aegyptia, studia monographica 8, 159–178. Göttingen, Universität Göttingen.

Haring, B. J. J. (2009) Workmen's marks on ostraca from the Theban Necropolis: a progress report. In B. J. J. Haring and O. E. Kaper (eds) *Pictograms or pseudo script? Non-textual identity marks in practical use in ancient Egypt and elsewhere. Proceedings of a conference in Leiden, 19–20 December 2006.* Egyptologische Uitgaven XXV, 143–167. Leuven, Peeters.

Hawass, Z. (2011) Excavation West of the Valley of the Kings near the Tomb of Thutmose III. In T. A. Bács, Z. Hawass and G. Schreiber (eds) *Proceedings of the colloquium on Theban archeology at the Supreme Council of Antiquities, November 5, 2009*, 57–71. Cairo, The American University in Cairo Press.

Kozloff, A. P. and Bryan, B. M. (1992) *Egypt's Dazzling Sun. Amenhotep III and his World. With Lawrence M. Berman and an essay by Elisabeth Delange*. Cleveland, the Cleveland Museum of Art and Indiana University Press.

Kunicki, C., Mariaud de Serres, J.-P., David, M.-C. *et al.* (eds) (2007) *Catalogue Pierre Bergé & Associés. Vente Archéologie, Art d'Orient, Extrême-Orient. Drouot Richelieu. Paris. Vendredi 27 Avril 2007, 14 heures. Samedi 28 Avril 2007, 14 heures.* Paris, Pierre Bergé & Associés.

McDowell, A. G. (1990) *Jurisdiction in the workmen's community of Deir el-Medîna.* Egyptologische Uitgaven 5. Leiden, Nederlands Instituut voor het Nabije Oosten.

Nagel, G. (1938) *La céramique du Nouvel Empire à Deir el Médineh. Documents de fouilles de l'Institut Français d'Archéologie Orientale du Caire 10.* Cairo, l'Institut Français d'Archéologie Orientale.

Peden, A. J. (2001) *The graffiti of pharaonic Egypt: scope and roles of informal writings.* Probleme der Ägyptologie 17. Leiden, Brill.

Peterson, B. E. J. (1973) Zeichnungen aus einer Totenstadt: Bildostraka aus Theben-West, ihre Fundplätze, Themata und Zweckbereiche mitsamt einem Katalog der Gayer-Anderson-Sammlung in Stockholm. *Medelhavsmuseet Bulletin* 7–8, 1–141.

Yoshimura, S. and Kondo, J. (1995) Excavations at the tomb of Amenophis III. *Egyptian Archaeology* 7, 17–18.